The past decade has witnessed a surge of pricing innovations in the US telecommunications industry. This volume systematically reviews recent innovations in the economic theory of pricing and extends results to conditions that characterize telecommunications markets. It then examines the implementation of normative pricing theory in selected US telephone tariffs. The experience accumulated in the United States provides a rich and diverse data base and a laboratory for examining the practical consequences of pricing innovations.

Throughout this volume the objective is to develop and illuminate the relationships between the normative economic theory of pricing – with its objectives of social welfare, economic efficiency, and fairness – and telecommunications pricing as it is practiced by businesses and regulators. In particular, the new pricing schemes are related to the theory of multiproduct and nonlinear pricing. The book describes the welfare and competitive properties of such pricing schemes and draws conclusions for future pricing problems in the areas of broadband networks and open network architecture. Many of the general theoretical pricing principles and lessons from US pricing experience should prove directly applicable to telecommunications services in other countries and to other industries, including electricity and natural gas supply, air and rail transportation, and postal and parcel services.

Telecommunications pricing

Telecommunications pricing
Theory and practice

Bridger M. Mitchell and
Ingo Vogelsang

A RAND research study
supported by WIK

Cambridge University Press
Cambridge   New York   Port Chester
Melbourne   Sydney

Published by the Press Syndicate of the University of Cambridge
The Pitt Building, Trumpington Street, Cambridge CB2 1RP
40 West 20th Street, New York, NY 10011-4211 USA
10 Stamford Road, Oakleigh, Melbourne 3166, Australia

First published 1991
Reprinted 1996, 1998

Printed in Great Britain by Athenæum Press Ltd, Gateshead, Tyne & Wear

A catalogue record for this book is available from the British Library

ISBN 0521 41667 1 hardback
ISBN 0521 42678 2 paperback

To the ones who gave us our first start,

especially our parents.

Contents

Figures

Tables

Acknowledgments

The concept of integrating within a single book the theory of telecommunications pricing and its practice in the United States was proposed to us by Karl-Heinz Neumann. To that end the Wissenschaftliches Institut für Kommunikationsdienste (WIK) of the German Bundespost, Bonn, supported the preparation of this book under a research contract to RAND. We are grateful for WIK's assistance and for the spirit of scientific inquiry with which Karl-Heinz Neumann, Dieter Elixmann, and Werner Neu have participated in all stages of this project.

Thorough and expeditious reviews of the first draft by Roger Sherman and Gerald Faulhaber have improved and extended our work. We have also benefitted from the careful readings and insightful suggestions of William Baumol, Larry Cole, Michael Crew, Alfred Kahn, Brenda Kahn, Dan Kelley, Steven Levinson, Dan Lundberg, Michael Murphy, David Salant, David Sibley, Mark Sievers, Daniel Spulber, Neal Stolleman, Glenn Woroch, and Ed Zajac.

The able and industrious assistance of William Lehr made it possible to include the material in Section 7.3, Chapter 11 and the Appendix.

I

PRICING AND TELECOMMUNICATIONS

1

Introduction

1.1 Telecommunications pricing

The last fifteen years have witnessed revolutionary technological and institutional changes in telecommunications. These developments – including fiber-optic cables and digital switches, cellular telephones, long-distance service competition, and the divestiture of the dominant US carrier – are having profound effects on the theory and practice of telecommunications pricing.

The economic theory of pricing has expanded substantially. New and modified methods of pricing natural-monopoly services have been developed, designed to achieve increased economic efficiency and acceptable distributive results. Increasingly, theoretical results have been extended to encompass entry and competitive supply in multiproduct markets.

Innovations in pricing theory, and their translation into ratemaking practice, have been examined systematically for electric power (Berg, 1983; Mitchell, Manning, and Acton, 1978); for telecommunications, a comparable assessment covers developments to about 1980 (Neumann, 1984). Since that time, many of the theoretical advances in pricing have been contributed by economists associated with the telephone sector, and some of these developments are found in Sherman (1989), Spulber (1989a), and Brown and Sibley (1986).

The broad principles of the theoretical literature on pricing are applicable to most regulated industries and public enterprises. However, the implementation of the theory varies significantly across industries. These variations – created by differences in cost, demand, and institutional conditions – call for a study that is devoted to telecommunications ratemaking.

In this volume we systematically review recent innovations in the

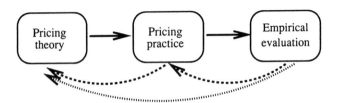

Figure 1.1
Innovation in theory and practice

theory of pricing and extend results to conditions that characterize
telecommunications markets. We then examine the implementation of
normative pricing theory in selected US telephone tariffs. In the United
States telephone services are highly developed, essentially ubiquitous,
and in many important markets supplied by several competing firms.
Regulatory authority is divided between federal and state governments;
as a result tariffs also differ by state. In all, the experience accumulated
in the United States provides a rich and diverse data base and a laboratory for examining the practical consequences of pricing innovations.

Many of the general theoretical pricing principles and lessons from US
pricing experience could be directly applicable to telecommunications
services in other countries. These theoretical pricing results will also
be of interest to a number of other industries, including electricity and
natural gas supply, air and rail transportation, and postal and parcel
services. Also, the practical experience in US telecommunications may
be relevant to future developments in these sectors as well.

1.2   Theory and practice

New developments in pricing arise from the interdependent nature of
innovations in the theory, practice, and evaluation of pricing, shown in
Figure 1.1.

One view of the process of innovation begins with theory – fundamental advances in the abstract characterization of markets and the
behavior of firms, consumers, and government institutions. Somewhat
later these discoveries may diffuse into industry and regulatory practices,
as firms' managers became aware of the new tools and incorporate them
into decisionmaking. Some of these pricing innovations succeed and be-

come widely used. Experience accumulates, and after several years firm and industry statistics reflect the impact of prices and enable the first quantitative evaluations to be conducted.

The pattern of theory $\longrightarrow$ practice $\longrightarrow$ evaluation is a plausible one. But the "feedback" effects shown by the dashed lines are of at least equal importance. Firms, particularly when faced with competition, are driven to innovate, introducing new services and pricing structures, even without reference to economic and marketing theories. Test-marketing, formal statistical experimental designs, and decentralized trials of management ideas may all contribute to tariff innovations that are first proposed in practical settings. Later, researchers observing real markets and seeking consistent explanations are impelled to extend available theories to accommodate successful innovation already in practice.[1]

The telecommunications sector is a fertile field in which to observe these bidirectional flows in pricing innovations. Throughout this volume our objective is to develop and illuminate the relationships between the normative economic theory of pricing and the practice of telecommunications pricing by businesses and regulators.

This study is therefore directed to practitioners – managers and staff in industry and public regulatory bodies – and to researchers, theorists, scholars, and students of telecommunications. More generally, many of the findings that emerge are also relevant to pricing in the energy and transportation sectors.

Economic theorizing about pricing is conducted primarily in the research environments of universities. In the United States this traditional source of innovation has been augmented by several institutions.

- One notable development that has fostered significant theoretical contributions was the establishment of an economics group at AT&T's Bell Laboratories and the founding of the *Bell Journal of Economics* (now the *RAND Journal of Economics*).

- Another feature of the US research environment is the activity of mature independent research institutes that conduct basic studies intended to inform the discussion of public policy issues, including RAND and the Brookings Institution.

[1] Faulhaber and Baumol (1988) describe the interactions between theory and practice that have occurred on some of the pricing issues discussed in this book – peak-load pricing, Ramsey pricing, and stand-alone cost tests.

- The Telecommunications Policy Research Conference was established in 1972 to bring researchers together with federal policy-makers in the telecommunications sector. This annual conference has subsequently expanded its reach to include state and international policy communities.

1.3   Overview

We have divided this study into four parts. In the next chapter (Chapter 2) of this introductory part we examine the fundamental technological conditions for producing telecommunications services and the nature of the costs of supplying telephone service. These factors are the backdrop for understanding the basic features of telephone pricing, and research on telecommunications demand and cost structures constitutes an important input of this work.

Part II is devoted to a tour of recent developments in the normative economic theory of tariffs. We first provide an overview of the major types of tariffs and establish the notation and conventions we need (Chapter 3). We then examine, successively, linear tariffs (Chapter 4), nonlinear tariffs (Chapter 5), and cost-based pricing (Chapter 6). This part, especially Chapters 4–6, is the most technical material of the study. It should be accessible to readers with a scientific, engineering, or economics background. Others may prefer to turn immediately to the following, case-study material.

Part III surveys the major types of rate structures found in US markets. We discuss governmental regulation and rates for retail services in Chapter 7, and follow this with a more extended examination of optional retail tariffs in Chapter 8. Pricing practices for services sold in volume to larger business and institutional customers are the topic of Chapter 9. Chapter 10 examines rates that one telecommunications carrier charges another for interconnection and transport services. Finally, in Chapter 11 we review "lifeline" and related social tariffs designed to assist selected telephone subscribers.

In the final part, we review the salient theoretical advances in the light of American practice and of the available evidence of the effectiveness of innovative pricing.

In an appendix we summarize trends in the prices of US telephone services and provide additional technical detail on price cap regulation.

2

Telecommunications production, costs, and pricing

This chapter presents a brief overview of the production of telecommunications services. Our purpose is to provide enough information to identify the most distinguishing economic features of this industry, yet to avoid the weight of excessive detail. We first examine the technology used in the telecommunications sector, emphasizing its most important economic characteristics and contrasting them with the salient features of other public utility services. Next, we summarize the institutional and regulatory arrangements that currently govern telecommunications in the United States. Finally, we briefly indicate the major types of tariffs that are found in American practice, many of which we examine in detail in later chapters. Readers who are already familiar with these topics may wish to turn directly to Chapter 3.

2.1 Stylized telecommunications technology

We may consider telecommunications to be the two-way exchange of information in the form of voice or data messages between two users at distinct geographic locations. Frequently it is useful to think of the users as terminal nodes in a network and the fundamental telecommunications service as simple telephone "calls" between nodes.[1] One method of supplying telecommunications is to provide a direct, dedicated link between each pair of nodes. With this technology the marginal cost of a link increases directly with the size of the network, and for more than a very

---

[1] Many elements of the voice telephone network are also used to supply data and video services. Enhanced information services are produced by combining selected transport, switching, and control features of the network with data storage and processing. Some message and data services are largely one-directional in nature, although their service standards usually require that confirmation of receipt be communicated to the originating node.

small number of nodes it becomes necessary to find ways to economize on links.

Switching networks perform this function. To take advantage of economies of scale, switching points concentrate calls that are destined for the same end node and bundle them together for bulk transport over a limited number of high-capacity links. Frequently, calls pass through intermediate switching points and additional links before they arrive at a terminating switch, where the calls are unbundled for final delivery. Today, telephone networks use *circuit switching* to reserve a single path for each call and dedicate it exclusively to that call. This technology contrasts with the *packet-switching* networks used to interconnect computers.

2.1.1 Network functions

A telecommunications network divides broadly into three functional parts as shown in Figure 2.1. Users (the terminal nodes of the network) are attached to the network by *access* facilities. The most common form of access is a twisted pair of copper wires from the user's telephone to a local switching office. This "local loop" has sufficient capacity to carry a voice telephone call or a limited volume of data, using analog transmission. Alternative access facilities include cellular radio, fiber-optic cable, and microwave radio.

The *switching* function is performed at the central office by automatic, computer-controlled electronic equipment (or, in older offices, by electromechanical switches). The switch establishes a communications path between the two user nodes, and reserves the needed capacity in shared switching and transport facilities for the duration of the conversation.

Except for the shortest-distance local calls – those between two nodes that access the same switch – a telephone call requires *transport* to one or more additional switching points before it reaches the destination node. The highest-capacity transport facilities are fiber-optic cables with their associated multiplexing electronics. Other facilities include microwave relay, communications satellites, and copper cables.

Digital technologies, using microelectronics, have proved the lowest-cost means of supplying most switching and transport functions. Analog transmission continues to be used in access facilities for the local loop links to individual subscribers.

Supply of the final product – telephone calls – requires a variety of

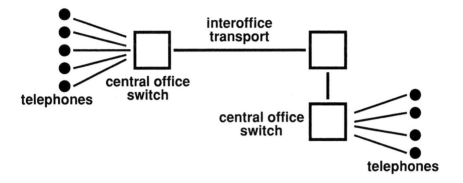

Figure 2.1
Stylized telephone network

associated services to supervise, maintain, and account for production. These related activities themselves make extensive use of the network.

2.1.2   Economic characteristics

In some respects telecommunications services strongly resemble other economic services delivered by networks. In telephone networks, components and facilities are geographically located in relation to final consumers. (Energy networks are located on the basis of the geographic positions of both final consumers and of energy sources.) Production is very capital intensive, and there is scant opportunity to store output in inventory in order to buffer differences in the timing of production and demand.

However, telecommunications also differs significantly from other types of network services. In telecommunications networks, production facilities have well-determined capacities, and the costs of operation are nearly independent of the flow of services through those facilities. Due to the extensive use of electronic components, maintenance and energy costs are mostly the result of simply operating a facility and are nearly independent of its actual use. Consequently (except for operator-assisted services) variable costs are very small.

Individual network components, although limited in their capacities, are frequently common resources in the production of several outputs. A local digital switch, for example, can process a maximum number of calls per hour, but within that constraint local calls and trunk calls are substitutes.

Telecommunications services are typically produced in a network that embodies more than a single technology. For example, to transport calls between several switching centers a network may use fiber-optic links of several speeds, microwave radio, and digital (T-1) carrier on copper cable facilities. These diverse systems enable a network to exploit economies of scale at different volumes of transport. With wide differences in the volumes of bundled demand on different network links, it is efficient to use fiber-optics for high-capacity backbone transmission but microwave radio in sparsely populated regions with high-cost terrain.

Multiple technologies also occur as the result of ongoing network modernization. Replacement of an older generation of equipment (for example, electromechanical switches) takes place gradually across the network. Modernization is economic when the rising repair and maintenance costs of a particular piece of equipment finally exceed the incremental investment cost of the new vintage. Once a facility has been installed in an operating network, most of the specific costs become sunk.

This side-by-side use of several technologies at different levels of output differs fundamentally from an apparently similar, "diverse-technology" practice, that of electricity supply. In the latter, efficient production to supply a time-varying demand for a given level of output leads to a balancing of production across several generating units having different capital/fuel cost ratios. Short-run marginal costs of generation then reflect the energy used by the marginal generating unit.

Using the current state of technology, telecommunications networks have some limited opportunities to substitute among productive inputs (labor, capital, energy) to produce telecommunications services. For example, directory assistance can be produced with the varying use of pre-recorded voice messages, and electronic switches can be maintained by fulltime local technicians or from a regional maintenance center. However, most opportunities for substitution take the form of combining alternative network activities to produce products. Once a user node has an access connection to the network, the network operator can supply a specific pairwise connection and thus produce a telephone call using any of several alternative routings through intermediate nodes. Although peak demands for individual routes are correlated, they are not fully coincident. As a result, especially in networks that span several time zones, it is possible to exploit production economies of scope.

2.1.3 Demand

Telecommunications demand is largely demand for two-way conversations and exchanges of information. As a result, telecommunications services must be produced in real time and are largely nonstorable. The exception is one-way message traffic (facsimile, data) that does not require immediate acknowledgment.

Although an individual consumer's telecommunications demand appears to an observer as stochastic, the market demand has strong regular daily and weekly patterns. In most urban markets, for example, local calling reaches its highest rate in late morning and mid-afternoon.

The infeasibility of storing production in inventory, combined with very small variable costs, poses the classic peak-load problem in its extreme form. Up to the available capacity, additional output can be produced at negligible additional cost. Thus, unlike energy and transportation networks, off-peak telecommunications services have nearly zero marginal costs.[2] Conversely, when demand exceeds capacity, output must be rationed by queueing or rejecting calls. In this case, congestion and rationing of available capacity by nonprice mechanisms results in a negative externality. Additional call attempts cause some high-valued demands not to be served.

The two-way nature of telecommunications demand gives rise to an important positive "network externality." The value of a network to a given user increases with the number of other users who have access to it. When a new node is added, the externality is reflected in the number of calls made between any existing nodes and the new node (not an increase in the calls between existing nodes).

As in transportation networks, demand is distributed across a large number of distinct markets – pairwise connections of end nodes. Aggregation across the markets (using total minutes, without weighting by distance as is customary, for example, in transportation) is useful for

---

[2] The current carrier-access charge system, which recovers some of the fixed costs of the local loop in per-minute prices, causes long-distance carriers to face significant off-peak variable costs.

obtaining industry-wide measures of supply. Nevertheless, the underlying diversity of individual markets is fundamental – a call to a different destination can rarely substitute for the intended connection.

The volume of demand is sensitive, in varying degrees, to the price of service. Broadly speaking, demand for network access is quite price-inelastic, and local calling is also relatively insensitive to price, whereas higher-priced and longer-distance services are more price sensitive. Overall, residential demand is more elastic than that of business customers. However, the demand for one supplier's services can be very price sensitive, especially from large business customers who have several communications options.

2.1.4   Technological change

The telecommunications sector has enjoyed a high, continuous rate of productivity increase, benefiting from rapid innovation in electronics, computers, materials, and processes.

Cost reductions have been particularly notable in long-distance transmission, where high-capacity fiber-optic cables and improved multiplexing have vastly increased capacity. In switching, digital-computer driven equipment has cut maintenance costs and software innovation has expanded the range of services. Within the network, these advances have allowed carriers to supply customers with specialized private networks composed of shared facilities under software control. Switching has also moved closer to the final user, with versatile private switches (PBXs) competing with local exchange carrier switches to supply a wide range of office communications services.

Access technologies have advanced less rapidly. For low volume nodes, the least-cost technology remains copper cable pairs, but fiber-optic distribution and microwave bypass are reaching larger office buildings. Cellular radio is enjoying explosive growth, primarily as an extension of access to new mobile nodes.

Terminal equipment has also enjoyed continuing innovation. Answering machines and facsimile devices have spread rapidly. Office equipment includes software-controlled PBXs and features such as least-cost trunk route selection. These developments stimulate both the volume and price sensitivity of telecommunications demand.

Continued advances in computer software and data storage technology have also led to process innovations throughout telecommunications.

Long-distance connections are now established and calls routed dynamically, according to the current availability of network links and switches. The service characteristics of an individual telephone number can be reprogrammed from a microcomputer terminal and, increasingly, by larger customers themselves.

Just over the horizon lie further technological advances. New low-power radio technologies promise to link subscribers via lightweight, vestpocket telephones. Broadband networks, incorporating high-speed switching and fiber-optic links to the consumer, may eventually provide a broad array of video, data, and personal communications services. Network technology will evolve to incorporate fault-tolerant ring and mesh topologies, more advanced packet- and connection-switching, and software advances to handle interconnections across different suppliers' networks and devices. Connected to these networks will be increasingly "intelligent" subscriber terminal equipment with easily programmed features.

2.1.5   Cost functions

The essential economic characteristics of telecommunications technology are represented by cost functions, which relate the total cost of production to the quantities of services produced. A cost function summarizes the firm's engineering knowledge about the least-cost method of producing the given levels of services. Several properties of telecommunications cost functions strongly influence pricing.

Economies of scale exist when a production function exhibits increasing returns to scale. A single-product firm that enjoys economies of scale at output level q will have decreasing average costs:

$$\frac{C(rq)}{rq} > \frac{C(q)}{q} \quad \text{for all } 0 < r < 1. \tag{2.1}$$

For a multiproduct firm producing $q = (q_1, \ldots, q_n)$ average costs are not clearly defined, so the concept of economies of scale cannot generally be represented by decreasing average cost. However, economies of scale can be represented by the more general concept of decreasing *ray* average cost, which is defined by:

$$C(rq) > rC(q) \quad \text{for all } 0 < r < 1. \tag{2.2}$$

A firm enjoying decreasing ray average costs can expand all outputs in proportion with a less than proportional increase in its total costs.

Table 2.1
Market shares, 1989

Switched and private line interstate services	Bulk-rate (WATS) services (forecast)
68.9% AT&T	44% AT&T
11.5% MCI	20% MCI
7.5% US Sprint	16% US Sprint
12.2% other carriers	20% other carriers

Source: Datapro Reports on Telecommunications, McGraw-Hill, 1989.

In telecommunications, large increases in volume in a single market may permit production with a higher-capacity technology and the achievement of scale economies. Over smaller ranges of output capacity is indivisible and output cannot be stored, leading to very low shortrun marginal costs whenever there is more than sufficient capacity to serve demand.

The cost function exhibits the property of natural monopoly when it is subadditive.[3] Thus, a single firm can produce any level of output more efficiently than two or more smaller firms:

$$C(q^1) + C(q^2) > C(q^1 + q^2). \tag{2.3}$$

Telecommunications cost functions appear to possess economies of scale and scope over at least initial levels of output. However, it is unlikely that telecommunications is a natural monopoly in the national long-distance market. Intercity carriers, which began competing with AT&T by entering selective markets, have expanded to provide nationwide service and have captured important market shares for both retail and bulk-rate services (Table 2.1). Most recently, these new carriers, which were initially advantaged by regulatory limits on AT&T's prices, have found it increasingly difficult to grow. AT&T has mounted a vigorous campaign of marketing and pricing innovations, using the pricing flexibility made possible by the shift to price cap regulation.

[3]Subadditivity is a mathematical property of a function defined by $f(\sum_i x_i) \leq \sum_i (f(x_i))$ for all combinations of $x_i \geq 0$. The standard work on natural monopoly is Sharkey (1982).

2.2   The US context

Prior to the settlement of the US antitrust suit against AT&T, US telecommunications was provided largely by a single, vertically integrated monopoly. Bell operating companies, owned by AT&T, supplied network access and local telephone service in each state (except Alaska and Hawaii) under exclusive local franchises. The AT&T Long Lines division supplied interstate long-distance service, and AT&T's Western Electric division manufactured network and subscriber equipment. Throughout the country, independent telephone companies, operating primarily in smaller communities and rural areas, also supplied local exchange services.

As a result of court orders and Federal Communications Commission (FCC) decisions, several new long-distance firms, led by MCI, had won the right to enter markets for intercity services and were competing with AT&T in most large city-pair routes.

Settlement of the suit (the Modified Final Judgment) required AT&T to divest itself of its local exchange operations. This process created seven Regional Bell Operating Companies (RBOCs), which received the local-service assets of AT&T. A total of 192 Local Access Transport Areas (LATAs) were defined around population centers, and the operating companies were prohibited from themselves providing services between these areas (interLATA services). AT&T reconstituted itself as an interexchange carrier (IXC), equipment manufacturer, and supplier of enhanced telecommunications services.

The vertical separation of firms in the industry is shown in schematic form in Figure 2.2. A local exchange carrier (LEC), a monopoly regulated by state commission, typically provides access and local calling in several communities within a LATA. It also supplies shorter-distance trunk calls. The LECs are the Bell operating companies plus GTE and a large number of much smaller independent telephone companies. Interexchange carriers interconnect with a LEC at a point of presence (POP) in each LATA, and supply trunk calls between those points.

Within the formerly integrated AT&T, long-distance rates had long been set at high levels to generate support for low access rates and local exchange rates. To replace this system, the FCC and state regulatory commissions established carrier access charges that IXCs were required to pay to local exchange companies to connect to their customers and to

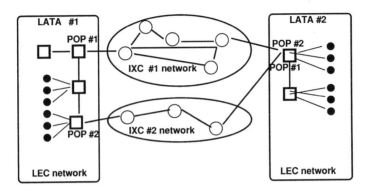

Figure 2.2
Local and trunk carriers

deliver their trunk calls to subscribers in other areas. In addition, local
rates were raised by the establishment of a nationally uniform Subscriber
Line Charge paid monthly by subscribers for each access line. This
increase was offset, however, by reductions in long-distance rates.

In the United States, regulation of telecommunications carriers is divided between federal and state authorities. Today, the FCC confines
its regulation at the retail level to the interstate services of the dominant carrier, AT&T. At the wholesale level, carrier access rates charged
by local companies are also subject to federal regulation. Until 1989,
AT&T's rates were regulated by an overall constraint on AT&T's rate
of return and a requirement that most services be priced with respect
to a fully distributed-cost standard. Beginning in 1989, AT&T has been
subject to price caps on three major groups of services, with built-in rate
reductions for productivity advances and the flexibility to reprice service subgroups up to ±5 percent annually (Chapter 7 and Appendix).
In 1991, the wholesale carrier access rates of the major local carriers
became subject to a similar price cap system.

The fifty states regulate local exchange and intrastate services through
state public utility commissions (PUCs). Policies toward competition,
market entry, and tariffs vary from state to state (Table 2.2).

The result of this divided federal/state regulatory jurisdiction is a
uniform nationwide pattern of tariffs for interstate services, and con-

Table 2.2
The US telephone market

Item	Market		
	Interstate	State and interLATA	Local and intraLATA
Services:	long distance	long distance	access, local calls
Firms:	IXCs— AT&T, MCI, others	IXCs— AT&T, MCI, others	LECs— Bell companies, independents, also IXCs in some states
Regulator:	FCC	state PUCs	state PUCs
Regulation:	AT&T price cap, open entry	from none to rate of return, limited entry permitted in some states	generally rate of return, entry barred in most states

siderable diversity of local and intrastate trunk call tariffs and market structures. In this study we focus predominantly on nationwide tariffs. Examples are drawn mostly from AT&T's rates, reflecting the market importance of that carrier and the availability of data. The rate structures of other major IXCs, who are free to change prices at any time, are broadly similar. Because these carriers do not formally file tariffs and data are more difficult to obtain, they receive less attention here. Some illustrations, particularly for social tariffs, are drawn from current LEC rates in several states.

2.3 Major tariff developments

The telecommunications sector in the 1980s has been characterized by substantial growth, regulatory and industrial restructuring, and the rise of effective competition. In this setting, telecommunications carriers have introduced a variety of new pricing structures and revised others. Here, we briefly survey major developments, several of which we will investigate in detail in later chapters.

For decades, basic long-distance service has been priced by the call and minutes of duration according to its distance and time of day. This standard rate structure has endured despite extensive changes in technology. There have been changes such as fewer distance bands and less price sensitivity to distance, and smaller differences between peak and off-peak rates.

Optional tariffs, offering simplified, uniform per-minute rates regardless of distance during night and weekend hours, have proved popular with residential and small business users. Carriers have expanded these plans, offering a variety of packages, some of which include discounts on standard rates in daytime and evening periods.

Innovations in the rate structures for larger users, almost entirely business customers, include a larger number of schedules, tailored to different volume segments of the market, and high-volume access arrangements that reduce rates.

For the largest corporate and institutional customers, carriers have developed special contracts that encompass nearly all the telecommunications services of a firm at its many locations. Technological innovation and new pricing arrangements have led major multiple-site customers to shift from self-managed, private networks that are assembled from leased private-line facilities to software-defined virtual private networks that are supplied by major carriers from their primary network facilities.

Carriers have also begun using pricing discounts and other incentives that encourage customers to purchase their entire bundle of telecommunications services from a single supplier.

Toll-free, 800-number services themselves constitute a form of pricing innovation that provides automatic call payment by the receiving customer. Increased network flexibility and volume-pricing plans have made this service attractive to a very wide size range of customers.

Customer-priced 900-number services enable customers to charge premium, individual per-call rates for information services that they themselves market, using the telecommunications carrier as a billing and collection service.

At the local exchange, US practice has seen two forms of rate innovation. Social tariffs, termed "lifeline" rates, have been established to offer lower-priced access to the network and local calling to selected groups of consumers. A variety of approaches have been developed in the different states. Second, many local exchange carriers have introduced some type of per-call or per-minute pricing for the most local calls by residential consumers, as an option or replacement to the often-standard fixed monthly rate charged for an unlimited number of local calls in most areas.

The explicit classification of customers into residential and business (non-residential) groups is a long-standing feature of local service tariffs. Monthly business rates are typically two to four times those for residential subscribers. The two classes are often supplied under different tariff structures, with residential service bundling access and local calls, while business customers are billed for each call. Other network services are generally classified only by type of access arrangement or other technical parameters. Although the labels "residential" and "business" are frequently used to designate the typical customers of particular services, these services (except in the case of local exchange service) are open to all users.

Billing for telephone calls using telephone credit cards has expanded greatly, promoted by interexchange carriers competing with AT&T. Most carriers offer such service and several incorporate calling-card calls into rate discount plans.

In 1989 the FCC shifted from rate-of-return regulation to price caps as its instrument for controlling AT&T's pricing of interstate services. Price caps have expanded AT&T's scope for introducing tariff changes, removed most regulatory lags, and accelerated pricing responses to changing market conditions.

Following the 1984 breakup of AT&T into seven regional companies who operate the majority of the local exchanges, AT&T and other interstate long-distance carriers pay uniform per-minute carrier access charges to the local companies for each minute of long-distance traffic that they transport. At the same time, residential and business subscribers pay fixed monthly subscriber line charges for each access line.

II

RECENT DEVELOPMENTS IN THE NORMATIVE ECONOMIC THEORY OF TARIFFS

3

Types of tariffs

3.1 The context

The following four chapters review the economics literature on public utility pricing with special reference to the telephone sector. We concentrate on major contributions made in the last ten years. We do, however, selectively make reference to earlier research, in particular if it is judged to be important and at the same time not well-known or not well-understood.

Our main objective in these chapters is to assess the relevance of the theoretical literature for setting telephone tariffs that move toward social optimality. In particular, we are interested in the compatibility of tariff proposals with the particular technology and demand conditions that are found in the telephone industry.

We also critically evaluate the assumptions under which results in the literature are derived. To do this, we make implicit assumptions explicit, extend some results by lifting restrictive assumptions or by adding more realistic constraints, and extrapolate results from one type of tariff to another. In presenting the progress made in the normative literature we also modify and extend results derived for a particular objective, such as profit maximization, to other objectives, such as maximization of social surplus, when those objectives appear to be more relevant for the study.

The last two decades have witnessed unprecedented progress in research on design and in implementation of public utility tariffs. Starting with Baumol and Bradford's (1970) paper on optimal departures from marginal-cost pricing and the initiation of the *Bell Journal of Economics and Management Science* (now the *RAND Journal of Economics*), a large number of scientific papers have dealt with this subject. By the end of the 1970s, peak-load pricing, cross subsidization, and Ramsey prices had become household words among economists; the theory of optimal two-part tariffs had been largely completed and work on general nonlinear prices, cost-axiomatic prices, and the sustainability of prices against entry was well under way. Since then, progress in the theoretical literature on tariffs has moved in several directions.

A first thrust, highlighted by Baumol, Panzar, and Willig's (1982) book on contestable markets, drives at the interaction between *tariffs and competition*, particularly competitive entry. This direction has obvious practical importance for the telecommunications sector, even though the conditions for contestability rarely hold in the telecommunications sector. Conditions for prices to be sustainable against (inefficient) entry have been derived in theory, and tests for their empirical significance have been designed (Fuss and Waverman, 1981). In particular, sustainable prices just cover minimum industry costs at the outputs demanded at these prices. Prices that are sustainable against potential entrants are also subsidy-free, and thus fair, in the sense that no subset of outputs generates more revenues than its stand-alone cost (Faulhaber, 1975). Potential competition and fairness considerations may therefore call for tariffs being squarely based on cost.

A closely related second direction encompasses *cost-axiomatic pricing*. Although subsidy-free prices may not exist, other plausible axioms for the relationship between prices and costs have been postulated in the literature. One set of such axioms leads to a particular type of average-cost prices (Aumann–Shapley prices, Aumann and Shapley, 1974) as the unique outcome. Such prices are guaranteed to exist under very general demand and cost conditions. While the first cost-axiomatic prices have been derived for a telecommunications application (Billera, Heath, and Raanan, 1978), their usefulness is seriously debated.

A third major direction is that of *nonlinear prices*. In terms of public utility pricing one might call the 1970s the decade of Ramsey prices while the 1980s appear to have been the decade of nonlinear prices. The literature on nonlinear prices provides additional tools for pursuing the objectives of equity and efficiency simultaneously. However, informational requirements for the implementation of some of the resulting pricing schemes have become successively heavier. Therefore, it is good to know that some of the (optional) pricing schemes can actually be used to generate this information (Spence, 1980; Maskin and Riley, 1984). For example, by giving customers the option between two combinations – a high access fee and a low usage fee, and a low access fee and a high usage fee – the supplier can make customers self-select into consumption size classes without having to know their specific demands. As the evidence on US tariff developments to be brought forward in Chapters 7-11 amply demonstrates, nonlinear pricing schemes are becoming more and more important in telecommunications.

A fourth direction that continues to be theoretically interesting and of utmost importance for telephone tariffs concerns *peak-load pricing* and related issues. Uncertainty and nonprice rationing have become major concerns, as has the pricing of services in view of lumpy capacity investment in an expanding sector.

A fifth direction deals with informational problems of implementation from a *principal-agent* perspective. It views government as a welfare-maximizing, uninformed principal and regulated firms (or public enterprise managers) as fully informed, utility-maximizing agents. Tariffs derived under this approach will typically deviate from tariffs derived under full information because the agent has to be induced to tell the truth (revelation principle). This literature has recently been applied specifically to the introduction of price caps by the FCC.[1]

In all, this is a rich, multifaceted, cross-cutting literature that could be examined in many different ways. We have chosen to organize the discussion of the contributions by types of tariffs. In Section 3.2 we introduce the normative framework in which we discuss objectives for tariff setting. The major objectives include maximization of a weighted welfare function and the observation of fairness constraints, and in the following chapters we systematically analyze (weighted) welfare-maximizing tariffs. Section 3.3 provides an introduction and overview of these tariffs.

Chapter 4 then concentrates on linear multiproduct tariffs. "Linear" here means that prices do not change with the quantity purchased; multiproduct means that services are differentiated by physical attributes and/or by consumer groups. Chapter 5 proceeds to nonlinear tariffs, meaning that price changes with quantity purchased. The subject of nonlinear tariffs includes most of the tariff innovations that have occurred in the US telephone industry over the past ten years. Under the heading of cost-based tariffs, Chapter 6 addresses the problem of constraints imposed by the objective of fairness and by the possibility of

---

[1]In addition to the literature on price caps, this literature includes the mechanism design literature. For overviews see Besanko and Sappington (1987) and Baron (1989).

entry and competition in regulated markets. In relation to Chapters 4 and 5, these additional constraints can require deviations from welfare-maximizing tariffs or the choice from a subset of the welfare-maximizing tariffs. It turns out that some of the cost-based tariffs call for deviations while others are a proper subset of welfare-maximizing tariffs.

3.2   Normative framework

3.2.1   General assumptions

Since the following chapters provide a literature review of the economic theory of telephone tariffs, we generally need to be able to accommodate various assumptions made in this literature. At this point we state general assumptions that will hold throughout unless stated otherwise.[2] We will make additional assumptions later when discussing specific models.

In emphasizing pricing in the telecommunications sector we abstract from all effects that telecommunications acitivities may have on other sectors of the economy. This partial equilibrium, rather than general equilibrium, approach is justifiable only if such effects of telecommunications tariffs on the rest of the economy are indeed small, diffuse, and unidentifiable. Since telecommunications deals with the interaction of people, the partial equilibrium assumption is a very strong one. For example, to the extent that telephone tariffs affect the introduction of new telecommunications technologies they will also affect other economic activities. In our models these other effects would all be covered by changes of consumer and producer welfare which in turn would lead to (diffuse) other activities. Our partial equilibrium approach implies that we consider economic agents only in their role as suppliers, regulators or planners, or consumers of telecommunications services.[3]

Firms.   Suppliers of telecommunications services are either regulated carriers or independent firms.   In line with most of the literature,

---

[2]Usually in footnotes.

[3]The literature has identified a number of general equilibrium qualifications that might be relevant for the setting of telephone tariffs. In this connection it is worth mentioning Peters' (1988) result that some input distortions are optimal under second-best pricing. The important question is whether such qualifications are of sufficient magnitude to make a difference and, in particular, whether this difference is larger than errors in measuring the required general equilibrium relationships.

regulated carriers are assumed to follow the same objective as their
regulator.[4] Independent firms are assumed to maximize profits

$$\pi = \sum_{i=1}^{N} R(q_i) - C((q_i)_N).\tag{3.1}$$

Here q_i is the vector of telecommunications services purchased by customer i. Unless stated otherwise, the set of services available is assumed
to be given. Usually, different services correspond to different markets.
There is a large antitrust literature on the correct definition of markets.
According to this literature, two services belong to the same market if
they are close substitutes in demand or supply, that is, if their cross-
elasticities of demand/supply are positive and sufficiently large. Sometimes, our definition of a service will be substantially narrower, requiring
only that a service can be priced differently from other services.

   The set of services purchased by all N customers is $(q_i)_N =
(q_1, \ldots, q_i, \ldots, q_N)$. The fact that we do not aggregate all quantities
to one sum reflects the multiproduct nature of telecommunications and
the possibility that there are customer-specific costs. If N is very large
we may assume a continuum of customers. In this case customer-specific
costs can be assigned to an additional output, "access," that is tied to the
purchase of one or all of the other goods. Then we may write $C((q_i)_N)$
as $C(\sum_i q_i)$. Assumptions on the cost function will vary substantially
from case to case. Except at output $q = 0$ and at capacity constraints we
will, however, assume that the total cost function is twice continuously
differentiable.

   $R(q_i)$ is the (possibly consumer-specific) outlay of customer i for the
quantity vector q_i. $R(q_i) = p'q_i$ in the case of a linear price vector p.
This will be our assumption throughout Chapter 4, where we also take up
the case of different price vectors for different classes of customers. However, linear tariffs are insufficient for characterizing the theory and practice of telephone tariffs. As mentioned above, both theory and practice
are dominated by nonlinear tariffs with the property that $R(q_i) \neq p'q_i$.
In this case $R(q_i)$ becomes a function stating the relationship between
outlay and quantity purchased. $R(\cdot)$ is called the outlay function (or
outlay schedule, if it is defined over discrete intervals of q). Because of
the nonlinearity of tariffs we will often refer to p as the "marginal price"

---

[4]For a discussion of problems behind this assumption see Section 7.1.

$p = \partial R/\partial q$. In Chapter 5 we make a number of assumptions about the shape of R. We will always assume $p \geq 0$, so that tariffs cannot become a money machine for enriching consumers.

Consumers. For a large part of our analysis we will simply look at the single-product case so that q_i becomes q_i. This is a simplification that can be generalized in some, but not in all, cases. Consumer i derives utility $U_i(q_i; q_i^*; y_i)$ from the consumption of telecommunications services; q_i^* is the quantity of other goods consumed by consumer i; and y_i is his income. We assume that the purchase of telecommunications services has no effect on the marginal utility of income and the marginal utility of these other goods, and we therefore drop q_i^* and y_i as arguments in i's utility function. This assumption requires either income effects to be negligible or, if they are not, that telecommunications services make up only a small fraction of consumer i's budget so their effect will be very small.[5]

The assumption also allows us to view the consumer's net utility from telecommunications services as the difference between gross utility and outlays: $U_i(q_i) - R(q_i)$. The consumer solves the maximization problem:

$$q_i = \arg \max \left[U_i(q_i) - R(q_i) \right]. \tag{3.2}$$

We will defer complications for consumer welfare that arise from the nonlinearity of R and for now assume $R(q) = pq$. Then the solution to consumer i's maximization problem leads to indirect utility $V_i(p)$ and to the consumer's demand function:

$$\frac{\partial V_i}{\partial p} = -q_i(p). \tag{3.3}$$

The demand function $q(p)$ and its inverse $p(q)$ are assumed to be downward sloping and twice continuously differentiable.[6] In the absence of income effects, consumer rationality requires that indirect utility $V(p)$ is convex. The indirect utility in the absence of income effects is the Marshallian consumer surplus, which can be expressed either as:

---

[5] As suggested by Zajac (1979), the prices derived under the assumption of no income effects often remain valid in the presence of certain income effects.

[6] In the multiproduct case, telecommunications services can be substitutes or complements.

$$CS = V(p) = \int_p^\infty q(p)\,dp,$$

or:

$$CS = V(p) = \int_0^q p(q)\,dq - p(q)q. \tag{3.4}$$

The first expression is usually convenient if we look at price setting behavior while the second expression is convenient for a quantity setting firm.

In the general multiproduct case the consumer surplus integrals have to be replaced by line integrals. Because of the absence of income effects the integrability conditions are met and the integrals are path-independent. In the special case where demands for various telecommunications services are independent of each other, the line integrals are replaced by the sum of consumer surpluses for the individual services.

How is our analysis of consumer welfare affected by the fact that many consumers are themselves firms rather than households? The properties of consumer surplus without income effects travel well into the world of profits. However, several caveats are in order. First, the regulator or planner may value consumers who are firms differently from those who are households. Second, firms may be large consumers with buying power (and bypass options) not available to households. Third, firms may compete with each other imperfectly. Under perfect competition the demand of a firm for telecommunications services is simply the demand derived from the demand for its own services. However, this is no longer true under imperfect competition. Any consequent problem will generally be ignored in our study, except that it will be treated in connection with the Pareto superiority of nonlinear tariffs.

A tariff R_k is said to be *Pareto superior* to another tariff R_l if at least one agent (consumer or supplier) is better off under R_k and no one is worse off. In this case R_l is said to be Pareto dominated. A tariff R_k is *Pareto optimal* (or Pareto efficient) if no tariff R_l Pareto dominates it.

Competition. The primary case of telecommunications carriers analyzed in the literature has been that of a regulated monopoly. However, the regulatory and market development in US telecommunications in the last two decades has increasingly required incorporating competi-

tion among carriers into the theory. Three types of competition are of
interest to us.

- Potential competition (or entry competition) has been analyzed
  in a natural monopoly situation. Here, the emphasis is on the
  existence and properties of tariffs that exclude inefficient entry.
  The literature concerned with this issue is discussed in Chapter 6.
  It emphasizes the extent to which potential entry reinforces or
  destroys desirable properties of tariffs.

- Actual competition is considered in an oligopoly or dominant firm
  model in which one firm is regulated and the others are unregulated. Here, the emphasis is on the interference between the
  objectives pursued by the other firms and by the regulator. This
  problem comes up in Chapters 4, 5, and 6.

- Actual (and potential) competition is considered in an oligopoly
  of unregulated profit-maximizing carriers. Here, the emphasis is
  on the degree to which competition can fully replace regulation
  in achieving regulatory objectives. The modelling of this kind of
  competition is done in Chapters 4 and 5. These models allow us
  to interpret oligopoly as a "monopoly" with adjusted elasticities,
  where the adjustment factor represents market share and competitive response. Thus, a small firm in a fiercely competitive market
  can be viewed as a monopolist in a highly elastic market. Using
  this adjustment the monopoly results can be extended to a class
  of oligopoly models.

In the last ten years game-theoretic models have increasingly come to
dominate oligopoly theory. For two reasons we have nevertheless re-
frained from introducing such models explicitly into our analysis of
oligopoly pricing in the presence of a welfare-maximizing firm. First,
in order to present these models we would have had to include a substantial amount of technical background material on the game-theoretic
concepts. Second, to the best of our knowledge there are few results on
welfare-maximizing pricing behavior. The results in Ware and Winter
(1986) are explained in Chapter 4 and are compatible with the more
traditional approach presented in the remaining analysis.

3.2.2   Objective functions for telephone tariffs

We view tariffs as instruments for pursuing policy objectives. The prime objective considered in the economics literature on optimal pricing has been efficiency in the sense of Pareto optimality or the maximization of surplus. The use of surplus is compatible with partial equilibrium analysis and the assumed absence of income effects.

Surplus is most often viewed as social surplus:

$$S = \pi + CS. \tag{3.5}$$

Sometimes only CS is maximized. Sometimes factor rents, managerial utility (or effort), taxes, and subsidies are also included in surplus. For specific types of tariffs, under both monopoly and competition, one strand of the literature concentrates solely on profit-maximizing prices. These analyses are nevertheless relevant for our study, either because profit maximization may be a relevant objective for us to consider or because in many cases profit-maximizing tariffs differ from welfare-maximizing tariffs by only a multiplicative factor.

In the last few years fairness and equity issues have received increasing attention. Fairness and equity can sometimes be expressed in the surplus concept by attaching differential importance to groups of economic agents affected by the tariff changes.

We shall focus primarily on the efficiency goal. A unifying approach can combine several objectives by applying weights to the various components of social surplus. Individual consumers are weighted implicitly by reciprocals of their marginal utilities of income in measures, such as consumer surplus, that accept the existing distribution of income. Some attention has been devoted to modifying these weights to achieve distributional objectives through pricing (Feldstein 1972a, 1972b), and we shall note efforts to apply welfare weights to the utility functions of various economic agents. Depending on those weights, consumer surplus maximization and profit maximization may then appear as polar cases of the weighting scheme. In particular, we may assume that the owners of the firm are not among its consumers. Then, maximizing a linear combination of profits and consumer surpluses (perhaps of various groups) with nonnegative welfare weights simultaneously achieves Pareto efficiency among these groups and the firm's owners. In this sense, weighted maximization in this form is convenient and also general.

An extreme case of weighting is implied by the Rawlsian *maximin principle* (Rawls, 1971) according to which the welfare of the most disadvantaged individual should be maximized. This means giving all the welfare weight to that individual. Since our objective function is in terms of aggregate surpluses rather than in terms of individual utilities, an application of the Rawlsian approach implies the leap of faith that the least advantaged individuals can, for instance, be identified as the consumers with the smallest purchase quantities, rather than being the ones with the least preferences for service.[7]

Weighting also has been used to take care of the shadow value of public funds, λ_g. This parameter summarizes the value of funds in government hands as opposed to their use to provide consumption. In most cases, $\lambda_g \neq 1$ is likely to obtain, because generating funds for governments is costly to society. Since raising taxes imposes an excess burden, any subsidies required (or profits provided) by a public enterprise would have the value λ_g (which is 1 + the excess burden) on pure efficiency grounds.[8] In Chapter 4 we will use λ_g as a justification for a budget constraint imposed on the supplier.

Yet a third justification for weighting, besides efficiency and income distribution, lies in the political economy of price setting. Telecommunications tariffs are often the result of political processes that can involve regulators, the judiciary, and elected politicians. The "objective function" expressed in this interaction can be mapped via welfare weights. These weights can be interpreted as implicit in the tariffs that are approved in the political process, or they can be set normatively, based on information about preferences of politicians or regulators. Methods for the calculation of implicit welfare weights have been devised by McFadden (1975) and Ross (1984).

[7]See in particular Section 5.6.5 on optional two-part tariffs.
[8]The "excess burden" was first estimated by Harberger (1964) and Browning (1976). For a discussion see Jones, Tandon, and Vogelsang (1990). The unifying approach is treated in Vogelsang (1990a). Shadow multipliers such as λ_g can take care of some of the general equilibrium implications of partial equilibrium analysis.

3.2.3   Fairness and competition

The unified weighting approach is able to deal with some of the main distributional and equity objectives of tariff setting. However, it is insufficient to deal with other important notions of fairness. These notions can be viewed as constraints in tariff space, which reduce the set of feasible tariffs from which to choose. Examples are the following:

1 A demand-related notion of fairness is that of an *economic right* to a particular service such as residential telephones (Zajac, 1982, 1985). This implies access to the service for everybody (universal service). Thus, the right normally takes the form of a constraint. To specify such a constraint requires definition of the scope of the right in terms of services (e.g., access to a telephone line for every household) and identification of the sources of finance (e.g., tax revenues or cross subsidies).

2 A presumption of fairness that rests on present arrangements may be called *status quo fairness* (related to Owen and Braeutigam, 1978; see also Baumol, 1986). The status quo can refer to producers and/or to consumers. Referring to both groups, status quo fairness would only allow tariff changes that are Pareto improvements. Again, fairness takes the form of a constraint, in this case a constraint on existing utility levels.

3 An element of fairness follows *cost causality* (inclusive of subsidy-free, anonymously equitable, and other fairness concepts).[9] Fully distributed-cost pricing is in this sense perceived as fair in that it prevents nonusers of a service from paying for it. As mentioned above, cost causality can be expressed in axioms leading to cost-axiomatic pricing. Cost causality is important not only because cross subsidization may be unfair but also because cross subsidization invites inefficient entry or bypass of the subsidizing services (cream-skimming). This third type of fairness generates constraints on prices with respect to cost concepts.

4 An aspect of fairness arises in the overall service *process* and the *opportunity* it affords. Free entry into a market is perceived as fair,

---

[9] These and other technical concepts will be defined in Chapter 6.

for example, in terms of offering equal opportunity to all potential entrants.[10] The resulting criteria for desirable tariffs strongly
overlap with those of the previous notion of fairness (sustainable,
supportable, second-best core, etc.). This is understandable since a
necessary condition for entry (including entry by bypass of incumbent suppliers by consumers themselves) is the ability to supply a
subset of consumers at costs that are below their outlay under the
incumbent's tariffs.[11]

Clearly, the four notions of fairness are not all mutually compatible.
The question then arises how tradeoffs should be struck and how fairness
should be balanced against (weighted) surplus maximization. We saw
that fairness usually leads to constraints. Incompatibility between the
different fairness concepts means that there is no feasible solution obey-
ing all fairness constraints. This issue becomes prominent in Chapter 6.
The tradeoff between fairness and surplus maximization comes out as
the difference between the unconstrained and the constrained surplus
maxima discussed in Chapters 4 and 5. As will be pointed out in Section 6.2 on cost-axiomatic pricing, the constraints may leave no room
for maximization because they lead to a unique feasible outcome.

3.3   Overview of tariff types

In the following three theoretical chapters we describe and analyze major
contributions made primarily in the last ten years, classified by types of
tariff.

Chapter 4 begins with the benchmark for all public utility tariffs,
marginal-cost prices, and exemplifies these under the heading of *peak-
load pricing*. Under the appropriate conditions marginal-cost prices are
welfare maximizing; they are firmly based on cost; and they, and the
rationale behind them, are easily understood. However, the simplicity of marginal-cost prices hides major conceptual difficulties, measurement problems, and potential inefficiencies. Potential inefficencies of

---

[10] Compatibility with the antitrust laws may be a requirement under this notion of
fairness.
[11] The fourth notion of fairness brings in competition as an objective in itself. Most
economists treat competition as a *tool* for achieving objectives, such as efficiency and
distributional equity, rather than as an *end* in itself. However, some policy-makers
clearly see competition as an objective in its own right.

marginal-cost pricing have mainly to do with the fact that marginal-cost prices, due to longrun excess capacity or due to economies of scale and scope, rarely cover total cost of service.

For reasons explained in Chapter 4, most of the literature goes on to assume that the firm's pricing must cover its total costs without external subsidies. We apply this postulate in the following section on *Ramsey prices*. The basic idea here is to find a set of prices for the firm's outputs such that a budgetary target is met with the smallest amount of overall distortion in consumers' quantity choices among the firm's products. In this case we therefore use a multiproduct approach to tariff setting by the regulated telecommunications carrier. Minimizing distortions may lead to prices with the property that different consumer groups buy the same quality and type of service at different prices, or that different services carry different relative markups of prices over marginal costs. In line with Phlips (1983) we define both these cases as "price discrimination", in spite of the pejorative connotation of this word, because they meet the terms of the definition. In these cases, however, price discrimination serves a social purpose. The relative markup of price over marginal cost:

$$L = \frac{p - MC}{p} \tag{3.6}$$

is known as the Lerner index. At the margin, L is a convenient measure of the inefficiency (and to some extent the exploitative nature) of a tariff. We also find this markup to be a highly convenient and intuitive way of characterizing various types of tariffs and in making them comparable, particularly if demands between services are *in*dependent of each other. If demands are *inter*dependent it may instead be more convenient to use the marginal effect of a price change on social surplus, $(p - MC)\partial q/\partial p$.

Subsequent sections of Chapter 4 extend the Ramsey pricing approach to problems of oligopolistic interaction, consumption externalities, customer group discrimination, and intertemporal pricing.

In general, Ramsey prices differ from marginal-cost prices. At the margin, one could increase social surplus (or Pareto-improve welfare) by selling additional units closer to, or at, marginal cost. This approach–selling different units of the same service to the same consumer at different prices–has been termed *nonlinear* (or *nonuniform*) *pricing*; it is the subject of Chapter 5. Nonlinear prices are widely applied in telecommunications. Their main advantage is that they can improve on Ramsey

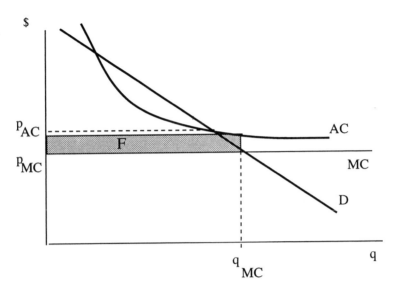

Figure 3.1
Average-cost and marginal-cost pricing

prices, yet allow the firm to raise enough revenue to cover costs. Their
main disadvantage is that their derivation requires more detailed information about individual demands.

The simplest types of nonlinear prices are *two-part tariffs*, consisting
simply of a (fixed) entry fee E and a (marginal) price p. The fixed fee
may exclude some customers from purchasing the service at all and can
lead to major inefficiency or unfairness even if the marginal units of
the service are sold at marginal cost. However, if everyone continues to
purchase the commodity in spite of the fixed fee imposed under a two-
part tariff, then the marginal-cost price can be charged and the firm's
budget can be covered simultaneously. Such first-best two-part tariffs
are called *Coase tariffs*.[12] In Figure 3.1 p_{AC} indicates the lowest price
that would allow the firm to break even, while at the marginal-cost price
p_{MC} the firm would incur a deficit of the size of the shaded rectangle F.
The Coase tariff would raise this deficit by a fixed fee $E = F/N$, where
N is the number of customers. The fixed fee of a Coase tariff acts as a

[12]Their virtue was shown by Coase (1946).

nondistortive head tax.[13]

Since Coase tariffs are infeasible for most services,[14] even two-part tariffs will contain distortions. We may be able to reduce the distortions, through various refinements, by increasing the nonlinearity of the tariffs, the extreme being a *smooth nonlinear tariff* that changes continuously with the quantity purchased. Smoothness may actually make such a tariff analytically and conceptually more tractable than the *multipart tariffs* that lie between the two-part and the smooth tariff. Multipart tariffs are hard to handle because the number of parts and their ranges have to be determined simultaneously. These are difficult problems, unless the parts of the tariff are naturally linked to specific consumer groups. In sequencing our exposition, we could alternatively have proceeded from two-part tariffs via multipart tariffs to smooth tariffs. Because of these difficulties, however, in Chapter 5 we will treat smooth tariffs immediately following two-part tariffs and then take up multipart tariffs. In order to keep the exposition tractable we do all this for the single-product case first. The multiproduct case is much less developed, and we explore it, less systematically, at the end of Chapter 5.

This overview of types of tariffs has started with marginal-cost pricing. In the last theory chapter, Chapter 6, we return to this beginning by linking pricing directly to cost. The main emphasis of the two other theoretical chapters is a link between cost and demand that can be used to maximize efficiency defined as some weighted sum of consumer and producer welfare. In Chapter 6 the emphasis is on compatibility of prices and cost rather than the maximization of such an objective function. The necessity for such compatibility is justified by issues of fairness and competition. We review traditional notions of *fully distributed-cost pricing* after examining the modern concepts of *cost-axiomatic, subsidy-free, sustainable*, and other game-theoretic approaches to cost-based pricing.

---

[13] In fact, from an allocative efficiency point of view, the fixed fee should be raised further to contribute to general tax revenues. However, from an income-distributional point of view this would be a regressive policy.

[14] Even in wealthy countries telephone penetration has yet to reach 100 percent.

4

Linear tariffs

4.1 Marginal-cost prices

4.1.1 Feasibility problems

The starting point and benchmark for all public utility tariffs in the literature have been *marginal-cost prices*: $p = MC$. Under the appropriate conditions marginal-cost prices are welfare maximizing; they are firmly based on cost; and they, and the rationale behind them, are easily understood. However, the apparent simplicity of marginal-cost prices hides measurement problems, potential inefficiencies, and major conceptual difficulties.

Measurement problems. Firms do not directly observe the cost changes attributable to marginal changes in output. Rather, firms observe cost changes over time. Their bookkeeping data are not designed to relate cost changes to output changes. Econometric techniques have been designed to do that. However, due to limitations in the number of observations and changes in cost functions over time, econometric results are imprecise and they lag behind technological and economic developments. Cost measurement on an engineering level overcomes some of these problems but is itself costly and time consuming (Mitchell, 1990).

Inefficiencies. Marginal-cost prices rarely cover the total cost of service, perhaps due to longrun excess capacity or due to economies of scale and scope. This failure to cover total cost has already been illustrated in Figure 3.1 above. Losses arising from marginal-cost pricing have to be covered from some other source. If this is done internally by the firm it requires some other source of finance, presumably through some deviation from marginal-cost pricing for a different service. Alternatively, if the firm is externally subsidized, taxes have to be raised or other government expenditure will have to be forgone. As mentioned in Section 3.2.2, the consequences of outside subsidies are some distortions or redistributions elsewhere in the economy, reflected in the government shadow multiplier λ_g. If such distortions for subsidies are deemed acceptable outside the firm they should also be acceptable for the firm's pricing, thus leading to deviations from marginal-cost pricing. In fact, in order to minimize overall distortions the marginal distortions should be equalized across economic activities both within and outside of the firm. However, in order to avoid the issue of external subsidies we will hereafter assume that the firm's pricing must cover its total costs without external subsidies.

Conceptual difficulties. Marginal-cost prices must be defined with respect to the time frame of output expansion. Should marginal cost be seen with reference to an immediate expansion of output using existing capacity (shortrun marginal cost), or with respect to a planned permanent expansion (longrun marginal cost), or with respect to some intermediate case? The first case clearly is well-defined, and causality can be clearly established. The problem is that, in telecommunications, shortrun marginal cost at less than full capacity utilization is close to zero. At the capacity limit it quickly moves to infinity. Of course, an infinite price is not achievable; rather, in times of capacity shortage, the price cannot exceed the one that rations demand at the capacity limit. Thus, pricing at shortrun marginal cost may lead to wildly fluctuating prices. In addition, at times of excess capacity, such prices may not even come close to covering capacity cost.

4.1.2 Peak-load pricing

When demand is anticipated correctly, marginal-cost pricing may cover total cost. In the classic formulation of peak-load pricing, demand is uniform in each of T periods of time, and the quantity demanded depends on the prices charged in each period:

$$Q_t = D_t(p_1, \ldots, p_T), \qquad t = 1, \ldots, T. \tag{4.1}$$

The T periods are assumed to form a cycle that is repeated indefinitely. There is a constant variable cost, b, and constant rental rate, β, per unit of capacity. Total costs of producing output Q_t in all periods is:

$$C = b \sum_t Q_t + \beta \max_t Q_t. \tag{4.2}$$

Fixed-proportion production is constrained by the quantity of variable resource, v, and the maximum productive capacity, K:

$$Q_t = \min_t(v_t, K), \qquad t = 1, \dots, T. \tag{4.3}$$

The welfare-maximizing prices are based on marginal costs. In the off-peak periods, when demand is less than capacity, price is equal to shortrun marginal cost:

$$p_t = b \qquad \text{for } t \text{ such that } Q_t < K . \tag{4.4}$$

In the peak period, demand is equal to capacity and price is equal to longrun marginal cost – variable cost plus the per-unit cost of expanding capacity:

$$p_t = b + \beta \qquad \text{for the } t \text{ for which } Q_t = K . \tag{4.5}$$

Furthermore, capacity is constructed to satisfy this demand:

$$K = \max_t D_t. \tag{4.6}$$

When capacity costs are large in relation to variable costs, as they are in telecommunications, the period having the maximum demand under a peak-load tariff may change from the period in which the maximum occurs under a uniform price. In such a case, the "shifting-peak" makes the above pricing rule inconsistent. The solution is to set price equal to variable cost when demand is less than capacity. In peak periods higher prices are set, such that in each peak period the demand is equal to capacity and the combined revenues from the peak periods cover longrun marginal costs:

$$\sum_t p_t = nb + \beta \qquad \text{for } t \text{ such that } Q_t = K, \tag{4.7}$$

where n is the number of periods for which $Q_t = K$.

The classical model has been extended to neoclassical, variable-proportions technology (Panzar, 1976) and to encompass production by a set of fixed-proportion technologies (Crew and Kleindorfer, 1979). Nevertheless, the empirically relevant assumption for telecommunications appears to be a single, fixed-proportions technology, which may change with the scale of output but not with the frequency distribution of hours of high demand (see Section 2.1.2).

4.1.3 Uncertainty and rationing

When demand (or reliability of supply) is uncertain, there is some probability of demand exceeding supply. The new issue in peak-load pricing derives from the introduction of uncertainty and the resulting possibilities of excess capacity and nonprice rationing. These issues are treated by Kay (1979), Sherman and Visscher (1982), Park and Mitchell (1987), and Sherman (1989).

Telephone demand distributions are very peaked even when different prices are charged during broadly defined day, evening, and night/weekend periods. To serve the absolute peak demand that occurs only for a few minutes, perhaps several times a year, would require additional capacity that would be almost always idle. Capacity engineering rules typically specify a blockage probability during "design busy hours" (.01 is commonly used for trunk lines). When excess demand does threaten, telephone systems customarily use various forms of quantity rationing to reduce effective demand to available capacity. Call attempts that arrive at the network switch are rejected with a circuits-busy tone or announcement.

If calls are placed randomly, then simply rejecting calls that are attempted when capacity is fully used amounts to random rationing. When a consumer dials a call she has no real-time indication that the network is congested, so that random arrival can be assumed for the first rationed call attempt a subscriber makes. Thereafter, redialing behavior may affect the distribution of willingness-to-pay of the subsequently rationed calls. Persistent redialing increases the probability of a successful call, but requires the subscriber to expend more time. To this extent calls that succeed after redialing are likely to be more valuable than the average rationed call. Subscribers with high time valuation will be more likely to purchase automatic dialing devices, but otherwise will be less prone to redial.

Park and Mitchell (1987) assume that quantity rationing is random and compare its welfare effects with pure price rationing. In practice, demand is not uniform within a pricing period. Feasible tariffs must be limited to only a few prices per day, with weekday and weekend regularities, so a period with a single price may include a range of demand levels. Therefore, even though demand is equal to capacity during some hours of a pricing period, there will be excess capacity in other hours.

As a result, some of the efficiency of marginal-cost pricing is foregone when peak-load pricing must satisfy feasibility constraints and positive prices deter additional calling in hours with excess capacity. For local calls Park and Mitchell find that quantity rationing (a fixed monthly rate and a zero price per call and no call measurement costs) may be at least as efficient as feasible time-of-day rates.

4.1.4   Priority rationing

Two improvements on the random nonprice rationing problem have been offered in the literature. The first one is to assume that nonprice rationing occurs in accordance with willingness-to-pay by consumers. This can be done by relating tariffs to the order in which customers will be served in the case of congestion (priority pricing as developed by Wilson, 1989a; Chao and Wilson, 1987; and Viswanathan and Tse, 1989). This approach differentiates the product by pricing quality of service (the probability of obtaining service or not being interrupted). The supply technology must be capable of serving customers' loads in a pre-determined order, and treatment of nonprice rationing has so far been developed in terms of applications to electricity services.

4.1.5   Real-time pricing

The second solution is to avoid nonprice rationing altogether by increasing and decreasing prices instantaneously, as congestion or slack occurs in the network. Real-time pricing was first proposed by Vickrey (1971).[1] In contrast to electricity supply, the prospects for such spot pricing in telecommunications appear to be mixed. The very nature of a telecommunications network – two-way communication – and the ease with which information-processing features can be incorporated into subscribers' terminal equipment should allow pricing and service quality information to be made available to consumers. On the other hand, the capacity requirements of a telephone network are inherently more diverse than those of electricity supply; additional capacity in a particular link or switch is useful to only a limited number of demanders, whereas an increase in electricity generating capacity can potentially supply any user attached to the network (Mitchell, 1983).

---

[1] Bohn et al. (1984) applied spot-pricing to electricity, and Pousette (1982) suggested its use in telecommunications. Such rates have also been proposed for computer networks (Gale and Koenker, undated; *Science*, 1989).

In addition, most economists agree that this type of (spot) pricing and the accompanying "correct" investment decisions are not currently feasible for solving problems of irregular demand fluctuations faced by a regulated public utility. Rather, under regulation tariffs will have to be steady and therefore based on anticipated longrun patterns of demand. This longrun nature of pricing decisions is the reason why we can use a static approach to pricing in most of this chapter. This does not mean that we will consistently apply the extreme concept of costs as longrun adjustments on an envelope cost function. Rather, our timeframe for the costs relevant for pricing decisions depends on the decisions at hand (Mitchell, 1990). As discussed in Chapter 2, sunk costs play a big role in telecommunications. Costs can be sunk for forty to sixty years or longer. If such costs result in excess capacity, then tariffs may have to be designed taking this excess capacity into consideration. This could, in particular, mean that capacity costs may not be recoverable through marginal-cost prices based on the time horizon with excess capacity. This may, for example, be a problem for the US fiber-optic trunk network for the foreseeable future.

Real-time pricing might develop to allocate "bandwidth on demand" in future ISDN and broadband networks. In addition, sophisticated price discrimination may be necessary to achieve wide penetration, given the high capital costs of establishing a broadband overlay network, combined with the high substitutability of data, video, and voice traffic that will defeat attempts to classify services by type of use.

4.2 Ramsey pricing (demand-oriented tariffs)

Linear tariffs are those in which the total consumer outlay is proportional to the quantity purchased. Optimal linear tariffs can exhibit some type of price discrimination across services and/or across consumers. Price discrimination by firms with market power is often viewed as unfair. From the point of view of social surplus, however, the judgment on price discrimination may be quite different. In the case of horizontal and perfect price discrimination by profit-maximizing firms, social surplus unambiguously increases.[2] In the case of third-degree price discrimina-

---

[2]This is in the absence of transaction costs caused by discriminating. Horizontal discrimination occurs by separately pricing the different units purchased by the same customer — what we call nonlinear pricing.

tion the judgment for profit-maximizing monopolists is mixed.[3] Roughly speaking, welfare goes up (down) if total output is increased (decreased).

We want to focus on the case of third-degree price discrimination, for a weighted surplus-maximizing monopolist. The objective of the regulator is to maximize $W = \pi + (1 - \gamma)CS = \gamma\pi + (1 - \gamma)S$ for a multiproduct monopolist.[4] Thus, γ can be viewed as the weight attached to profit, while the weight attached to *social* surplus is $(1 - \gamma)$. Alternatively, profit receives weight 1 and *consumer* surplus receives weight $(1 - \gamma)$. For the time being we interpret these weights as the preferences of the regulator or social planner. Assuming that the integrability conditions hold we can write the maximization problem as: Find $p = (p_1, \ldots, p_m)$ such that:

$$p = \arg\max \left\{ \left[\sum_{i=1}^{m} p_i q_i - C(\sum_{i=1}^{m} q_i) \right] + (1 - \gamma) \oint_p^{\infty} q(p)\,dp \right\}. \qquad (4.8)$$

Here consumer surplus is a line integral. Its gradient with respect to p is $\nabla V(p) = -q$, where q is the output vector. Now, we can write the first-order conditions of this problem in compact form as:

$$\left(p - \frac{\partial C}{\partial q}\right)\frac{\partial q}{\partial p} = -\gamma q. \qquad (4.9)$$

Here $\partial C/\partial q$ is the *vector* of marginal costs and $\partial q/\partial p$ is the *matrix* of partial demand derivatives. Equation (4.9) says that prices should be set such that the marginal increase in social surplus from further price reductions is proportional to the quantities demanded at those prices. The proportionality factor is the weight given to profits. If cross derivatives are zero we can write (4.9) as a set of m independent equations of the form:

$$\left(p_i - \frac{\partial C}{\partial q_i}\right)\frac{\partial q_i}{\partial p_i} = -\gamma q_i, \qquad i = 1, \ldots, m. \qquad (4.10)$$

Dividing both sides of (4.10) by p_i and $\partial p_i/\partial q_i$ gives us the familiar formula:

$$\frac{p_i - \frac{\partial C}{\partial q_i}}{p_i} = -\frac{\gamma}{\epsilon_i} \qquad \text{for all } i, \qquad (4.11)$$

---

[3]Third-degree price discrimination occurs by segmenting the market into different submarkets – what we call customer-class pricing.

[4]This is Schmalensee's (1981) weighted welfare function.

where $\epsilon_i = (\partial p_i/\partial q_i)(q_i/p_i)$ is the demand elasticity for q_i.

Since the weight γ is assumed to be the same for all i, this equation establishes the *inverse elasticity rule*:

> All relative deviations of prices from marginal costs should be inversely proportional to the corresponding demand elasticities.

The crucial parameter γ is known as the *Ramsey number*. It determines the firm's general price *level* (while demand elasticities determine the price *structure*) needed to meet the budget constraint.

Weighting enterprise profits may be seen as a substitute for the budget constraint usually imposed under the Ramsey pricing approach. A budget constraint of the form $\pi = B$ leads to a maximization problem of the form:

$$\max \mathcal{L} = \pi + V(p) + \lambda(\pi - B). \tag{4.12}$$

In our formulation it turns out that at the optimum $\lambda/(1 + \lambda) = \gamma$. Thus, the weighting approach and the approach using budget constraints are formally similar. Instead of distributional weighting by γ we could also have weighted profits by λ_g, the shadow value of public funds, and weighted consumer surplus by 1. This would be appropriate if the regulated telecommunications carrier is a public enterprise. The budget constraint then corresponds to a particular value of λ_g, and λ_g turns out to be related in a simple way to the Ramsey number. The implicit λ_g can therefore be used to evaluate whether from the point of view of optimal taxation the budget constraint for the Ramsey problem has been set at an appropriate level. Usually, in the literature on public-utility pricing a balanced-budget constraint $B = 0$ is set in order to assure financial independence of the enterprise with no more than competitive returns for investors.

The intuition behind the inverse elasticity rule in case of a budget constraint $\pi = B$ and independent demands is brought out in Figure 4.1. This figure uses the property of Ramsey prices that quantities deviate *approximately proportionately* from the quantities demanded under marginal-cost prices.[5] In Figure 4.1 two services with the same marginal

[5]The quantity deviations are only approximately proportional because the elasticities provide only local information about quantity changes, which themselves are discrete.

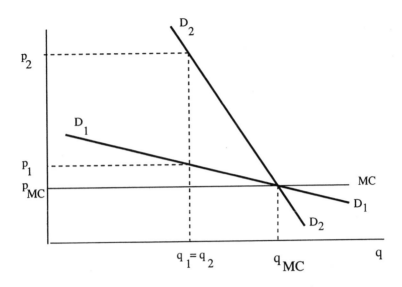

Figure 4.1
Ramsey pricing

costs and the same demand at marginal-cost prices are superimposed.
However, demand for service 1 is more elastic than demand for service 2. If we now want to raise a certain amount of net revenues through
profits we have to trade off profit increases against reductions in social
surplus. These tradeoffs are as follows: For output 1 a reduction in
quantity from q_{MC} to q_1 leads to a reduction in social surplus by the
small right-angled triangle and an increase in profit by $(p_1 - p_{MC})q_1$.
For output 2 the same quantity reduction leads to the surplus reduction
represented by the larger right-angled triangle, while profits increase by
$(p_2 - p_{MC})q_2$. Thus, the larger social surplus reduction in the less elastic
market is compensated for by a larger profit increase that can be used
to satisfy the budget constraint. From the size of the two triangles it is
clear that the increase in profit per unit of reduction in social surplus is
equal for the two services at equal outputs.

If demands are interdependent, then cross derivatives do not vanish.
In this case these cross effects appear in the form of nonzero off-diagonal
terms in the matrix $\partial q / \partial p$. Then (4.9) takes the form:

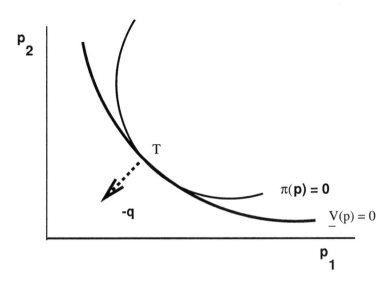

Figure 4.2
Geometry of the Ramsey optimum

$$\sum_{j=1}^{m} \left(p_j - \frac{\partial C}{\partial q_j}\right) \frac{\partial q_j}{\partial p_i} = -\gamma q_i, \qquad i = 1, \ldots, m. \tag{4.13}$$

For the case of a decreasing-cost industry there is a simple graph provided by Figure 4.2 that illustrates the geometry of the Ramsey optimum (Vogelsang and Finsinger, 1979). Due to the property of decreasing cost, the zero-profit constraint will be binding at the Ramsey optimum. This has two implications: First, we can replace the relevant welfare indicator, constrained social surplus $W(p)$, with consumer surplus $V(p)$. Second, the optimum has to lie on the zero-profit contour $\pi(p) = 0$. Instead of the familiar illustration of profits and welfare in quantity space, Figure 4.2 is in price space. The zero-profit contour could also have other shapes than the one indicated in the figure, but it will be downward sloping in the relevant part of its range. $V(p) = \underline{V}$ indicates a social indifference curve in price space. It is convex if the axioms of revealed preference hold and if $V(p)$ is consumer surplus with no income effects. Contrary to social indifference curves in quantity space, consumer welfare in price space increases in the direction of the origin. Now, the indicated point of tangency T between the social indifference

curve and the zero-profit contour is the Ramsey optimum. It is the point
with the highest level of consumer surplus compatible with nonnegative
profit. We also know that differentiating consumer surplus with respect
to prices yields $\nabla V(p) = \partial V(p)/\partial p = -q$. Together with (4.12) this
implies that at the Ramsey optimum the demand vector is perpendicular
to the social indifference curve and to the zero-profit contour.

Another way of improving the intuition behind (4.13) is to follow
Rohlfs (1979) and define "superelasticities" Υ_i as:

$$\Upsilon_i = \sum_{j=1}^{m} r_{ji} e_{ji}, \tag{4.14}$$

where $r_{ji} = p_j q_j / p_i q_i$ and $e_{ji} = 1/\epsilon_{ji}$, with ϵ_{ji} the elasticity of the
demand for i with respect to the price of j. Then an equation similar to
(4.11) is obtained for the case of interdependent demands:

$$\frac{p_i - \frac{\partial C}{\partial q_i}}{p_i} = -\frac{\gamma}{\Upsilon_i} \qquad \text{for all } i. \tag{4.15}$$

Note that, due to demand complementarities between the firm's outputs,
superelasticities can be positive for some i, so it is possible that p_i can
be less than MC_i for some i.

Ramsey prices are hard to implement politically if they imply a price
structure that is quite different from the status quo. For example, suppose that initially prices deviate proportionally from marginal cost. Under Ramsey pricing, consumers with inelastic demands would be called
on to pay higher prices while consumers with elastic demands would pay
lower prices. Apart from this change, which violates status quo fairness,
Ramsey prices could be viewed as unfair because they ask consumers
to contribute different amounts above the direct costs that they cause.
However, as can be seen from Figure 4.1, the consumers with the inelastic demand, in spite of the price difference, enjoy a comparatively higher
amount of consumer surplus than the consumers with elastic demand.

4.3   Ramsey pricing with competition

In the last ten years important contributions to Ramsey pricing were
made by Braeutigam (1979 and 1984). Braeutigam's 1979 paper
deals with Ramsey pricing for a regulated firm operating under scale
economies and facing intermodal competition from a competitive fringe

of small firms. He differentiates two major cases, *Totally Regulated Second Best* (TRSB) and *Partially Regulated Second Best* (PRSB). Under TRSB the regulator can set prices and entry restrictions for both the competitive fringe and the regulated firm, while under PRSB the competitive fringe firms remain unregulated. In both cases the regulated firm faces a balanced-budget constraint. The main conclusions are that, under TRSB, entry restrictions and price regulation for the competitive fringe will be such that Ramsey numbers are the same for all modes, including the one with economies of scale. The information requirements for this solution are enormous.

Under PRSB (treated simultaneously by Sherman and George, 1979) the regulator will typically apply Ramsey pricing by ignoring the competitive fringe. While important, these results may be more appropriate for sectors other than telecommunications, because until now competition in this sector is not materially affected by a competitive fringe.[6]

4.3.1 Homogeneous services

In natural oligopoly (even in the single-product case) there is room for *second-best pricing policies* just as in the natural monopoly case. The reason is that economies of scale can prevail at the outputs produced by some of the oligopolists in equilibrium.[7] If the government has full control over all firms in the natural oligopoly industry and can set an overall budget constraint, then it can treat these firms as if they were different plants of a single enterprise. This leads to what Baumol, Panzar, and Willig (1982) have called a *Viable Industry Ramsey Optimum* (VIRO). Since this approach treats the different regulated firms like parts of one firm, it may not be feasible under natural oligopoly. If it is, this would provide for a nice possibility to avoid diseconomies of scale that eventually arise and we would be back in the world of (weak) natural monopoly.

In practice, to avoid diseconomies of scale may require the financial independence of the different regulated firms. In this case, separate budget constraints would have to be imposed on the individual firms.

---

[6]The presence of small resellers and arbitrageurs in telecommunications markets might contradict this statement. Such firms limit the amount of feasible price discrimination and therefore do have a competitive impact. We believe, however, that this impact is largely limited to the nonlinear prices treated in Chapter 5.

[7]Natural oligopoly is defined by the property that the welfare-maximizing number of firms is small, but larger than 1. This means that there are some diseconomies of scale (or scope) that prevent a monopoly from being cost-minimizing. For further explanation see Vogelsang (1990a), upon which the following paragraphs are based.

To illustrate, let the government regulator maximize welfare over the output of two firms operating in the same market under the constraint that both firms at least break even. Prices and outputs solving this problem are called a *Viable Firm Ramsey Optimum* (VFRO) in the Baumol–Panzar–Willig terminology. Thus:

$$\max \mathcal{L} = \int_0^Q p(Q)\,dQ - C(q_1) - C(q_2)$$
$$+ \lambda_1 \left[p(Q)q_1 - C_1(q_1) \right] + \lambda_2 \left[p(Q)q_2 - C_1(q_2) \right]. \quad (4.16)$$

Here $Q = q_1 + q_2$ is total market output. First order conditions are:

$$\frac{\partial \mathcal{L}}{\partial q_i} = (1 + \lambda_i)\left(p - \frac{\partial C_i}{\partial q_i} \right) + \frac{\partial p}{\partial Q} \sum_j \lambda_j q_j$$

$$= 0 \qquad \text{for } i, j = 1, 2. \quad (4.17)$$

In case of two nonbinding constraints $(\lambda_1 = \lambda_2 = 0)$, equations (4.17) imply marginal-cost pricing. Otherwise:

$$\frac{p - \frac{\partial C_i}{\partial q_i}}{p} = -\sum_j \frac{s_j \lambda_j}{(1 + \lambda_i)\epsilon}, \quad (4.18)$$

where s_j is the market share of firm j. This is exactly analogous to Ramsey pricing for the single firm case, except that the markup over marginal cost (in case of a binding constraint) is multiplied by the weighted sum of the firms' market shares and there may be a different Lagrangian multiplier λ_i for each firm i. This result easily extends to the multimarket multifirm case. It corresponds to the *Autarkic Ramsey Optimum* in Baumol, Panzar, and Willig (1982).

Equation (4.17) implies that pricing above marginal cost by firm i will help relax the binding constraint for firm j. If only one of the two constraints in (4.16) is binding, the other firm may still have to price above marginal cost. Also note that total cost of producing the market output is not necessarily minimized because markups, and therefore marginal costs, of the two firms may differ.

4.3.2 Heterogeneous services

For telecommunications, Braeutigam's 1984 paper is more relevant than his 1979 paper, because the 1984 paper treats imperfectly substitutable services offered under economies of scale. Each service is now assumed to be produced by only one firm. Demands for the different services produced by the same firm are assumed to be independent of each other, while the demands for services produced by different firms may either be independent, or they may be weak gross substitutes. For this constellation of heterogeneous oligopolies Braeutigam looks at the cases of VIRO and VFRO. Both are described as multifirm Ramsey problems, with a joint budget constraint (side payments allowed) under VIRO and a separate budget constraint for each firm under VFRO.

Under the VIRO solution the joint budget constraint will be binding, and there will generally be revenue transfers between firms. In fact, as mentioned above, VIRO may be interpreted as the Ramsey solution for a multiplant firm.

In contrast, the VFRO is quite complicated. Due to the large number of budget constraints (equal to the number of firms) there can be corner solutions in which certain firms do not produce. However, assume that all firms produce at the optimum. Then (due to economies of scale) the budget constraint will be binding for at least one firm, but not necessarily for all firms. For firms with binding budget constraints all prices will exceed marginal cost. And for firms with a nonbinding budget constraint there may be cases where price must equal marginal cost. For such firms prices will exceed marginal cost only for those services that are competing with services offered by a firm with a binding budget constraint.

Writing down the exact pricing rules requires some notation. We let first indices denote firms and second indices denote services. Superscripts identify variables as belonging to firms and services, and subscripts indicate partial derivatives. For services that are independent of each other we get the familiar inverse elasticity rule:

$$\frac{p^{is} - C^i_{is}}{p^{is}} = -\frac{\lambda^i}{(1+\lambda^i)\epsilon^{is}}, \tag{4.19}$$

where ϵ^{is} is the own elasticity of demand by firm i for for service s.

The more intriguing rule appears for services with demand interdependence. It is:

$$\frac{p^{ij} - C^i_{ij}}{p^{ij}} = -\frac{\lambda^i}{(1+\lambda^i)\epsilon^{ij}} - \sum_{k \neq i} \frac{\lambda^k e^{kj}_{ij}}{(1+\lambda^k)}, \tag{4.20}$$

where e_{ij}^{kj} is the cross-quantity elasticity of demand of firm k's price for service j with respect to the quantity of firm i's service j. Since the last term in (4.20) is positive, (4.19) and (4.20) imply that the ratio of markups between noncompeting and competing services is larger than the inverse ratio of the corresponding demand elasticities. If own elasticities are the same in all markets, then the optimal markups are lower for those services of firm i which have no substitutes produced by a firm k.

4.3.3 Competition between a regulated and an unregulated firm

Competition among regulated telecommunications carriers is quite rare. More interesting is the case where government refrains from regulating price and entry and instead uses the dominant regulated firm as its only instrument to maximize welfare in an oligopolistic market otherwise populated by unregulated profit-maximizing firms. To simplify matters we assume a homogeneous duopoly with one regulated (welfaremaximizing) and one unregulated (profit-maximizing) firm. Both firms face the same cost function $C(q_i)$, $i = 1,2$, with subscript 1 for the regulated and subscript 2 for the unregulated firm. The inverse demand function is $p(Q)$ with $Q = q_1 + q_2$. The unregulated firm therefore will maximize $\pi_2(q_2) = p(Q)q_2 - C(q_2)$.

Now assume that the regulator wants to maximize unweighted social surplus for the regulated firm. In doing so it has to accept profit maximization by the unregulated firm (PRSB). This can be modelled in several ways. One way is to assume that both firms behave as in any other duopoly situation, except that their objectives differ. In this case it is most convenient to use a simple conjectural variations model. Welfare is:

$$W(Q) = V(p(Q)) + \pi_1(q_1, q_2) + \pi_2(q_1, q_2). \tag{4.21}$$

The regulator would maximize (4.21) with respect to q_1, the output of the regulated firm.

In equilibrium, first-order conditions for both firms would have to hold simultaneously. The first-order condition for profit-maximizing firm 2 is:

$$\frac{p - \frac{\partial C}{\partial q_2}}{p} = -\frac{k_2 s_2}{\epsilon}, \tag{4.22}$$

where ϵ is the market demand elasticity and $k_2 = dQ/dq_2$ is the conjectural variation that firm 2 faces. This means that k_2 includes the expected reaction of firm 1 to firm 2's output increase.

At the same time the first-order condition for the welfare-maximizing firm is:

$$\frac{p - \frac{\partial C}{\partial q_1}}{p} = (1 - k_1)\frac{p - \frac{\partial C}{\partial q_2}}{p}. \tag{4.23}$$

We would expect $0 \leq k_2 \leq 1$ in (4.22) because, from the competitor's viewpoint, the regulated firm is seen as a welfare maximizer who neither colludes ($k_2 > 1$) nor acts perversely ($k_2 < 0$). Again, one can exclude collusion. Therefore $k_1 \leq 1$ in (4.23).

The simple equilibrium consisting of (4.22) and (4.23) brings out some fairly strong features. Assuming that firm 2 does not react in some perverse way ($k_2 < 0$) and that both firms face the same cost functions, then the regulator will always want the regulated firm to be the larger one. She will prescribe marginal-cost pricing only under special conditions.

First, marginal-cost pricing by the regulated firm is optimal if $k_1 = 1$. This is the case of Cournot behavior in a partial-equilibrium second-best model. The regulator wants to correct a distortion caused by the socially inefficient behavior of the other duopolist. To achieve this she would be willing to reduce the regulated firm's output in order to induce the other firm to increase its output. However, if she believes she has no influence on the other firm, then she might as well fully optimize without regard to the other firm.

The second case for optimality of marginal-cost pricing by the regulated firm occurs under constant marginal cost and $k_1 \neq 1$, in which case $\partial C/\partial q_1 = \partial C/\partial q_2$, and the regulated firm's first-order condition implies $p = \partial C/\partial q_1$. But the same cannot hold for firm 2 unless $s_2 = 0$. In this case the regulator would price the unregulated firm 2 out of the market. This is not surprising, since constant marginal cost usually means at least a weak natural monopoly. Furthermore, marginal-cost pricing and monopoly also hold for the case of declining marginal cost.

The conjectural variations model can be used to gain a simple extension of our multifirm Ramsey result. In this case the regulator would maximize a welfare function like (4.16), but only with respect to the regulated firm's output, taking reactions of firm 2 into account. One then gets the Ramsey pricing result:

$$\frac{p - \frac{\partial C}{\partial q_1}}{p} = -\frac{k_1 \lambda_1 s_1}{\epsilon(1 + \lambda_1)}[k_1 \lambda_1 s_1 - (k_1 - 1)k_2 s_2]. \qquad (4.24)$$

Since the unregulated firm is assumed to pursue a competitive strategy ($k_1 \leq 1$), this means that the regulated firm's markup over marginal cost will be lower than in the case in which the prices of all firms are regulated.

A solution for the Ramsey pricing problem of welfare maximization in a multiproduct setting in the presence of a profit-maximizing rival firm has also been provided by Ware and Winter (1986). They consider a differentiated oligopoly that consists of a public two-product firm that is competing with a private single-product firm. Each firm is a monopolist in its own markets but with a positive cross elasticity between one of the public enterprise products and the private product. Ware and Winter characterize this as a game-theoretic problem in which the government, instead of choosing welfare-maximizing prices, seeks an optimal outcome by affecting equilibrium configurations.

Ware and Winter characterize the game between the public enterprise and the private firm as one in which both firms simultaneously select prices. The public enterprise chooses prices to maximize social surplus, whereas the private firm chooses a profit-maximizing price. While the authors find no unambiguous results on prices compared to the VFRO, two interesting propositions emerge. The first is that the optimal public-enterprise price always exceeds marginal cost for the good which has a substitute privately-produced under imperfect competition. This is because the private monopolist always prices above marginal cost. By the envelope theorem a small deviation from marginal-cost pricing in the public enterprise market will reduce welfare there by very little, while it will appreciably increase welfare in the market for the privately produced good. As a corollary the public firm's balanced-budget constraint may not be binding even though price exceeds marginal cost. The second result is that, from an initial position of marginal-cost pricing in the private market, a small increase in market power improves welfare if the public firm's budget constraint is binding. The reasoning is the same as before, only the envelope theorem here applies to the private pricing.

4.4 Ramsey pricing with consumption externalities

Network externalities are among the distinctive features that differentiate the theory of telephone tariffs from other areas of public utility pricing, such as electricity tariffs.

4.4.1 Network externalities

The importance of network externalities for POTS ("plain old telephone service") has been reduced as penetration rates approach 100 percent of all households in high-income economies. Nevertheless, they have remained a major issue for certain consumer groups and for new services, such as facsimile. In the presence of network externalities, Ramsey prices may have to be adjusted so that more customers are being served. The issue of lifeline rates, which we discuss in Chapter 11, is also connected with the network externality, and the introduction of lifeline rates (with an accompanying increase in prices for the remaining customer groups) could actually be Pareto-improving.

The following items have to be considered for externality pricing: there is a *call* externality and a *network* externality. The call externality is the benefit of a call to the party that does not have to pay for the call (usually the party being called). The network externality, which results from adding a new consumer, is the aggregate benefit that other subscribers enjoy by being able to call, or to be called by, the new subscriber. The network externality can therefore be assumed to equal the sums of consumer surplus changes of other customers who call and who are called by the new customer.[8] Both of these changes are reflected in the change in the (derived) demand for access by all the other consumers; that is, by the shift in the market demand function for access. This demand function includes all (expected) consumer surpluses from use (that is, CS from calling and from being called).

This is essentially the argument by Willig (1979, pp. 113-14) on the use of incremental consumer surplus as a measure for the network externality. Willig considers the change in consumer surplus that results as the number of subscribers increases from N to $N + \Delta N$, leading to a shift in the demand curve for calls from $Q^*(p, N)$ to $Q^*(P, N + \Delta N)$.

---

[8]It is debatable whether there is an "option value" contributed by a new subscriber in addition to the actual (expected) consumer surplus increases.

Willig uses the "conditional" demand curve (conditional on the number of customers).[9] Now, the problem is that the conditional market demand curve may never be observable since, with the exception of those points that coincide with the unconditional market demand curve, the conditional demand curve consists only of disequilibrium points. As Pyatt (1972) and Squire (1973) note, the observed demand curve is going to be a curve connecting equilibrium points, that is $N = N(p)$ and the function $Q^*(p, N)$ is not equal to the function $Q(p, N(p))$.[10] In other words, in order to observe the conditional demand curves, the econometrician would have to be able to change price and hold the number of subscribers constant (or change number of subscribers independently if he wants to trace all conditional demand curves). In reality, however, a change in price triggers a change in the number of subscribers.

Equilibrium demands need not form a well-defined market demand function $Q(\cdot, \cdot)$. Rather, Rohlfs gives an example (1974, p. 28), illustrated in Figure 4.3, where the equilibrium set of consumers, $N(p)$, follows the p-axis and an inverted parabola. The firm (and consumers) would generally be best off on the downward sloping part of the parabola. However, since these are all equilibrium points and the framework is static, there is no method (short of simultaneous contracts conditioned on the number of customers) to get consumers to this part of the equilibrium user set.

Now, what are the implications of the network externality for pricing? For simplicity, let us assume a two-product firm that offers a network service, for which it charges only an access fee, and some other nonnetwork product with independent demand. (This other product only serves as a benchmark and helps make the budget constraint of the Ramsey problem nontrivial.) The π-max and W-max monopolies would yield similar (Ramsey) pricing structures if the externality were fully expressed in the demand function for access, $Q = Q(p, N(p))$, where $N(p)$ is the total number of customers.

However, as explained above, the relevant incremental consumer sur-

---

[9] Squire (1973) calls this the "conceptual" demand curve.
[10] These equilibrium points are derived from what Rohlfs (1974) has called equilibrium user sets. Rohlfs uses a fairly general framework in which the demand of each consumer for access depends on the subscription and calling by other consumers. The special case in which this information can be comprised in the number N of other subscribers is what he calls a uniform calling pattern, in the sense that any subscriber makes the same number of calls to any other subscriber.

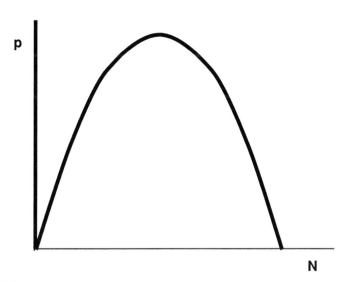

Figure 4.3
Equilibrium subscriber set

plus that equals the externality effect EX is given by the shaded area in
Figure 4.4 created by the shift in the conditional market demand curve
from $Q^*(p, N)$ to $Q^*(p, N + \partial N/\partial p)$, that is:

$$\frac{\partial EX}{\partial p} = \int_p^\infty Q^*(p, N)\, dp - \int_p^\infty Q^*\left(p, N + \frac{\partial N}{\partial p}\right)\, dp, \qquad (4.25)$$

or:

$$\frac{\partial EX}{\partial p} = \int_p^\infty \frac{\partial Q(p, N)}{\partial N} \frac{\partial N}{\partial p}\, dp. \qquad (4.26)$$

In this case the pricing condition for the W-max monopolist is:

$$(p - MC)\left(\frac{\partial Q}{\partial p} + \frac{\partial N}{\partial p}\frac{\partial Q}{\partial N}\right) = -\frac{\lambda Q + \frac{\partial EX}{\partial p}}{1 + \lambda}. \qquad (4.27)$$

Here $(\partial Q/\partial p) + (\partial N/\partial p)(\partial Q/\partial N)$ is the observed (or perceived) slope
of the (unconditional) demand curve $Q\big(p, N(p)\big)$ in Figure 4.4. Note that
$\partial N/\partial p$ is negative.[11]

---

[11] The shift in demand due to network externalities resembles the demand shifts
caused by the firm's advertising. Such shifts can be welfare improving if a budget
constraint prevents the firm from pricing at marginal costs. The relationship between
second-best pricing and advertising is treated in Vogelsang (1990a) and Kaserman
and Mayo (1991).

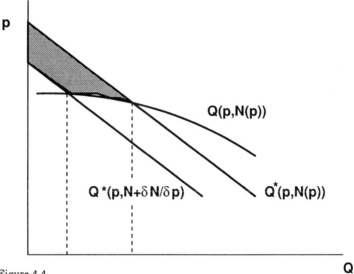

Figure 4.4
Access externality

In terms of this demand curve the result for the π-max monopolist remains as if there were no externality:

$$(p - MC)\left(\frac{\partial Q}{\partial p} + \frac{\partial N}{\partial p}\frac{\partial Q}{\partial N}\right) = -Q. \tag{4.28}$$

However, as is apparent from Figure 4.4, the externality makes the observed demand curve $Q(p, N(p))$ more elastic than the conditional demand curve $Q^*(p, N)$. This causes the profit-maximizing monopolist to have a lower price/cost margin for the service with network externality than for the other service if (conditional) demand elasticities for both services are the same. Thus the monopolist internalizes one part of the externality.

Now consider the case of oligopolistic competition. For profit-maximizing firms facing demand with a network externality the problem arises: What is the natural assumption on the strategic variable? In the simple Cournot case with q_i as the strategic variable for firm i and for an interconnected network we get basically the same result obtained for the profit-maximizing monopolist, only altered by multiplying the right-hand side of (4.28) by the market share weight s_i. This is quite surprising, because it means that oligopolists have at least some incentive to internalize the externality. It comes about because in both monopoly and oligopoly the firms consider the effect of their pricing behavior on what they perceive as their demand. The profit-maximizing firm knows only the equilibrium demand curve, while the welfare maximizer has to know the conditional demand curves as well.

Our expression of the network externality effect in Ramsey pricing differs from the literature in the following way: Willig and Bailey (1977) treat the network externality simply as the difference between private and social cost of the network service. Thus, by substituting marginal social cost for marginal (private) cost, the Ramsey formula (4.11) becomes the same for the network service as for the other service. This is not entirely correct, however, because the budget constraint of the constrained-welfare maximization problem should be formulated in terms of private cost rather than social cost. The budget constraint is a *financial* constraint that is imposed to ensure the viability of the firm, rather than a part of the objective function.[12] When the maximization problem uses private cost in the constraint and social cost in the objective function, the correct formula is obtained:

$$\frac{p - MC}{p} = -\frac{\lambda}{(1+\lambda)\epsilon} - \frac{[\frac{\partial EX}{\partial Q} - 1]}{(1+\lambda)}. \tag{4.29}$$

Thus (4.29) resembles Ramsey pricing in (4.11) except for the externality effect. Here this effect enters in a different form and receives a different weight than marginal cost.

This also becomes apparent in Rohlfs (1979) and Griffin (1982), who define an externality effect, $ex = (p + \partial EX/\partial Q)/p$, as the ratio between marginal social benefits and marginal private benefits of an additional subscriber. They then proceed to substitute ex for p in the welfare-maximization problem for access. For the case of independent demands between access i and all other services j Griffin derives the correct first-order conditions:

$$\frac{\epsilon_j(p_j - MC_j)}{p_j} = \frac{p_i - \frac{MC_i}{ex}}{p_i} \frac{\epsilon_i ex}{\epsilon_i(1 - ex) + 1}. \tag{4.30}$$

In spite of the simplifying assumption of independent demands these conditions are quite forbidding. A version that is simpler to interpret is:

---

[12]Under weighted welfare maximization the externality factor may receive extra weight.

$$\frac{\epsilon_j \left(p_j - MC_j \right)}{p_j} = \frac{\frac{\epsilon_i(p_i - MC_i)}{p_i} - \epsilon_i(1 - ex)}{\epsilon_i(1 - ex) + 1}. \tag{4.31}$$

The left-hand side of (4.31) is the Lerner index for service j multiplied by service j's demand elasticity. On the right-hand side the denominator is ≥ 1. The first term in the numerator is the Lerner index for service i multiplied by i's demand elasticity, and the second term is negative. Clearly, for $ex = 1$ we get the familiar Ramsey condition. For $ex > 1$ the interpretation is less transparent. For the same demand elasticity $\epsilon_j = \epsilon_i = \epsilon$ the Lerner index for services j and i are related as follows:

$$\frac{p_j - MC_j}{p_j} = \frac{\frac{p_i - MC_i}{p_i} - (1 - ex)}{\epsilon(1 - ex) + 1}. \tag{4.32}$$

Since the Lerner index is smaller than $1/|\epsilon|$, the Lerner index for service i has to be smaller than the Lerner index for service j whenever $ex > 1$.

4.4.2 The interaction of call and network externalities

Unlike network externalities, which are large numbers problems, call externalities are strictly a problem of two economic agents. That is why Littlechild (1975) assumed away call externalities. However, the Coase theorem does not apply to the internalization of call externalities because negotiations that would lead to internalization themselves require telephone calls (see Acton and Vogelsang, 1990). Willig (1979) finds call externalities hard to deal with if they are not easily related to other variables in his model (e.g., to outgoing calls, other purchases, or number of subscribers). This is partly due to the fact that demand for incoming calls is not observable (except at a zero price, under 800-number calls).

However, if one switches from a model of demand for calling to a model of demand for access, then the problem of the value of call externalities can be greatly simplified. A consumer's value of access is the total consumer surplus from calling and being called, including the value of the call externality. Thus, a shift in the demand curve for access that results from an increase in the number of subscribers should lead to the relevant incremental consumer surplus. In other words, the effects of call externalities are captured by that part of the shift in demand for access that is not explained by the increase in the consumer surplus due to the increment in use.

The simultaneity of call externality and access externality as a problem of optimal pricing has been analyzed by Einhorn (1990) in the context of bypass of a network. Since Einhorn chooses to treat this as a two-part tariff problem and since his derivation uses assumptions from the literature on two-part tariffs, we will come back to his model in Section 5.3. The main result that can be derived in this context is that the importance of the call externality relative to the network externality increases with subscriber penetration. Hence, the price/marginal-cost markup for calls, relative to that for access, should decrease as penetration rate increases.

4.5 Definition of services

So far we have taken the basket of services as given. What do we mean by a basket of services? As explained in Chapter 2, telephone calls represent a heterogeneous set of commodities. Calls at different times and with different connections are rarely interchangeable. Thus, as an extreme we may view all units of output as distinct from each other. Nevertheless, there are good practical reasons to reduce the number of distinct services to just a few. One is the fact that services may be close substitutes in supply. This is true, for instance, for services that share the same facilities. The second is that, in aggregate terms, demands for certain services share certain common characteristics that allow an economist to characterize an aggregate demand function. We now take up the issue of definition of services with respect to geographic characteristics.

4.5.1 Local versus long-distance services

An example of separate market demand functions can be seen in local services and long-distance services. Demand appears to become more elastic with distance (Taylor, 1980). The implication would be that, in percentage terms, rate differences for successive distance bands should be smaller than differences in marginal cost. For a long time, however, the reverse has been true in practice.

In terms of definition of services, the issue is whether higher elasticities are only the result of higher prices associated with longer distances. We could be sure about the elasticity differences only if demand curves were iso-elastic. Suppose that, on the contrary, demand curves are linear.

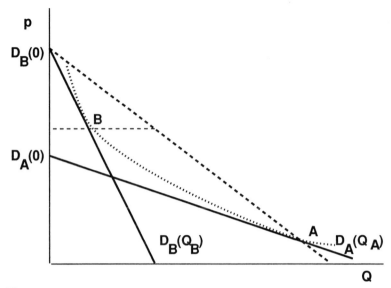

Figure 4.5
Distance-related demand curves

Then elasticities on the same demand curve increase with price, and
since price increases with distance, we would also find that demand
elasticities increase with distance. Now, we know that both iso-elastic
and linear demand curves cannot be globally correct descriptions of true
demand. Rather, true demand curves are likely to be convex and lie in
between these two extremes.

One way to check whether the higher elasticities at greater distances
are due solely to higher prices is to see whether linear demand curves
would imply larger or smaller distance-related elasticity increases than
those that are observed. How this can be done is shown in Figure 4.5.
Assume that we observe point A for local calls and point B for long-
distance calls. Obviously, point A represents a smaller price and a much
larger quantity than point B. The larger quantity could be the result
of the lower price, but much more likely it is the result of denser communications channels between people living closer together. We have
to adjust for this size effect if we want to see whether local and long-
distance demand can be aggregated to a single demand function. Now,
linear demand curves with the same elasticity but different sized markets

cut the p-axis at the same point. If we know the demand elasticities at A and B, we can draw linear inverse demand curves $D_A(Q_A)$ and $D_B(Q_B)$ through these points. In order for the two demand curves to represent the same elasticities (although different market sizes) it must be true that $D_A(0) = D_B(0)$. However, if $D_A(0) < D_B(0)$, then the linear local demand would be more elastic than the linear long-distance demand, which is empirically refuted. This observation, however, would be compatible with an aggregate convex demand curve in which both services would be merged (e.g., the dotted curve through A and B). Another way of testing the distance dependence of elasticities is to see if narrowing price differentials lead to narrowing elasticity differentials.

The consequence of a single demand curve would be that at the same cost the optimal prices would be the same. Differential pricing by distance derives from the fact that costs, demand functions, and the level of competition in telecommunications are likely to vary with distance. In the absence of competition, a Ramsey pricing model would be appropriate for analyzing efficient pricing by distance (Willig and Bailey, 1977).

An interesting feature of distance is that it is a continuous variable and that cost of supply increases monotonically with distance. Given that distance-related pricing involves extra metering and information costs, the issue of the optimal number and size of distance zones has to be solved. So far this has not been accomplished in the literature.[13]

In terms of cost trends we note that the increase in costs with distance has become less important. This should have two effects. One is that the optimal rate difference between different distances should narrow. Second, the number of different rate zones should decrease. As pointed out in Chapters 7-10, this trend is clearly observable in the United States.

4.5.2 High density versus low density (urban–rural) services

Services could also be defined and differentiated by the region of the country. This appears to be a natural consequence of differential regulation between American states. However, it is politically off-limits for federally regulated interstate telecommunications services.

Regional price differentiation is related to the customer-class price dis-

---

[13]Ray Rees (1976, Chapter 5) has looked at the formally similar problem of determining the optimal number T of time-of-day rates in a peak-load problem.

crimination, which we discuss in the next section. In addition, the effect of uniform pricing across high-density and low-density regions and markets comes under this heading. Since this involves cross-subsidization, it raises severe bypass and cream-skimming issues which are discussed in Chapter 6.

The appropriate density concept is volume on a pairwise route connecting two nodes i and j. This is *correlated* with geographic (population) density. Note the difference from electricity supply, where density occurs in a single location, and the similarity to air transport.

4.6   Customer-class pricing

Price discrimination by customer class differs from Ramsey pricing because customers are classified on institutional grounds rather than by separating customers neatly according to their demand elasticities. For the case of distributional weighting of customer classes, Bös (1983) distinguishes between pricing by services, by income, or by group affiliation. While distributional pricing by income classes would appear to be cleanest, it may require unpopular and costly certification procedures.[14] Also, as Bös (1985a) has pointed out, problems with means-tested pricing arise at the income threshhold levels that trigger lower prices. Consumers at a threshhold level may want to adjust their incomes so that they benefit from the lower prices. In extreme cases this could lead to a gap in the income distribution.

Distributional pricing by services replaces the procedure of certifying eligibility by one of self-selection. It uses correlation between income and demands for specific services, such as first-class rather than economy-class travel, as a means of price discrimination. In this case, services purchased predominantly by the poor would receive higher weights in the welfare-maximization problem than services purchased predominantly by the rich. As a result the Ramsey numbers will differ between services. Bös (1983) points out that, contrary to the intentions of such a weighting scheme, prices paid by the poor can end up higher than under the unweighted Ramsey pricing problem – if demands for the luxury services are more elastic than those for necessities purchased by the poor,

[14] See Chapter 11.

or if elasticities or marginal costs change with the quantities produced. We discuss self-selection under optional tariffs in Chapter 5.

Institutional affiliations make customer separation easier to achieve (Bös, 1983). Typically, institutionally separated customer classes show some homogeneity. Classes differ by both their demand characteristics and by the costs of serving them. For example, business calls typically concentrate on workdays between 8 a.m. and 5 p.m., while household calls peak in the early evening hours. However, businesses among themselves are very heterogeneous. For example they vary tremendously in size. Both the interclass variance and the intraclass variance in demand should be reflected in price structures. Empirically, it is therefore important to identify the relevant characteristics of customer classes. The following could be relevant characteristics: size of consumer in terms of consumption quantity, demand elasticity, time pattern of consumption, and geographic pattern of consumption.

The theoretical analysis of customer-class pricing draws on Ramsey pricing and rate-of-return regulation. In the constrained optimal pricing problem defined on customer classes, a complete analog to the Ramsey pricing formula emerges (Eckel, 1985). This is because customer classes can be treated like different services in the Ramsey problem. Thus, we may reinterpret (4.11) in such a way that the subscript i denotes customer class i rather than service i.[15]

Also, Eckel derives the effect of rate-of-return regulation on the price structure chosen for the different customer classes. She comes up with a bias toward capital-intensive services similar to that of Averch and Johnson (1962), and with an excessive dependence of prices on demand elasticities relative to Ramsey prices.

An interesting aspect of customer-class pricing is taken up by Eckel and Smith (1990) who consider economies of scope due to the stochastic nature of demand.[16] The authors assume that a public utility has to commit to building production capacity before demand is known. Customer classes differ by the variance of their demand and by the co-

---

[15] Customer classes often have to be characterized as buying *bundles* of services rather than single services. In this case the simple Ramsey pricing analogy does not hold. The distinction between single services and consumption bundles is also at the heart of the distinction between subsidy-free prices and anonymously equitable prices defined below in Section 6.1.1.

[16] The title of this paper "Multiproduct Pricing and Capacity Choice with Correlated Demands" is misleading. The authors clearly deal with a single product in the sense that outputs can be summed as $\sum q_i = Q$ in the demand and cost functions.

variance between their demand and market demand. Eckel and Smith exploit the similarity of this feature with that of the stochastic nature of capital markets. They come up with a "beta" concept like the one used in capital asset pricing models. The major further assumptions are that, in addition to the profit constraint, there is a reliability constraint, due to capacity limitations imposed ex ante, combined with uncertain demands. Consequently, the authors derive a Ramsey pricing formula like (4.11). However, on the right-hand side there is an additional term that contains the beta coefficients, the shadow price of capital, and the Lagrange multiplier of the reliability constraint. Two main results emerge. First, as long as demands are not perfectly correlated, there will be economies of scope from joint production. Second, demands that covary negatively with market demand are charged lower prices than demands that covary positively with market demand.[17]

4.7 Dynamic pricing

4.7.1 Dynamic externality pricing

In the static problem of pricing with network externalities discussed earlier in Section 4.4 the network had been assumed in equilibrium at all times. Consumers responded instantaneously to price changes by joining or leaving the network. At any point in time each consumer, when making her subscription decision, was assumed to know the subscription price and the number of other subscribers. In reality, there exists no instantaneous coordination mechanisms that would allow such a Nash equilibrium in subscriptions to emerge instantaneously. Rather, consumers base their subscription decision on expectations about the future number of subscribers, which in turn is likely to depend on current subscription levels, past trends in subscriptions, and the expected subscription price. Also, subscriptions often entail entry and exit costs in addition to rental rates. Hence, decisions about subscribing cannot costlessly be reversed.

These problems have led to a strand of literature on dynamic externality pricing that takes into account adjustments over time to equilibrium subscriber levels. Dynamic pricing models have been treated by Dhebar

[17]This paper bears some similarity to papers on bundling by Adams and Yellen (1976), Schmalensee (1984), and McAfee, McMillan, and Whinston (1989). See also Chapter 5.

and Oren (1985a), Xie and Sirbu (1988), and Woroch (1989). Dhebar and Oren's and Xie and Sirbu's highly sophisticated models are for a profit-maximizing monopolist. It remains to be shown to what extent their methodology and results carry over to the welfare-maximizing case. However, Dhebar and Oren (1985b) analyze welfare maximization with network externalities in a dynamic nonlinear pricing framework, which we discuss in Chapter 5.

4.7.2   New products and network externalities

The pricing of new services poses two problems. First, new services may be accompanied by large network externalities. Second, there may be cumulative economies of scale (learning by doing). This second problem is treated by Faulhaber and Boyd (1989). Their main conclusion (which, with some modification, would also hold for network externalities) is that new services may require introductory prices that are lower than subsequent period prices. Traditional regulatory pricing, which does not allow for such lower prices, may therefore discourage innovation.[18]

Faulhaber's and Boyd's paper is of interest to us because it can be extended to the issue of pricing in the presence of large one-time investments that are sunk, e.g., fiber-optic cables. The authors use a two-period learning-by-doing framework for a single-product monopoly, without discounting. Production in period 1 is accompanied by firm or consumer learning. This learning leads to either lower production costs or increased consumer demand in period 2. The cost function for output in the current period is denoted by $C(q, q_{-1})$ and the inverse demand function by $p(q, q_{-1})$, where q refers to the current period output and q_{-1} to the previous period output. Learning effects imply $\partial C / \partial q_{-1} \leq 0$ and $\partial p / \partial q_{-1} \geq 0$.

In the absence of discounting a profit-maximizing monopolist would maximize:

$$\pi = p(q_1, 0)q_1 + p(q_2, q_1)q_2 - C(q_1, 0) - C(q_2, q_1). \qquad (4.33)$$

In the absence of intertemporal effects, (4.33) would read:

$$\pi = p(q_1)q_1 + p(q_2)q_2 - C(q_1) - C(q_2). \qquad (4.34)$$

[18]Faulhaber and Boyd (1989) do not discuss competitive services in this connection. In the presence of (potential) competition it may be difficult to distinguish between efficient introductory pricing and inefficient predatory pricing.

The first-order condition for (4.34) would imply the well-known monopoly rule:

$$\frac{p_i - \frac{\partial C}{\partial q_i}}{p_i} = -\frac{1}{\epsilon_i} \qquad \text{for } i = 1, 2. \tag{4.35}$$

In contrast, the first-order condition to (4.33) for period 1 leads to:

$$\frac{p(q_1, 0) - [\frac{\partial C(q_1, 0)}{\partial q_1} + \frac{\partial C(q_2, q_1)}{\partial q_1}]}{p(q_1, 0)} = -\frac{1}{\epsilon_1} - \frac{\epsilon_{12}}{\epsilon_1 \epsilon_2} \frac{p(q_2, q_1)q_2}{p(q_1, 0)q_1}, \tag{4.36}$$

where $\epsilon_{12} = (dq_2/dp_1)(p_1/q_2) < 0$ is the *demonstration elasticity* that measures the period 2 demand response to a period 1 increase in price. The bracketed term on the left-hand side of (4.36) represents *dynamic marginal costs* of period 1 production. These dynamic marginal costs consist of regular period 1 marginal costs and the *reduction* in period 2 costs caused by the period 1 output expansion. Contrary to demand and cost interactions in static models, in dynamic models the interactions only go in one direction – forward in time. Consequently, the first-order condition to (4.33) for period 2 is similar to (4.35).

We now turn to the problem of constrained welfare maximization corresponding to (4.33). The budget constraint in this case could be required to hold period by period or over both periods together. The period-by-period budget constraint appears to be more in line with regulatory traditions in the United States and elsewhere, requiring regulated firms and public enterprises to stay within their budget constraints each year. However, intertemporal effects are often captured in capitalization and depreciation rules that allow regulated firms to shift costs from one period to the next. So, the joint period budget constraint is not utterly unrealistic.

Faulhaber and Boyd assume that the firm maximizes welfare over both periods' outputs:

$$\max \int_0^{q_1} p(x, 0)\, dx - C(q_1, 0) + \int_0^{q_2} p(x, q_1)\, dx - C(q_2, q_1), \tag{4.37}$$

subject to a joint budget constraint for both periods.

The first-order condition for (4.37) for first-period pricing is:

$$\frac{p(q_1,0) - [\frac{\partial C(q_1,0)}{\partial q_1} + \frac{\partial C(q_2,q_1)}{\partial q_1}]}{p(q_1,0)}$$

$$= -\frac{\lambda}{1+\lambda}\left[\frac{1}{\epsilon_1} + \frac{\epsilon_{12}}{\epsilon_1\epsilon_2}\frac{p(q_2,q_1)q_2}{p(q_1,0)q_1}\right]$$

$$-\frac{1}{1+\lambda}\frac{1}{p(q_1,0)}\int_0^{q_2}\frac{\partial p(x,q_1)}{\partial q_1}\,dx. \tag{4.38}$$

Aside from the usual Ramsey number $\lambda/(1+\lambda)$, equation (4.38) differs from the profit-maximizing condition (4.36) by the last expression, which captures the benefits received by inframarginal consumers from learning about the product. This effect is irrelevant for the profit-maximizing firm because it would not affect that firm's profit.

Equation (4.38) can lead to pricing below conventional marginal costs, both because of the additional consumer benefits and because of the future cost reduction resulting from increases in period 1 outputs. Also, price in period 1 will be below price in period 2. This contrasts with the case of period-by-period budget constraints under which price in period 1 will be above price in period 2 because costs go down with output and learning. If the regulator cannot ex ante commit to a two-period set of prices and a two-period budget constraint, then after period 1 is over the regulator would want to set the period 2 price below the period 1 price (an instance of dynamic inconsistency).

4.7.3 Dynamic Ramsey pricing

Explicitly incorporating longrun investments in the pricing decision of the firm leads to two further problems besides peak-load pricing. First, the investments may come in lumpy sizes. Second, there may be adjustment costs caused by the new investment.

The first of these problems goes back to a conjecture by Boiteux (1964). It is further treated in the literature by Starrett (1978), Rees (1986), Park (1989), and Woroch (1985). The main implication of this literature is that, with steady growth of demand, lumpy capacity investment will lead to some kind of longrun peak-load pricing. Price would have to increase smoothly over time during the interval between investments, reaching its peak right before the new investment comes

on stream. At that moment price should take a discrete drop and thereafter again increase smoothly. Such a price schedule suggests that it
may be optimal to have consumers contribute to investment financing
before and during construction in progress rather than afterwards. We
refrain from reviewing this literature and concentrate on the case of
investments with adjustment costs. This issue may become of major
importance with the introduction of integrated services digital network
(ISDN) and broadband technologies.

The problem of adjustment costs caused by investment is treated by
Brock and Dechert (1985) and by D. Salant and Woroch (1989). The
two papers have in common that they use a concept of dynamic marginal
costs in order to derive a dynamic Ramsey pricing solution. We concentrate on Salant and Woroch.

These two authors assume that the firm starts out with an initial
capacity $\hat{q}_0 \geq 0$ which deteriorates at a geometric rate δ. Denot-
ing gross investment in period t by $I_t \geq 0$, capacity at t is $\hat{q}_t =
I_t + (1 - \delta)\hat{q}_{t-1}$. Investment cost in any period is an increasing, convex
function $C(I)$ with $C(0) = 0$. Adjustment costs are buried in the convexity of $C(I)$. Average variable costs v are assumed to be constant, and
output q is constrained by capacity.[19] The firm's cash flow in period
t is $\pi_t = (p_t - v)q_t - C(I_t)$. We denote the discount factor by
$\rho = 1/(1 + r)$ where r is the interest rate. Dynamic marginal costs can
now be defined by:

$$MC_t = v + \frac{\partial C}{\partial I_t} - (1 - \delta)\rho \frac{\partial C}{\partial I_{t+1}}. \tag{4.39}$$

Here the first two terms are marginal operating and investment costs.
The last term deducts the discounted savings in investment next period
that are made possible by the depreciated investment in the current
period.[20]

---

[19] Due to capacity limitations there could be excess demand at price p. Since there
is no uncertainty in this model and since price can be adjusted instantaneously, it is
never optimal to have nonprice rationing.

[20] The definition of dynamic marginal costs by Brock and Dechert is quite different
and requires knowledge of the initial capital stock plus the investment plans for the
capital stock in the two subsequent periods. They do not derive an explicit formula
for Ramsey optimal prices.

The regulator maximizes:

$$W_0 = \sum_{t=1}^{\infty} \rho^t \left[V(p_t) + (1+\lambda)[(p_t - v)q_t - C(q_t - (1-\delta)\hat{q}_{t-1})] \right.$$

$$\left. + \mu_t(q_t - \hat{q}_t) \right]. \tag{4.40}$$

The fact that λ has no time subscript indicates the assumption that the profit constraint of this Ramsey problem only holds for the discounted present value of all cash flows. The Lagrange multiplier of the capacity constraint is μ_t, and I_t can vary from period to period. For the absence of excess capacity ($q_t = \hat{q}_t$) Salant and Woroch derive a period-by-period inverse elasticity rule:

$$\frac{p_t - MC_t}{p_t} = \frac{\lambda}{(1+\lambda)\epsilon_t}. \tag{4.41}$$

When the system starts out with excess capacity, the firm will optimally not invest until capacity depreciates to the level that is demanded at $p = v$. The authors do not discuss further properties of pricing with excess capacity.

To vastly simplify the broadband/ISDN pricing issue, consider the following problem of providing a one-time investment that has a life of T periods. Such a one-time investment is preferable to many small investments over time if the investment function $C(\hat{q})$ is concave. Instead of assuming growth in demand we assume stationary demand and a deterioration (i.e., reduction) in capacity of $\delta\hat{q}_t$ per period. Using the same notation as before, the problem becomes one of maximizing:

$$W_0 = \sum_{t=1}^{T} \rho^t \left[V(p_t) + (1+\lambda)(p_t - v)q_t + \mu_t(q_t - \hat{q}_t) \right] - (1+\lambda)C(\hat{q}_0) \tag{4.42}$$

Here $\hat{q}_t = \hat{q}_0(1 - \delta)^t$. At time T the capacity is assumed to become worthless. We further assume that there is never any nonprice rationing at the optimum. This is realistic for the problem at hand because, for the same quantity, surplus under nonprice rationing is never higher than under price rationing. First-order conditions are:

$$\frac{\partial W_0}{\partial \hat{q}_0} = -\sum_{t=1}^{T} \mu_t(1-\delta)^t \rho^t - (1+\lambda)\frac{\partial C}{\partial \hat{q}_0} = 0, \tag{4.43}$$

and:

$$\frac{\partial W_0}{\partial p_t} = \rho^t \left[\lambda q_t + (1+\lambda)(p_t - v)\frac{\partial q_t}{\partial p_t} + \mu_t \frac{\partial q_t}{\partial p_t} \right] = 0. \tag{4.44}$$

In periods where the capacity constraint is binding we have $\mu_t < 0$ while in periods with nonbinding constraints $\mu_t = 0$. Now, condition (4.44) implies:

$$\frac{p_t - v + \frac{\mu_t}{1+\lambda}}{p_t} = -\frac{\lambda}{1+\lambda}\frac{1}{\epsilon_t}. \tag{4.45}$$

Equation (4.45) is the usual inverse elasticity rule where $\mu_t/(1+\lambda)$ is the shadow price of capacity in period t. Note that this price is dependent on the budget constraint.

Combining equations (4.43) and (4.44) we get:

$$\frac{\partial C}{\partial \hat{q}_0} = \sum_{t=1}^{T} \left[[(p_t - v) + \frac{\lambda}{1+\lambda}\frac{p_t}{\epsilon_t}](1-\delta) \right] \rho^t. \tag{4.46}$$

Equation (4.46) says that the marginal cost of additional capacity should be equated to the discounted sum of the marginal profit contributions generated by this capacity plus the discounted sum of an adjustment factor that contains an inverse relationship between price and elasticity.

4.8   Conclusions

In this chapter we first discussed the concept of marginal-cost pricing with an application to the peak-load pricing problem. Budget constraints on the regulated telecommunications carrier or differentiated welfare weights in the objective function then lead us to various versions of Ramsey pricing and of the inverse elasticity rule. The rule says that relative markups of prices over marginal costs for the various services offered should deviate in inverse proportion to the respective demand elasticities. This rule can be adapted in various ways to cases of interdependent demands, competitive situations, situations involving consumption externalities, and dynamic settings. Also, it holds for both welfare-maximizing and profit-maximizing behavior. Thus the inverse elasticity rule, properly interpreted, is a surprisingly robust concept. Consumption externalities and learning-by-doing, however, lead us to additional terms in the pricing equation under welfare maximization, terms that are absent under profit maximization.

5

Nonlinear tariffs

5.1 The consumption framework

Nonlinear tariffs involve price discrimination in the sense that different units of a homogeneous output are sold at different prices. They share with linear price discrimination the property that nonlinear tariffs can only be used under certain market conditions. In particular, the supplying firm has to have some market power; perfect arbitrage (resale without transaction costs) must not be possible; customer purchases have to be monitored; and disaggregated demand data have to be available.

In order to analyze linear tariffs in Chapter 4, in either a multiproduct or a peak-load context, it was sufficient to know properties of market demand curves (including cross elasticities between services or time periods). Nonlinear and optional tariffs, however, can only be analyzed with additional knowledge about individual demand curves. This is so because price p now becomes dependent on the quantity q purchased by an individual consumer: there is a price schedule $p(q)$ leading to an outlay schedule $R(q)$ with $p(q) \equiv dR/dq = R'(q)$. Since it is entirely unrealistic for a supplier or for a social planner to know the individual demand curves of all customers and since calculation of optimal nonlinear prices becomes extremely complicated even with this knowledge, some regularity assumptions have to be made and new types of aggregation procedures have to be devised.

The now conventional approach in the literature has been to assume that individual demand curves do not cross and that consumers can be characterized by a single-dimensional type parameter τ.[1] In Figure 5.1 the noncrossing assumption is illustrated for three consumer types de-

---

[1] Multidimensional consumer types are handled in a few papers, e.g., Maskin and Riley (1984) and Laffont, Maskin, and Rochet (1987).

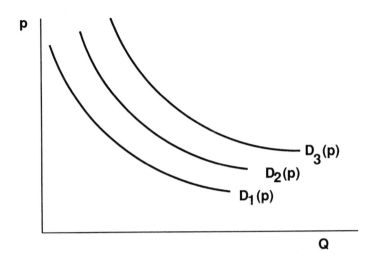

Figure 5.1
Noncrossing demand curves

noted by $\tau = 1, 2, 3$. The noncrossing assumption means that consumer surplus increases in τ, or $\partial^2 U / \partial q \partial \tau > 0$ for all q. Noncrossing ensures that consumers can be uniquely ranked by the quantity purchased at any given (linear) price; the assumption of a type parameter ensures that they can be identified and grouped. Usually, a statistical distribution $F(\tau)$ of types is assumed, and its density is denoted by $f(\tau)$. Without loss of generality, τ can be assumed uniformly distributed with $0 \leq \tau \leq 1$. Then τ refers to percentiles in the population, and smaller τ's refer to consumer types with lower demands at all prices.

The question is: How restrictive is the assumption of noncrossing? An example, in which the assumption is violated, would be the case where residential telephone customers are ranked by income y and household size n. Clearly, demand for telephone services increases in both components. Could one now construct a one-dimensional index $I(y, n)$ such that $q(p, I)$ has the noncrossing property? Most likely not. The rich bachelor may at low prices consume less telephone services than the poor family of ten, while at high prices he may consume more.

A critical role in the analysis of nonlinear prices is played by the *marginal consumer* who is indifferent between buying and not buying at a given price schedule $p(q)$. Due to the noncrossing assumption the marginal consumer is assigned a unique τ. The analysis is then separated into the effect of a price schedule change on marginal consumers (for whom there usually is a discrete jump in quantity purchased) and the effect on inframarginal consumers. The role of marginal consumers is particularly relevant for two-part tariffs, where the fixed fee usually excludes some customers. Under the noncrossing assumption the marginal consumer will always consume less than the average consumer.[2]

Consumer surplus in the absence of a fixed fee ($E = 0$) can now be written as a function of p and τ, $CS = V(p, \tau)$, and quantity demanded by type τ is $q = q(p, \tau)$. As before, $\partial V / \partial p = -q$. The effect of paying a positive fixed fee is that consumer surplus is reduced by the amount of that fee. In the absence of income effects, quantity purchased is only affected by E if $V(p, \tau) < E$. In this case a consumer stops purchasing.[3] Thus, in two-part tariff models the marginal consumer type τ_0 is defined by $V(p, \tau_0) = E$. In Figure 5.2 this τ_0 is approximately the consumer group with demand D_2. At price p these consumers purchase q_2, resulting in a consumer surplus triangle equal to the fixed fee E given by the dark rectangle. For consumers with demand D_1 the surplus triangle at q_1 is smaller than E, while consumers with D_3 would keep a positive surplus at q_3 even after paying the fixed fee E.

We can now state a number of relationships (Schmalensee, 1981):

$$\frac{\partial \tau_0}{\partial E} = \frac{1}{\frac{\partial V}{\partial \tau}} > 0, \quad \text{and} \tag{5.1}$$

$$\frac{\partial \tau_0}{\partial p} = \frac{q(p, \tau_0)}{\frac{\partial V}{\partial \tau}} = q_0 \frac{\partial \tau_0}{\partial E} > 0. \tag{5.2}$$

[2]Instead of noncrossing demands, Schmalensee (1981) assumes that consumer surplus increases with τ in the relevant range. By doing so, he combines uniqueness of the marginal consumer with the possibility that the marginal consumer consumes more than the average consumer. We do not believe that the occurrence of the latter is empirically very relevant. Since Schmalensee's is the more general assumption, our discussion under noncrossing of demands follows as a special case.

[3]The absence of income effects is a particularly strong assumption in the case of two-part tariffs, where the fixed part is a direct reduction in income. Income effects of nonlinear tariffs are treated by Goldman, Leland, and Sibley (1984). They point out that in the presence of income effects optimal pricing takes on the role of optimal redistributive taxation.

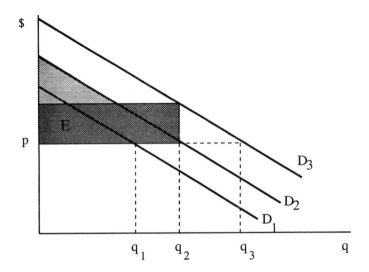

Figure 5.2
Fixed fee and three types of consumers

Equation (5.1) means that an increase in E has to be compensated for by an equivalent shift in the demand curve. In contrast, (5.2) means that an increase in p has to be compensated for by a shift in the demand curve multiplied by the quantity affected by the price increase.

The quantity of customers in the market, N, and the quantity purchased, Q, are given by:

$$N(p, E) = \int_{\tau_0}^{1} f(\tau)\, d\tau \quad \text{and} \quad Q(p, E) = \int_{\tau_0}^{1} q(p, \tau) f(\tau)\, d\tau. \qquad (5.3)$$

The inframarginal substitution effect in the absence of income effects is:

$$\sigma = \int_{\tau_0}^{1} \frac{\partial q}{\partial p} f(\tau)\, d\tau. \qquad (5.4)$$

Recall that $\tau_0 = \tau_0(p, E)$. Then demand derivatives are related as follows (Schmalensee, 1981, Proposition 1):

(a) $\qquad \dfrac{\partial N}{\partial p} = q_0 \dfrac{\partial N}{\partial E} = \dfrac{\partial Q}{\partial E}, \qquad\qquad\qquad (5.5)$

and:

(b) $\quad \dfrac{\partial Q}{\partial p} = q_0 \dfrac{\partial N}{\partial p} + \sigma.$ $\hfill (5.6)$

The first equality, (5.5), says that a price increase of one unit has the same effect on the number of buyers as the equivalent increase in the fixed fee per unit of purchase by the marginal customers. The second equality, (5.6), translates this feature into total quantities purchased. Equality (5.6) simply sums the inframarginal substitution effect and the effect of losing marginal customers.[4]

We can sometimes assume that the number of consumers is very large so that N can be taken as a continuous variable. Derivatives of the aggregate consumer welfare $V(E, p)$, with respect to access fee E and price p, are then $\partial V / \partial E = -N$ and $\partial V / \partial p = -Q$.[5] This says that the burden of a marginal increase in E is carried by all consumers affected and that the burden of a marginal increase in p is carried by all consumption units affected.

An entirely different approach to demand under nonlinear pricing has been taken by Spence (1977, 1980). He assumes that there is a finite number N of customers or customer groups whose gross benefit and demand functions are known to the regulator. The regulator then picks an optimal consumption/outlay pair for each customer group, resulting in an outlay schedule as a vector of outlays and quantities (R, q). This approach does not require any ordering of customer groups by types and does not impose a noncrossing condition. However, it does require that certain incentive-compatibility and self-selection conditions (to be discussed in Section 5.6.4) are satisfied. In Chapter 6 we refer to Spence's approach as the *consumption outlay model*.

5.2   Two-part tariffs

Two-part tariffs are defined by the pair $(E, p) \geq (0, 0)$ where E stands for the fixed fee (or entry fee), payment of which is a prerequisite for buying consumption units at a constant price p. Since E can be zero, two-part tariffs are a generalization of linear prices, and it trivially follows that

---

[4] If income effects are nonnegligible, then an inframarginal income effect has to be subtracted from the right-hand side of (5.6) and added to the right-hand side of the second equation in (5.5).

[5] In the presence of income effects these derivatives would hold only if income distribution were adjusted optimally so that the marginal utility of income would be 1 for all individuals.

optimal two-part tariffs are (weakly) superior to optimal linear prices.
Starting points for the analysis of two-part tariffs are the papers by Coase
(1946), Oi (1971), Ng and Weisser (1974), and Schmalensee (1981).

As mentioned in Section 3.3 above, Coase two-part tariffs are first-
best. They allow the monopolist to raise, through a uniform fixed fee,
any deficit that would result from marginal-cost pricing. A more equitable solution would weight consumers in relation to their marginal
utilities of income. This is an approach following the lead of Feldstein
(1972b) who analyzes two-part tariffs for a fixed number of consumers.[6]
Although assuming a fixed number of consumers is not usually empirically relevant, it is when a Coase two-part tariff is feasible. Then no one
who is willing to pay more than marginal-cost prices is excluded by the
fixed fee, and therefore Feldstein's result will apply: if smaller consumers
get more weight than larger consumers, then the optimal price p is above
marginal cost and the fixed fee E is lower than for the Coase two-part
tariff. The reason is that the fixed fee acts as a regressive head tax
that can be lowered through an increase in the price. Such an increase
hurts the large customers more than the small customers, while both
types pay the same fixed fee. Auerbach and Pellechio (1978) modified
Feldstein's approach to allow for a change in the number of consumers.

Oi (1971) provided the modern framework for analyzing two-part tariff
monopolies. By eschewing the noncrossing assumption he derives the
dilemma that a profit-maximizing Disneyland monopoly may have to
set the price below marginal cost in order to be able to raise the fixed
fee. From a social point of view, such a monopolist would appear to
produce too much output per customer.

Ng and Weisser (1974), also foregoing the noncrossing assumption,
lay out and solve the problem of two-part tariffs that maximize welfare
under a balanced budget constraint for the monopolist. They make this
problem nontrivial by assuming that the number of customers changes
with the access fee and the price charged by the monopolist. In the case
of constrained optimal two-part tariffs, the markup of the variable price
over marginal cost depends on the relation between consumption of the
marginal consumer and average consumption, while the optimal access

[6] If one thinks of "in relation to" as "reciprocal of," then consumer surplus provides
the correct weighting. Feldstein departs from the income-neutral weighting by reciprocals of marginal social utilities of income and allows for discriminatory entry fees.

fee depends on the elasticity of participation by the marginal consumer only. Again, it can happen that pricing below marginal cost is optimal if there are crossing demand curves.[7]

Schmalensee (1981) comes closest to the conditions present in telecommunications by including a separate cost of access for each consumer. He compares results under profit-oriented and social surplus-oriented policies. Cost of customer access has the implication that in general $C(\sum_i q_i) \neq C(\sum_j q_j)$ even if $\sum_i q_i = \sum_j q_j$ where subscripts i and j denote different partitions of consumers. For simplicity Schmalensee assumes constant access costs F per customer and constant variable costs v per unit of output. Unweighted social surplus can then be expressed as:

$$S(p, E) = \int_{\tau_0}^{1} [V(p, \tau) - F + (p - v)q(p, \tau)] f(\tau) \, d\tau. \tag{5.7}$$

Maximizing $S(p, E)$ with respect to E and p yields first-order conditions:

$$\frac{\partial S}{\partial E} = (E - F)\frac{\partial N}{\partial E} + (p - v)\frac{\partial Q}{\partial E} = 0, \tag{5.8}$$

and:

$$\frac{\partial S}{\partial p} = (E - F)\frac{\partial N}{\partial p} + (p - v)\frac{\partial Q}{\partial p} = 0. \tag{5.9}$$

Both of these conditions are satisfied by marginal-cost prices $p = v$ and $E = F$ (and in this case second-order conditions are satisfied as well). Schmalensee then considers the weighted welfare function:

$$\Gamma(p, E) = \gamma\pi(p, E) + (1 - \gamma)S(p, E) \text{ with } 0 \leq \gamma \leq 1. \tag{5.10}$$

This weighting procedure is equivalent to weighting aggregate consumer surplus by $(1-\gamma)$ and profit by 1, yielding maximization of profit and maximization of social surplus as the extreme cases.[8]

First-order conditions can be written as:

[7]Brown and Heal (1980) treat two-part tariffs in a general equilibrium setting. They remind us of the fact, first pointed out by Guesnerie (1975), that under increasing returns to scale Pareto-efficient marginal-cost pricing equilibria and two-part tariff equilibria may only exist for certain initial endowments.

[8]For a derivation of optimal two-part tariffs with distributional weights applied to the Portuguese telephone sector see Cabral (1990).

$$[E - F + (p - v)q_0]\frac{\partial N}{\partial E} + (p - v)\left[\frac{\partial Q}{\partial E} - q_0\frac{\partial N}{\partial E}\right] = -\gamma N, \qquad (5.11)$$

and:

$$[E - F + (p - v)q_0]\frac{\partial N}{\partial p} + (p - v)\left[\frac{\partial Q}{\partial p} - q_0\frac{\partial N}{\partial p}\right] = -\gamma Q. \qquad (5.12)$$

Here q_0 is the quantity demanded by the marginal consumer.

From these equations and the demand properties stated earlier, Schmalensee derives the following propositions:

1 Profits provided by the marginal customer are strictly positive for $\gamma > 0$. Since Schmalensee has chosen a constant-returns-to-scale framework, overall profits are strictly positive as well in this case.

2 $(p - v)$ has the sign of $\bar{q} - q_0$, where $\bar{q}$ is average consumption of the subscribing customers.

3 If demands are noncrossing, $(p - v) > 0$, which means that average consumption exceeds that of the marginal customer.

4 $(E - F)$ has the sign of $[(\bar{q} - q_0)\frac{\partial Q}{\partial E} - \sigma]$.

5 Under noncrossing demands the sign of $(E - F)$ is ambiguous. The larger the difference between $\bar{q}$ and q_0 the more likely that it is optimal to set E below F. However, E is bounded by 0, because otherwise nonconsuming subscribers would be subsidized.

Another way of viewing Schmalensee's case with $F > 0$ is as a two-product monopoly, where the demand relationships between the products are given by (5.1) to (5.6). The two-product interpretation of two-part tariffs is one of tied sales where usage can only be purchased in conjunction with access. The demand properties establish a special kind of complementarity such that $p < v$ is possible if a consumer with low demand for access (the marginal consumer) demands a larger quantity of usage than the average of the consumers with higher demand for access. This is in contrast to the noncrossing assumption, under which consumer types continue to be one-dimensional, and under which higher demands for access are accompanied by higher demands for usage.

5.3   Two-part tariffs with consumption externalities

As mentioned in Chapter 4, the interaction between network externalities and call externalities can be seen as a two-part tariff problem or as one of two products: access, A, and usage, U. The market quantity of access is N (the number of subscribers) and price is p_A. The quantity of usage is Q and price p_U. Following Einhorn (1990) we assume that the firm's cost function is $C = F + zN + cQ$. Thus, z and c represent the respective marginal costs. We assume that N is a continuous variable, meaning that there is a continuum of consumers. Intensity of demand for access and usage in the consumer population is perfectly correlated and is indexed by τ in increasing order of preference;[9] τ is continuously distributed with density $f(\tau)$ and distribution $F(\tau)$ over support $[0, 1]$.

Following Einhorn (1990) we also provisionally make the assumption of uniform calling patterns (Rohlfs, 1974). This means that for each subscriber the consumer surplus for all her outgoing calls is the same and that each consumer distributes her calls evenly among all other subscribers. Therefore, each consumer receives the same number of phone calls $r_\tau = Q/N = r(Q, N)$, while the number of outgoing calls per customer, q_τ, is an increasing function of τ. Furthermore, each consumer receives the same call-externality benefit e from being called by any other subscriber. At p_A and p_U there will be a marginal customer type τ_0 such that for all $\tau < \tau_0$ access and usage are zero and for all $\tau \geq \tau_0$ access and usage are positive. A customer τ's benefit from calling is the indirect utility $V_\tau^u(p_U)$, assumed to be of the form $V_\tau^u(p_U) = N v_\tau^u(p_U)$. The call externality from being called is $er(Q, N)$ for each customer and eQ for the sum of all customers. A customer τ's benefit from access is:

$$V_\tau^a(p_A, p_U, N) = V_\tau^u(p_U) + er(Q, N) - p_A. \qquad (5.13)$$

The access externality EX created when a customer of marginal type τ_0 joins the network is:

$$EX = \int_{\tau_0}^1 f(\tau) v_\tau^u(p_U) \, d\tau + e q_{\tau_0}, \qquad (5.14)$$

where q_{τ_0} is the quantity of calls made by the marginal consumer. Thus, the first term in (5.14) is the consumer surplus of all those subscribers

[9]This corresponds to the noncrossing assumption. Note that, because the demand for access is a derived demand, we only need the noncrossing assumption for usage and for the call externality.

calling the marginal subscriber, while the second term is the call externality created from being called by the marginal subscriber.

We now consider a regulator who maximizes total consumer surplus plus profits with respect to p_U and p_A and subject to a zero-profit constraint. Since the willingness to pay for access is derived solely from the consumer surplus from calling and from being called, total consumer surplus is the consumer surplus for access. The regulator therefore maximizes:

$$\mathcal{L} = \int_{\tau_0}^{1} f(\tau) V_\tau^a(p_A, p_U, N) \, d\tau + (1 + \lambda)\pi, \tag{5.15}$$

with $\pi = (p_A - z)N + (p_U - c)Q - F$.

The first-order conditions are:

$$(p_A - z)\frac{\partial N}{\partial p_U} + (p_U - c)\frac{\partial Q}{\partial p_U} = -\frac{\lambda Q + e\frac{\partial Q}{\partial p_U} + EX\frac{\partial N}{\partial p_U}}{1 + \lambda}, \tag{5.16}$$

and:

$$(p_A - z)\frac{\partial N}{\partial p_A} + (p_U - c)\frac{\partial Q}{\partial p_A} = -\frac{\lambda N + e\frac{\partial Q}{\partial p_A} + EX\frac{\partial N}{\partial p_A}}{1 + \lambda}. \tag{5.17}$$

Here the partial derivatives are the *observed* demand effects discussed in Section 4.4.1.

What happens to (5.16) and (5.17) if we relax our provisional assumption of a uniform calling pattern and instead assume that for each consumer the quantity of incoming calls is a function of τ just like the quantity of outgoing calls, while the call externality e remains the same for all calls? Then the aggregate call externality is eQ, just as before. However, for each consumer type τ total utility and the distribution of utility between outgoing and incoming calls change. Thus, (5.16) and (5.17) remain formally the same, while parameter values change.

In order to improve our intuition on (5.16) and (5.17), we now consider the most restrictive case where cross effects $\partial N/\partial p_U$ and $\partial Q/\partial p_A$ vanish.[10] In this case (5.16) and (5.17) become:

$$\frac{p_U - c}{p_U} = -\frac{\frac{\lambda}{\epsilon_U} + \frac{e}{p_U}}{1 + \lambda}, \tag{5.18}$$

and:

[10] By (5.5), if one of the cross effects vanishes then so does the other.

$$\frac{p_A - z}{p_A} = -\frac{\frac{\lambda}{\epsilon_A} + \frac{EX}{p_A}}{1 + \lambda}. \qquad (5.19)$$

Equations (5.18) and (5.19) say that prices for access and usage follow an inverse elasticity rule modified by externality effects. Assuming, for illustrative purposes only, that both elasticities are the same ($\epsilon_U = \epsilon_A = \epsilon$) the ratio of Lerner indices for usage and access, L_U/L_A, is given by:

$$\frac{L_U}{L_A} = \frac{\frac{e}{p_U} + \frac{\lambda}{\epsilon}}{\frac{EX}{p_A} + \frac{\lambda}{\epsilon}}. \qquad (5.20)$$

Here e/p_U and EX/p_A are the externalities per dollar spent on calling and access, respectively. Since λ/ϵ is negative, (5.20) says that the service with the larger externality per dollar would receive the lower markup (which could become negative).

We may now return to (5.16) and (5.17). They can be interpreted in terms of superelasticities. The result is again that, for the same superelasticities, the service with the larger externality effect per dollar receives the larger *correction* in the markup relative to the inverse elasticity rule.

Now, what does the relative externality effect per dollar depend on, and can the call externality effect be larger than the network externality effect? Departing from the specific assumptions chosen to derive (5.16) and (5.17), we can say that the network externality effect depends on the elasticity of entry of marginal consumers and on the interaction of marginal consumers with all the other consumers. In contrast, the call externality effect depends on the interaction between *all* consumers. So the call externality effect can be larger than the network externality effect, and this will occur at some sufficiently high level of market penetration. In a large population, as penetration reaches 100 percent, the call externality effect has to exceed the network externality effect. Thus, the presence of call externalities somewhat offsets equity justifications for reducing the price of access. In the extreme case where a Coase tariff is feasible, the access price would have to be *above* the marginal cost of access and the usage price *below* the marginal cost of usage.

5.4 Discriminatory two-part tariffs

A set of constrained optimal two-part tariffs for the various outputs of a telecommunications carrier can be substantially more efficient than simple (one-part) Ramsey prices. However, the access fees of such tariffs may exclude customers who are willing to pay more than the cost of services (or who would be included under such Ramsey prices). This deficiency raises two issues: First, how can efficiency be increased? Second, is exclusion equitable and if not, how can equity be improved?

The answer to both questions may lie in discriminatory two-part tariffs. Clearly, if the firm (or regulator) is fully informed about demand by every type of customer, then perfect price discrimination can be mimicked by using distinct type-specific two-part tariffs that have a variable price equal to marginal cost and an access fee equal to consumer surplus for each consumer type at the marginal-cost price. This result, while it maximizes social surplus, would give consumers no surplus at all. In the absence of income effects, an allocatively equivalent solution would reduce the access fees so that profits of the regulated firm would vanish. This reduction in access fees could be proportional for all consumer types, or it could be related to the marginal utilities of income of consumers in support of some income distributional goal (Feldstein, 1972b). This then could lead to some of the social tariffs described in Chapter 11.

Brander and Spencer (1985) take up the issue of customer-class pricing in a constrained optimal two-part tariff framework. They assume that there are L customer groups designated by superscripts l. Within each customer group demands and consumer surplus properties are described by (5.1)–(5.6) by attaching superscript l to all demanded quantities, prices, etc. Costs are assumed to be a function of aggregate demand only.[11] Brander and Spencer maximize a function:

$$W[(p, E)] = \sum_l CS^l[(p, E)] + (1 + \lambda)\pi[(p, E)], \qquad (5.21)$$

where $(p, E) = ((p^1, E^1), \ldots, (p^L, E^L))$ and λ is the Lagrange multiplier of the balanced-budget constraint.

They derive first-order conditions:

$$(p^l - \frac{\partial C}{\partial Q})\frac{\partial Q^l}{\partial p^l} + E^l\frac{\partial N^l}{\partial p^l} = -\frac{\lambda}{1 + \lambda}Q^l, \qquad (5.22)$$

and:

[11] It would be easy to introduce a fixed cost per investment as done by Schmalensee (1981).

$$(p^l - \frac{\partial C}{\partial Q})\frac{\partial Q^l}{\partial E^l} + E^i\frac{\partial N^l}{\partial E^l} = -\frac{\lambda}{1+\lambda}N^l \qquad \text{for all } l = 1,\ldots,L. \qquad (5.23)$$

These conditions lead to the following propositions:

1 If $\partial N^l/\partial E^l = 0$ holds at the optimum for some group l with positive subscribership, then $\lambda = 0$ and $p^l = \partial C/\partial Q^l$.

This says that, if membership in group l is independent of a change in E^l, then E^l can be used as a lumpsum transfer to finance marginal-cost pricing.

2 If $\lambda > 0$, then the sign of $(p^l - \partial C/\partial Q)$ is the same as that of $(\bar{q}^l - q_0^l)$. Here $\bar{q}^l$ is individual consumption by the average consumer in group l, and q_0^l is the individual consumption by the marginal consumer in that group. This property parallels the one derived by Schmalensee (1981).[12]

Relevant for customer-class pricing may be that demand curves *between* customer groups cross, while *within* groups the noncrossing assumption holds. (Such crossings may result from multidimensional type parameters which, for all practical purposes have to be reduced to one dimension.) If that holds, prices will exceed marginal costs.

5.5 Smooth nonlinear tariffs

In principle, a nonlinear tariff can be smooth in the sense that it corresponds to a differentiable outlay schedule for consumers. The outlay schedule can have many different shapes. In particular, a single outlay schedule can include convex sections (quantity premia) and concave sections (quantity discounts). The properties of social surplus-maximizing smooth nonlinear tariffs have been analyzed by Goldman, Leland, and Sibley (1984), Mirman and Sibley (1980), and Wilson (1989b).

5.5.1 A consumption framework using demand profiles

Recently, Wilson (1989b, based on Oren, Smith, and Wilson, 1982, and related to Brown and Sibley, 1986) has suggested a somewhat unusual demand framework for analyzing nonlinear prices. He uses the concept of a *market demand profile* rather than the market demand curve. The

---

[12]See proposition 2, page 80.

market demand curve $Q(p)$ gives the relationship between (linear) price and total quantity demanded. In contrast, the market demand profile $N(p, q)$ gives the number of customers who will buy at least quantity q at a (linear) price p. In the following we will sometimes treat N as an integer, and sometimes as a continuous variable so that $N(p, q)$ can be differentiated. This is less legitimate the smaller the number of customers becomes. The demand profile defined in this way is restricted to the case of no income effects and can be applied only for nonlinear price schedules that cut the conventional demand curve only once, from below. The latter property precludes the application of the demand profile to two-part tariffs, which also cut the demand curve at zero quantity. The absence of income effects is necessary to ensure that the inframarginal parts of nonlinear price schedules do not themselves affect the demand of a given consumer type.[13]

For a given price p, the number of customers N is a declining function of q because everyone who consumes a large quantity must also consume the small quantity, but not vice versa. Increases in p cause the function to shift inward. The quantity demanded in the market at price p can be expressed in terms of the market demand profile as the sum (integral) of $N(p, q)$ over all q:

$$Q(p) = \sum_{q=0}^{\infty} N(p, q). \tag{5.24}$$

This equation holds because $N(p, q)$ are all customers consuming in the increment between $q-1$ and q. Conceptually (as, e.g., Brown and Sibley, 1986) we can treat this increment as a small market which serves $N(p, q)$ consumers.[14] Summing over all of these increment markets gives us the total market demand.

Alternatively:

$$Q(p) = -\sum_{q=0}^{\infty} \frac{\partial N}{\partial q} q. \tag{5.25}$$

---

[13] Wilson (1989b) also introduces a concept of general demand profiles that allow for the presence of income effects. However, this concept is extremely cumbersome, and its properties are not well worked out.

[14] There is a problem of inferring willingness to pay from demand profile information: $N(p, q)$ cannot readily be inverted so that $q(p, N)$ could be used.

This equation holds, because $-\partial N/\partial q = n$ gives us the number of customers consuming precisely q, and market demand is the sum of quantities consumed by all customers. This also suggests expressing the
demand profile as:

$$N(p,q) = \sum_{x \geq q} n(p,x) = 1 - \Phi(p,q). \tag{5.26}$$

The second equality normalizes the total customer population to be 1.
$\Phi(p,q)$ is therefore the cumulative distribution function of customers
consuming at most q.

An important concept in nonlinear pricing is the *price elasticity of
the demand profile*, $\epsilon_{Np}(p,q) = (p/N)(\partial N/\partial p)$, which is evaluated at
q. This is the relative change in the number of customers consuming q
divided by the relative change in p. How is this elasticity related to more
familiar demand elasticities? Since we have expressed market demand
in terms of the market demand profile, we can also express the market
demand elasticity, ϵ_{Qp}, in terms of the demand profile elasticities:

$$
\begin{aligned}
\epsilon_{Qp} &= \frac{\partial Q}{\partial p}\frac{p}{Q} = \sum_{q=0}^{\infty} \frac{\partial N(p,q)}{\partial p}\frac{p}{Q} = \sum_{q=0}^{\infty} \epsilon_{Np}(p,q)\frac{N}{Q} \\
&= \sum_{q=0}^{\infty} \epsilon_{Np}(p,q)\frac{N(p,q)}{\sum_{x=0}^{\infty} N(p,x)} \\
&= \sum_{q=0}^{\infty} \epsilon_{Np}(p,q)w(q), \tag{5.27}
\end{aligned}
$$

where $w(q)$ is the profile weight of q in Q. Thus, the market demand
elasticity is a weighted average of the demand profile elasticities, where
the weights are proportional to the demand profiles. This means that,
the more elastic is the market demand, the more elastic, on average, are
the demand profiles. In this sense we can extend our intuition from market demand to the demand profiles. On the other hand, there is some
distinct structure in demand profile elasticities. Recall that on ordinary
demand curves the quantity is q, whereas on the demand profile the
quantity is N. The *larger* is q, the *smaller* is the N of the corresponding demand profile $N(p,q)$. Hence, in constrast to ordinary demand
curves, we can also expect the demand profiles to become more elastic

the larger the corresponding q. In particular, the profile elasticity for the largest consumption increment q is infinite, because, at that increment, all remaining consumers drop out of the market.

Now consider the relationship between demand profile elasticity and individual demand. To do this, we assume that consumers can be ranked as customer types τ by their intensity of demand. We assume τ to be a one-dimensional variable and make the noncrossing assumption for demand curves. Then individual demand D is a function of price and of consumer type: $D(p, \tau)$.[15]

Total market demand is the aggregate of individual demands:

$$Q(p) = \sum_{\tau=0}^{T} D(p, \tau) f(\tau), \tag{5.28}$$

where $f(\tau)$ is the mass (density) of τ. Consequently, the relationship between individual and market demand elasticities is:

$$\epsilon_{Qp} = \sum_{\tau=0}^{T} \epsilon_{Dp} \frac{D}{Q} f(\tau), \tag{5.29}$$

again a weighted average. Here the weights are the demands of consumer type τ in the total market demand.

Assuming that τ is a continuous variable, the relationship between individual demand elasticities and the market demand profile elasticity is given by Wilson (1989b, p. 112) as:

$$\epsilon_{Np} = \epsilon_{Dp} \frac{\epsilon_{F\tau}}{\epsilon_{D\tau}}. \tag{5.30}$$

This expression can be interpreted as follows: The market demand profile elasticity evaluated at q and p equals the individual demand elasticity of the marginal consumer type multiplied by the ratio between the relative frequency of this type, $\epsilon_{F\tau} = f\tau/F$, and the relative shift in individual demand as consumer types change, $\epsilon_{D\tau} = (\partial D/\partial \tau)(\tau/D)$. The denominator here results from the fact that there is no natural metric for consumer types.

Another way of stating the market demand profile elasticity is:

---

[15] The demand profile need not be continuous at $q = 0$. Suppose that $D(p(0), \tau(0)) = 0$ at a price schedule $p(q)$, then $\lim_{q \to 0+} N(p, q) = 1 - F(\tau(0)) < 1$, whereas $N(p(0), 0) = 1$.

$$\epsilon_{Np} = p \left[\frac{f(\tau)}{1 - F(\tau)} \right] \frac{\partial \tau}{\partial p}. \tag{5.31}$$

Here the fraction in brackets is the *hazard rate* of the type distribution. Moving along the cumulative distribution function of types, the hazard rate is the conditional probability for consumers of type τ of being passed by.[16] Wilson (1989b) assumes that the hazard rate is increasing in τ, which is compatible with $f(\tau)$ decreasing.

In order to discuss consumer welfare in terms of the demand profile we go to a continuous change in q. Market demand Q evaluated at p becomes the integral under the market demand profile evaluated at p:

$$Q(p) = \int_0^\infty N(p, q)\, dq. \tag{5.32}$$

Consumer surplus is then the integral between price and the demand curve:

$$CS(p) = \int_p^\infty \int_0^\infty N(p, q)\, dq\, dp. \tag{5.33}$$

We know that in the absence of income effects Roy's identity becomes:

$$\frac{\partial CS}{\partial p} = -Q(p) = -\int_0^q N(p, q)\, dq. \tag{5.34}$$

This is a property that we can use in interpreting results. Also, since there are no income effects, $CS(p)$ is convex. This property allows us to use linear approximations of consumer surplus changes under a piece-meal policy of the type to be described in Section 5.9.

Using the demand profile rather than consumer types has two distinct advantages: First, the demand profile can in principle be estimated from aggregate data about the distribution of purchase quantities. Second, straightforward and intuitively appealing inverse elasticity rules for nonlinear tariffs emerge as optimality conditions.

5.5.2 The inverse elasticity rule for smooth nonlinear tariffs

We can now state the main result on nonlinear tariffs for a single service. Defining $R(q)$ as the outlay schedule and $p(q) \equiv dR/dq$ as the price schedule, the problem is to find $R(q)$ such that:

---

[16]See Tirole (1988), p. 156.

$$R(q) = \arg\max \left[CS\big(R(q)\big) + (1 + \lambda)\big(R(q) - C(q)\big) \right]. \tag{5.35}$$

As first-order conditions Wilson (1989b) derives, for all values of q:

$$\frac{p(q) - MC(q)}{p(q)} = -\frac{\alpha}{\epsilon_{Np}}, \tag{5.36}$$

where $\alpha = \lambda/(1 + \lambda)$ is a parameter between 0 and 1 that is the same for all q. For the profit-maximizing monopolist $\alpha = 1$. In case of unconstrained welfare maximization, $\alpha = 0$. In case of budget-constrained welfare maximization and oligopolistic competition $0 \leq \alpha \leq 1$. An alternative formulation of (5.36) is:

$$\big(p(q) - MC(q)\big)\frac{\partial N(p, q)}{\partial p(q)} = -\alpha N(p, q). \tag{5.37}$$

The left-hand side of this equation gives the surplus reduction from a marginal change in the price schedule at q. Following from Roy's identity the right-hand side is α times the corresponding decrease in consumer surplus.

Equation (5.36) is the inverse elasticity rule for nonuniform pricing:

> At each point on a nonuniform outlay schedule $R(q)$, the percentage markup between marginal price and marginal cost is inversely proportional to the elasticity of demand for an increment of consumption at that point with respect to the marginal price at that point.[17]

The main lesson from this is that *quantity premia and discounts may be justified by differences in demand elasticities, as well as by cost differences.* Due to its perfectly elastic demand profile the largest output unit purchased is associated with a marginal-cost price $p(q) = MC$.[18]

Contrary to Brown and Sibley (1986), Wilson (1989b) assumes that outlay schedules are concave so that the marginal outlay $p = dR/dq$ is nonincreasing. He makes this assumption in order to prevent arbitrage opportunities from occurring for a customer who might otherwise pretend to be two or more customers. Wilson's assumption, however, is more restrictive than needed for this purpose. The assumption can be

---

[17]Brown and Sibley (1986), p. 128.
[18]To the best of our knowledge this rule was first formulated by Goldman, Leland, and Sibley in a 1977 working paper that was published as Goldman, Leland, and Sibley (1984).

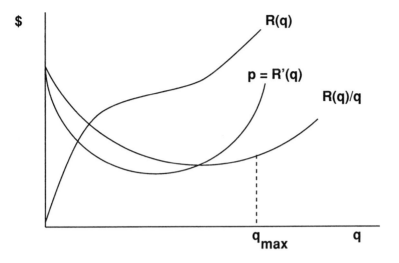

Figure 5.3
Subadditive outlay function

relaxed to the subadditivity assumption that $R(\sum q_i) \leq \sum \left(R(q_i)\right)$ for all combinations of q_i.[19] This assumption allows for all functional forms that have been identified as cost functions under natural monopoly. For example, the schedule shown in Figure 5.3 would be feasible over the range $[0, q_{max}]$.

On the other hand, it is true that, for a wide class of consumer type distributions (with increasing hazard rates), utility functions, and cost functions, the optimal outlay schedule involves quantity discounts and is therefore concave.[20] However, this is a *result* rather than an *assumption*. The main reason for this result lies in consumer self-selection: Under nonlinear outlay schedules consumers can choose average outlays as a function of quantity. It then turns out to be optimal to associate high-demand consumers with lower average (and marginal) outlays and with larger quantities. This is definitely true for the largest consumers who pay a marginal outlay equal to marginal cost.

---

[19] In Section 2.1.5 we used the subadditivity assumption to describe the natural monopoly property of a cost function.
[20] See Maskin and Riley (1984), Proposition 6, pp. 185-6.

5.5.3 Dynamic nonlinear pricing with network externalities

As mentioned in Section 4.7.1, Dhebar and Oren (1985a), Xie and Sirbu (1988), and Woroch (1989) have constructed dynamic pricing models with network externalities. In each case the firm would offer a price path for achieving optimal penetration over time. Dhebar and Oren (1985b) introduce the additional feature that at any moment in time there is a smooth nonlinear outlay schedule so that the instantaneous price for usage is quantity dependent. This is somewhat different from other presentations of network externalities, where access is viewed as a commodity separate from use. In Dhebar and Oren (1985b) the two are integrated into one outlay function $R(q, t)$, where t represents time. The outlay function then has two components; $s(t)$ is the subscription charge and $p(q, t)$ the marginal price of use. The schedule has at most one fixed charge at $q = 0$ and is otherwise twice continuously differentiable. A consumer τ has an instantaneous surplus:

$$CS(q, \tau, N) - R(q, t), \tag{5.38}$$

where N is the total number of subscribers. The noncrossing assumption applies to demand as a function of q and N. There is no setup cost for joining, and no exit cost for leaving, the network. There is a marginal subscriber τ_0 with the property:

$$CS(q, \tau_0, N) - R(q, t) = 0. \tag{5.39}$$

The demand for network access is in equilibrium if the marginal subscriber has zero consumer surplus at her optimal consumption volume. Equilibrium thus defines the equilibrium subscriber set in the sense of Rohlfs (1974). Following Rohlfs the set of equilibria can be characterized in a price/quantity diagram by the null set ($N = q = 0$ for all p) plus an inverted parabola (Figure 4.3, p. 57). The upward sloping part of the parabola is unstable, in the sense that small perturbations of N around the equilibrium path lead away from these equilibria. It turns out that the null set and the downward sloping portion of the inverted parabola are stable equilibria for $p(q, t) \neq 0$.

Given that there are no entry and exit costs for the consumers, anticipations of future price schedules do not affect current subscription and consumption decisions. However, the authors assume that individual consumers anticipate growth of subscribership and that consumers base their current subscription decision on an anticipated subscriber set characterized by type indices in the interval $[\nu\tau + (1 - \nu)\tau_0, 1]$, where τ_0 is the marginal user class and ν is a *growth anticipation* parameter. Thus, the subscriber set is not assumed to be in equilibrium at all times. While the possibility of disequilibria in a dynamic setting adds welcome realism to the model, it is debatable whether the particular assumption about consumer anticipations is the best one to make. In reality, the costs of changing network access decisions certainly play a role.

The subscription demand expressed as the set of consumers wishing to subscribe is denoted by d^ν. The authors adopt a generic diffusion model in continuous time. The network growth dynamics are characterized by a diffusion function $G[N(t), d^\nu(N, R)]$ with the properties:

1 $\partial G/\partial d > 0$. The network expands faster, the higher subscription demand.

2 $G \geq 0$ for $d^\nu \geq N$. If subscription demand exceeds subscribership, then the network grows.

3 $\partial G/\partial d = -\partial G/\partial N$ for all $d^\nu = N \geq 0$. No growth occurs on the equilibrium subscriber set.

Cost is assumed to be of the form:

$$C(Q, N, \frac{\partial N}{\partial t}) = \int_{\tau_0}^{1} C_1(q_\tau)\, d\tau + C_2(N, \frac{\partial N}{\partial t}). \tag{5.40}$$

Here C_1 and C_2 are the quantity-related and network size-related cost components, assumed to be stationary and twice continuously differentiable.

The cost function defined in equation (5.40) is unusual in two respects. First, it additively separates network costs from usage costs. Second, usage costs depend on total usage, and network costs depend on a dynamic adjustment cost factor $\partial N/\partial t$. The additive separability may be restrictive in the telecommunications application, since usage costs here may depend on the size of the network (number of nodes). Otherwise (5.40) appears to be appropriate.

The regulator chooses the $R(q, t)$ that maximizes the discounted weighted sum of total surplus and profits, applying weights γ and $(1-\gamma)$, respectively, and using a discount rate δ. This objective function contains profit maximization ($\gamma = 0$) and surplus maximization ($\gamma = 1$) as limiting cases.

The maximization problem can be decomposed into two nested problems. The price setter's first problem is to find an optimal consumption pattern which implies an optimal usage charge schedule $p^*(q,t)$. The second optimization problem requires the determination of optimal trajectories $s^*(t)$ and $N^*(t)$. Solving these problems the authors derive the *instantaneous inverse elasticity rule* for nonlinear price schedules:

$$\frac{p(q) - \frac{\partial C_1}{\partial q}}{p(q)} = -\frac{1 - \gamma}{\epsilon_{\tau_0, p(q)}}, \tag{5.41}$$

where $\epsilon_{\tau_0, p(q)}$ is the marginal price elasticity of the market demand for the qth unit of the product. This corresponds to the profile elasticity defined earlier.

Given the optimal instantaneous usage outlay function and consumption pattern, the remaining optimization is an optimal control problem with $N(t)$ as the state variable and the trajectory $s(t)$ as the control variable. Dhebar and Oren state three regimes for $s(t)$:

$$(a) \qquad s = 0, \tag{5.42}$$

$$(b) \qquad 0 < s < CS(q, \tau_0, N) - p^*(q^*), \quad \text{and} \tag{5.43}$$

$$(c) \qquad s = CS(q, \tau_0, N) - p^*(q^*). \tag{5.44}$$

In case (a) subscription is free, and all consumers will subscribe. In case (b) the marginal subscriber has a positive consumer surplus, and spontaneous network growth will occur. In case (c) the marginal subscriber has zero consumer surplus. Dhebar and Oren (1985a) show that a steady-state equilibrium cannot be reached under case (c). Hence, only (5.42) and (5.43) can be relevant for approaching steady-state equilibria. Starting out with case (a) involves a *bang-bang policy* in which the subscriber fee jumps from zero to the steady-state equilibrium value. According to Dhebar and Oren, this policy is restricted to the case of a linear Hamiltonian in $s(t)$. Instead, Dhebar and Oren consider a concave Hamiltonian leading to an optimal feedback policy that is triggered by market penetration rather than by the progression in time.[21] The network is monotonically increasing over time, converging to the optimal

---

[21] Since their analytical formulations and results are highly complex, Dhebar and Oren conclude their paper with numerical examples.

steady state. The optimal steady-state network size is shown to decrease in the discount rate and increase in the growth anticipation, while the opposite holds for the optimal steady-state subscription price s.

5.6 Discrete multipart and optional two-part tariffs

5.6.1 Introduction

It is fairly straightforward to characterize the properties of optimal smooth nonlinear tariffs, as we have done above. However, in practice such tariffs seem to be used rarely. Instead, one frequently observes tariffs consisting of several discrete parts, usually called *blocks*. As shown in the step function in Figure 5.4, these blocks are discrete quantity intervals within which the same (marginal) price holds. There appear to be several reasons for the lack of smooth tariffs:

- Consumers rarely comprehend formulas, yet they do understand tariffs consisting of several parts. However, some smooth types of tariffs are actually very simple, for example linearly increasing quantity discounts.

- Firms lack information about costs and demands. In particular, data may only come in discrete form, or there may only be discretely identifiable consumer types. A piecewise-linear approximation may then be just as good as a smooth curve.

- Even when full information is available, approximations do very well (according to Wilson, 1989b).

- Piecewise-linear tariffs may be the result of a combination of optional two-part tariffs, which themselves may be the result of regulatory restrictions on tariff setting. *Optional tariffs* are alternative rate structures that apply to the same consumption conditions, one of which the consumer may choose for billing. Under an *ex ante* optional tariff the consumer must declare the tariff before choosing the consumption quantity. Under an *ex post* tariff the choice can be declared after the consumption quantity is known, and in this case the choice can be replaced by having the supplier select the tariff that is best for the consumer for the consumer's chosen quantity.

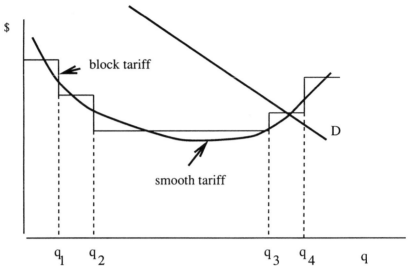

Figure 5.4
Block and smooth tariffs

- A further reason, brought out by Goldman, Leland, and Sibley (1984), is that there may be gaps in smooth outlay schedules, for instance, if the constraint $d\tau/dq \geq 0$ is binding.

5.6.2 Pareto superiority of optional tariffs

Whereas optional tariffs can be interpreted simply as special types of nonlinear tariffs, there is one particular feature that has made them stand out in the literature. As developed extensively first by Willig (1978) optional tariffs can be designed in such a way that they are Pareto-superior to tariffs without the optional part. In technical terms, an $(n+1)$-part tariff can be made Pareto-superior to an n-part tariff. Specifically, a supplier can offer an additional tariff as one option while keeping the old, existing tariffs as the other option.

Clearly, by revealed preference all customers choosing the new tariff must be better off. For the firm (or the regulator) the major task then remains to find an additional tariff that makes the firm at least as well off as before. This can often be done without any specific knowledge of demand, as long as the firm's (marginal) costs are known.[22]

5.6.3 Problem of intermediate goods

There is a restriction, however, first noticed by Ordover and Panzar (1980), which calls into question the Pareto superiority of optional tariffs. The restriction is that Willig's result only holds unambiguously for buyers who are final consumers. If the buyers of telephone services are themselves firms, then these services become intermediate inputs. Now, the optional tariffs usually result in quantity discounts which will affect competition between these firms. It may then be impossible to design Pareto-superior optional tariffs.

Ordover and Panzar (1980) construct an example to illustrate this impossibility. They assume that a monopolistic supplier sells its output to two types of buyers, l and h, who use this service as an input and who compete on the same output market. This latter market is assumed to be perfectly competitive. The only difference between the two types of firms is that the l-firm has access to a lower cost technology (or some scarce input) than the h-firm, with $\partial C_l / \partial q_l < \partial C_h / \partial q_h$ for all outputs q of the downstream firms. The number of l-firms cannot be expanded. If the monopolist offers its service at a profit-maximizing linear price $p > MC$, then equilibrium requires that h-firms break even at marginal-cost prices in the downstream market while l-firms earn a rent. Also, the l-firms will be larger than the h-firms. If the monopolist now offers a nonlinear outlay schedule with a marginal price for the larger purchases that is below the linear price, then this will lead to an expansion of the l-firms and a market exit of h-firms (even taking into consideration that the expansion of the l-firms might allow the monopolist to reduce the price to the h-firms as well). Ordover and Panzar show that this strategy can never be profitable to the monopolist.

The essence of Ordover and Panzar's example is the specific kind of interaction in demand between the two types of buyers. Due to call externalities and network externalities, demand interactions could also appear between final consumers of telecommunications services, not just between intermediate goods buyers of telecommunications services. However, restricting attention to firms as buyers, there is another aspect

---

[22] As described in Section 10.4, Heyman, Lazorchak, Sibley, and Taylor (1987) neatly illustrate this possibility and apply the principle to customer access charges proposed for New York.

that does not come out in Ordover and Panzar's example: due to nonlinear prices, some buyers may lose their rents. In the above example
this would have been the case if the h-firms had also earned rents in the
initial equilibrium with the linear price but had been forced out of the
market due to the price change.

If no Pareto-superior nonlinear outlay schedule exists, then optional
tariffs may actually hurt some consumers. One way out of this problem (chosen in the United States) appears to be to allow resale which
would make these tariffs indirectly available to disadvantaged consumer
groups. As explained below in Section 6.4.2, this reduces sustainable
rate differences to the cost of arbitrage. However, Pareto superiority
may still be unachievable. In the most favorable case for sustainability, with zero transaction cost of resale, the outlay schedule will have
to be linear and there will be no Pareto-improving change. With positive transaction costs some buyers will be excluded from the benefits of
quantity discounts, and that gives room for competitive disadvantages
of these buyers compared to larger buyers.

5.6.4 Incentive compatibility and self-selection constraints

Optional two-part tariffs represent a type of price discrimination between
groups where customers, through their choice of tariff, self-select the
group into which they belong. Under rationality and full information
each consumer prefers the tariff chosen over the tariffs not chosen. This
does not mean that the consumer prefers the chosen tariff over its entire
range, but just at the preferred consumption level. Thus, if two-part
tariffs are indexed by subscripts k and l, then incentive compatibility
requires that indirect utility levels for consumers choosing tariff k be:

$$V\big((p_k, E_k)\big) \geq V\big((p_l, E_l)\big) \text{ for all tariffs } l = 1, \ldots, L. \tag{5.45}$$

We now index consumers and the tariffs chosen by these consumers
by $\tau = 1, \ldots, T$. If the noncrossing assumption holds, then (5.45) is
implied by two constraints (Sharkey and Sibley, 1991)—the *downward
incentive compatibility* constraint:

$$V_\tau\big((p_\tau, E_\tau)\big) \geq V_\tau\big((p_{\tau-1}, E_{\tau-1})\big) \tag{5.46}$$

and the *upward incentive compatibility* constraint:

$$V_\tau\big((p_\tau, E\tau)\big) \geq V_\tau\big((p_{\tau+1}, E_{\tau+1})\big). \tag{5.47}$$

Hence under noncrossing demands we only have to be concerned about incentive compatibility between adjacent customer groups. Also, any tariff chosen has to obey the *participation constraint*:

$$V_\tau\big((p_\tau, E_\tau)\big) \geq 0. \tag{5.48}$$

In fact, due to the incentive compatibility constraints the participation constraint only has to be imposed on the marginal consumer group τ_0.

In addition, Faulhaber and Panzar (1977) derive *self-selection constraints*. Under the noncrossing assumption, optional tariffs must have the property that the lower envelope of a set of two-part tariffs is concave:

$$p_\tau \geq p_{\tau+1} \text{ and } E_\tau \leq E_{\tau+1} \text{ for } \tau = 1, \ldots, T-1. \tag{5.49}$$

If these inequalities did not hold, then a consumer type τ might be induced to purchase a smaller quantity than a consumer type $\tau - 1$. This quantity would be cheaper under (p_τ, E_τ) than under $(p_{\tau-1}, E_{\tau-1})$, but then it would also be preferred by the consumer with $\tau - 1$.

5.6.5 Welfare weights

Sharkey and Sibley (1991) analyze optional two-part tariff with welfare weights for different consumers. The transaction cost advantage of optional two-part tariffs over other discriminating two-part tariffs is that consumers self-select into consumption categories – no certification of needs is required. However, there are two disadvantages as compared to certification. First, self-selecting tariffs correspond to concave outlay schedules. This feature reduces the regulator's ability to improve the welfare of the smallest customers. Second, regulators (or firms) have to know the type distribution in the population, and types have to be one-dimensional (to avoid hopelessly complicated derivations). Sharkey and Sibley allow for either decreasing or constant, or increasing, welfare weights. Decreasing (increasing) welfare weights mean that the smallest (largest) customers get the highest weight.

Besides the usual noncrossing assumption and simplifying assumptions on the firm's cost $\big(C(Q) = C(\sum_k Q_k)\big)$, Sharkey and Sibley assume that the number of optional two-part tariffs, L, equals the number of homogeneous consumer types, T. Had the authors assumed $L > T$ the number of different tariffs would still have been bounded by T. The assumption of $L = T$ is not restrictive because pooling is always a possibility. *Pooling* of tariffs means that two distinct (adjacent) consumer groups are charged under the same tariff. Assuming $L = T$ initially implies that consumers who are different only get the same tariff if pooling of tariffs is optimal. In particular, consumers with the largest τ $(= T)$ will always face a marginal price equal to marginal cost.

Sharkey and Sibley's analysis generates these interesting results:

- As the extreme case of decreasing welfare weights consider Rawlsian tariffs, defined as those where the smallest customers receive all the weight. Then, in spite of all the welfare weight going to the smallest consumers, larger customers will nevertheless receive more consumer surplus than smaller customers. Also, the general set of optional two-part tariffs will consist either of the Coase two-part tariff, with the same fixed fee for everyone and the variable price equal to marginal cost, or it will consist of a choice between several two-part tariffs where the largest customers pay a variable price equal to marginal cost and the small customers pay a variable price in excess of marginal cost. In the latter case the small customers will pay a smaller fixed fee than the larger customers, but in both cases the small consumers will pay a higher *average* price.

- If large users get higher welfare weights than small users, then the largest users may face a marginal price below marginal cost. Also, if Coase tariffs are not feasible, then the group of smallest consumers will be left with zero consumer surplus.

Thus, compared to linear tariffs, optional tariffs appear to be a good tool to redistribute welfare in favor of large consumers, whereas they are a much weaker instrument for shifting the distribution in favor of small consumers. However, if optional tariffs are already in use in a market, different welfare weights may have significant redistributional effects.

5.6.6 Optional versus nonlinear tariffs

In most of the literature (starting with Faulhaber and Panzar, 1977) optional and nonlinear tariffs are treated as *equivalent* to each other in the sense that under certain (usually assumed) conditions any arbitrary (linear or nonlinear) tariff combined with a set of optional tariffs can be

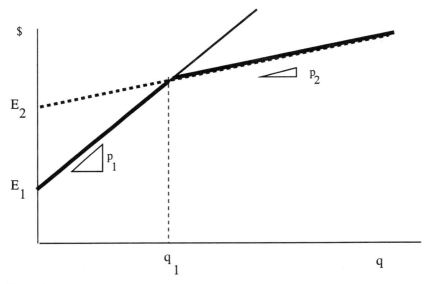

Figure 5.5
Optional and multipart tariffs

replaced by some other nonlinear tariff that, for all distributions of demand, gives the same outcome for consumers and the firm. Usually, this equivalence is only stated explicitly for a set of optional self-selecting two-part tariffs. Note that the implication only goes in one direction: A set of optional two-part tariffs implies a nonlinear outlay schedule consisting of the undominated parts of the 2 two-part tariffs. This is the bold lower envelope of the two-part tariffs drawn in Figure 5.5. Due to the fact that the outlay schedule for each of the two-part tariffs is affine linear and upward sloping, the resulting nonlinear schedule is concave. This means that the reverse implication does not hold, because a nonconcave outlay schedule cannot be represented by a set of optional two-part tariffs – there does not exist, for every nonlinear tariff, a set of optional tariffs that could generate this nonlinear, nonconcave tariff.

The equivalence result requires that several assumptions hold. Consumers must have perfect information about their individual demands, and suppliers must be informed about demands of groups of homogeneous consumers. Also, there must be no intermediate demand, no transactions costs, and no competition between suppliers. If the implementation of optional tariffs implies additional costs, then optional tariffs must have a compensating advantage to be preferred. The fact that, in spite of additional transactions costs, optional tariffs are observed in practice leads to the conclusion that at least one of the other assumptions needed for the equivalence of optional and nonlinear tariffs is violated. We take up this issue in further detail in Chapter 8 when discussing optional calling plans for residential customers.

From a fairness perspective optional tariffs may be viewed as preferable to other tariffs that lead to the same surplus results. Optional tariffs are procedurally fair by providing consumers with choices that include the status-quo tariff. Even if the consumer makes the wrong choice, this could be preferred to the correct choice imposed on the consumer by the telecommunications supplier.

5.6.7 Nonlinear tariffs with discrete blocks

If there is a finite number T of discrete homogeneous consumer types, then we can essentially sort these consumers by a T-part block tariff. With T homogeneous consumer groups the optimal T-part tariff turns out to be as good as the optimal smooth tariff. But what about a $(T-1)$-part tariff? Such a tariff is welfare dominated by the optimal T-part tariff. Nevertheless, we may want to restrict ourselves to a tariff with fewer parts than the number of distinct consumer types. The main reason for this is a tradeoff argument. The additional gain from adding another block to a multiblock tariff is a Harberger triangle. The more blocks are added, the smaller these additional triangles become.[23] At the same time, additional blocks increase the cost of metering by the supplier and the cost of optimization and comprehension by the buyers. Thus, decreasing marginal benefits tend to be outweighed by increasing transaction costs.

In previous sections we looked at the problem of piecewise linear tariffs as one of choosing T self-selecting two-part tariffs. That problem is a somewhat more restricted one, because having each of the self-selecting two-part tariffs available over the whole range of quantities imposes concavity on the resulting equivalent nonlinear outlay schedule. Concavity of the outlay schedule (that is, quantity discounts) is optimal under

---

[23] This problem of the optimal number of blocks formally resembles the one of finding the optimal number of periods for peak-load pricing. For an attempt to solve this particular peak-load pricing problem see Rees (1976).

certain conditions on the distribution of preferences (and the cost function). In particular, an increasing hazard rate of the distribution $f(\tau)$ of consumer types is sufficient for the optimal nonlinear schedule to be concave.[24] However, if the number of types T is discrete, then this condition is violated, and therefore the optimal nonlinear schedule may not be implementable as a set of optional tariffs (Tirole, 1988, p. 157). In the following, however, we assume that it is possible. This condition is fulfilled if larger purchases are accompanied by more elastic demands.

We consider the case of a smaller number of blocks than consumer types. The blocks could then correspond to consumer groups, but each group would be defined as a discrete interval of the type distribution. In particular, we may want to combine a given linear tariff p with only one optional two-part tariff (E_1, p_1). We know that, if the group of consumers choosing the optional part is homogeneous, then the welfare-optimal marginal price to these consumers will have to equal marginal cost. Conversely, if this group of large consumers is not homogeneous but nevertheless pays a common price, then the optimal marginal price will have to *exceed* marginal cost for all consumers. This definitely holds for the case of a continuous distribution of types with a finite number of optional two-part tariffs (Faulhaber and Panzar, 1977). The main reason is that, within the group of largest consumers, the size of the fixed fee is restricted by those types with smaller willingness to pay. Lowering the fixed fee and increasing the marginal price in this final block only will slightly reduce the contribution of these types to profits while at the same time it increases the contribution of the types with the largest willingness to pay. This latter contribution thus allows the firm to induce more consumers to choose the optional part of the tariff.

We now apply this insight to our case of a given linear price combined with an optional two-part tariff. The reason for beginning from a preexisting tariff may lie in a price cap rule, limited information by regulators, or fairness considerations (universal service). Assume that cost can be covered with the linear price p alone. The total number of customers is given by the number who consume under the linear price. Thus, the two-part tariff (E_1, p_1) only changes the relative contributions of these customers. Assume that a Coase two-part tariff is not

---

[24]For the hazard rate see Section 5.5.1.

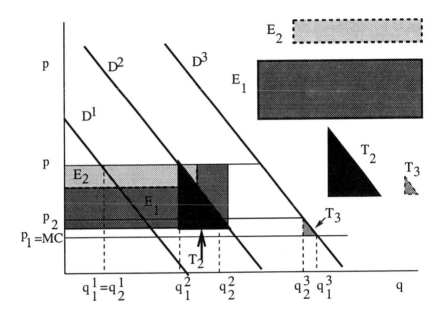

Figure 5.6
Nonoptimality of marginal-cost price

feasible.[25] Average costs must be declining. Otherwise, total cost could
not be covered under the combination of tariffs. Also assume that there
is a continuous distribution of types.

Then the nonoptimality of $p_1 = MC$ can be seen by an argument
based on the envelope theorem. This is illustrated in Figure 5.6. Assume that the budget constraint is binding and that initially $p_1 = MC$.
Since $E_1 > 0$, the marginal and average price have to be lower for consumers choosing the optional tariff than the linear price p. Otherwise no
one would buy under the optional tariff. Customers buying under the
optional tariff (E_1, p_1) are represented by demand curve D^3.

Now there is no price distortion for the larger types who buy under the
two-part tariff while there is a distortion of $p - p_1$ per unit for the smaller
types buying under the linear tariff p. The largest of these types buying

[25] Otherwise the linear tariff would, over the whole range, be dominated by the two-
part Coase tariff.

under the linear tariff are represented by D^2, leading to an efficiency loss T_2. These consumers have to be indifferent to the two-part tariff. Now we can construct a small increase from p_1 to p_2 combined with a decrease from E_1 to E_2 such that a small fraction of additional consumers can be induced to switch from the linear to the two-part tariff. Since the larger types were at the optimum with $p_1 = MC$, such a small increase in p causes only a tiny distortion represented by the triangle T_3. However, the distortion for the switching customers is reduced substantially, that is, by the large triangle T_2. Hence, as long as p is sufficiently above marginal cost and as long as there are sufficiently many customers at the margin of switching to the two-part tariff, it pays to raise p_1 above marginal cost.[26]

5.7 Tying/bundling versus unbundling

5.7.1 Multiproduct issues in nonlinear pricing

The literature on nonlinear pricing is largely restricted to single products, although there are some multiproduct interpretations of several nonlinear-pricing results. For example, two-part tariffs can be viewed as the two prices for access to and the use of a service. The demand for access is then derived from the consumer surplus from use. Also, we saw that the incremental quantities purchased under a nonlinear outlay schedule can be interpreted as multiple markets for quantity increments. However, these markets are for goods with a very specific structure. Use of a service presupposes access to it. Purchase in the market for quantity q presupposes purchase in the market for quantity $q - 1$. Also, this interpretation turns a single product *nonlinear* pricing problem into a multiproduct *linear* pricing problem.

The general multiproduct *nonlinear* pricing issue concerns pricing goods and services that do not have such a naturally hierarchical relationship. In this case consumers would buy a basket of services represented by a vector $q = (q_1, \ldots, q_m)$. Not all results found for single-product nonlinear pricing carry over to the general multiproduct case. Issues that are still unresolved for multiple goods include the characterization of Pareto-dominating tariffs.

---

[26] If the linear tariff alone would just cover costs and if $C = F + cQ$, then under a continuous distribution of types an optional two-part tariff $E_1 + p_1 q$ with $p_1 = c$ may not be cost-covering unless it is chosen only by the largest customer type.

Mirman and Sibley (1980) assume the same consumer type distribution for all products. This results in consumers purchasing outputs in fixed proportions so that the multitude of products is in effect reduced to a single bundled commodity. It is not clear, however, that consumer types can be characterized by a single type parameter τ with respect to output vectors for multiple commodities. Wilson (1989b, Chapter 13, and 1991) tries to deal with this problem of multiple type parameters in a setting of smooth nonlinear tariffs. His derivations become extremely messy and the results intuitively hard to grasp.

A specific, but potentially relevant multiproduct issue has been taken up by Srinagesh (1990). He combines the linear pricing of one product with the nonlinear pricing of a second. Based on Mirrlees' (1976) theory of optimal taxation Srinagesh shows that the marginal price for the nonlinearly priced good will be above marginal cost if the two goods are substitutes in consumption and will be below marginal cost if the two goods are complements. This holds for both the profit-maximizing and the surplus-maximizing monopolist. The main reason for this is that, due to substitutability (complementarity), a price increase of one product leads to a demand increase (decrease) for the other product. With no demand interaction the marginal price of the nonlinearly priced good equals marginal cost. Hence complementarity leads to an optimal marginal price below marginal cost and substitutability to an optimal marginal price above marginal cost.[27]

5.7.2   Tying and bundling under monopoly

Most of the multiproduct nonlinear-pricing issues are handled under the more specialized heading of bundling. Tying and bundling of services is commonplace in the telephone sector. It has received little attention, however, in the normative theory of pricing. Rather, most of the literature on tying and bundling is concerned with the issue of monopolistic price discrimination and antitrust. The particular issue discussed concerns the incentive for monopolists to use bundling and tying to achieve

---

[27]Under the combination of linear and nonlinear tariffs another interesting issue emerges that is different from multiproduct linear pricing. Even if there are no demand and cost interdependencies between the two products the two-product firm will price differently from two single-product firms. In particular, the multiproduct firm will lower the linear price because the resulting higher utility allows the firm to extract more surplus under the nonlinear price (via the incentive-compatibility and participation constraints of the nonlinear pricing problem).

price discrimination that would otherwise not be feasible. This literature applies to profit-maximizing monopolists only (Adams and Yellen, 1976; Schmalensee, 1982; McAfee, McMillan, and Whinston, 1989). In that context price discrimination is usually seen as something bad for society. We investigate whether and to what extent this literature can be extended to welfare-maximizing firms. When welfare maximization is the objective, additional opportunities for price discrimination could be used to increase welfare.

Bundling occurs when two services are offered in fixed proportions. *Pure bundling* means that consumers cannot buy the individual services separately, while under *mixed bundling* consumers have access to both the bundle and to the individual services. *Tying sales* and pure bundling share the property that the individual services cannot be bought separately. However, under tying sales quantity proportions can vary.

Adams and Yellen (1976) showed that it may be advantageous for a monopolist to package two or more services in bundles rather than offering them separately, even if there are no economies of scope in production and even if the services are not complements in the consumer's consumption. Rather, bundling serves here as a way of extracting additional surplus from consumers if other possibilities for price discrimination are unavailable.

Adams and Yellen provided examples for the occurrence of bundling, while Schmalensee (1984) and McAfee, McMillan, and Whinston (1989) provide general characterizations of conditions under which bundling is profit maximizing. Based on Adams and Yellen the latter authors consider two services produced at constant marginal cost c_1 and c_2. Each consumer desires at most one unit of each good, and the willingness to pay is given by $(v_1, v_2) \geq 0$. The joint distribution function $F(v_1, v_2)$ in the population has density $f(v_1, v_2)$; $g_i(v_i|v_j)$ and $h_i(v_i)$ denote the conditional and marginal-density functions derived from $f(\cdot, \cdot)$. $G_i(v_i|v_j)$ and $H_i(v_i)$ denote the conditional and marginal distribution functions $(i, j = 1, 2)$, with $v_i > c_i$ at least for some positive measure of consumers. Resale by consumers is prohibited. McAfee, McMillan, and Whinston show that in their model pure bundling is always dominated by mixed bundling. To see this, assume that under pure bundling the price for the bundle is p_b. Then mixed bundling with a price of p_b for the bundle and $p_i = p_b - c_j$ $(i, j = 1, 2)$ weakly dominates pure bundling. Hence, one can concentrate on the case of mixed bundling.

Mixed bundling is nontrivial only if $p_b < p_1 + p_2$. The main feature
of mixed bundling is therefore that it is less costly for consumers to buy
the bundle than the individual services. Otherwise the bundle would
always be dominated by individual purchases. This property of the
outlay function is similar to the economies of scope property of a cost
function. The bundling property of an outlay schedule R therefore may
be defined by $R(q_1, 0) + R(0, q_2) > R(q_1, q_2)$.[28]

McAfee, McMillan, and Whinston (1989) show that mixed bundling
dominates unbundled sales in terms of profits if the following condition
on the distribution of preferences holds:

$$
\begin{aligned}
0 \; < \; \int_0^{p_i^*} & \left[[1 - G_j(p_j^*|s)] - g_2(p_j^*|s)(p_j^* - c_j)\right] h_i(s) \, ds \\
& + (p_i^* - c_i)[1 - G_j(p_j^*|p_i^*)] h_i(p_i^*), \quad i, j = 1, 2
\end{aligned}
\tag{5.50}
$$

and where (p_1^*, p_2^*) are the optimal nonbundling prices.

Condition (5.50) is fairly complex. It includes the case of *independent*
distributions of willingness to pay for goods 1 and 2. What is definitely
excluded, however, is perfect correlation between the willingness to pay
for both goods. This is easily understood. If consumers have the same
ordering for their valuation of good 1 and good 2, then they also have
the same ordering for their valuation of the bundle. Hence, bundling
cannot be used to differentiate between consumer x with low valuation
of good 1 and a high valuation of good 2, and consumer y with intermediate valuations of both. If correlation of preferences for the services
is imperfect, then both may have the same valuation for the bundle but
x would prefer to buy only good 2 even if its price is higher separately
than its implicit price as part of the bundle.

McAfee, McMillan, and Whinston derive condition (5.50) by starting
out with the optimal nonbundling prices and a bundle price equal to
the sum of these prices. They then consider marginally increasing the
price of good 1, and show that this will lead to an increase in profits
if condition (5.50) holds. Alternatively, and from their point of view

---

[28] If $p_b > p_1 + p_2$, then consumers would buy the bundle only if they could not
buy both commodities separately. If the seller can "monitor" consumers' purchases,
he can prevent individual consumers from acquiring the bundle by purchasing the
services one at a time. If monitoring is feasible, mixed bundling dominates unbundled sales for virtually all joint distributions of willingness to pay. This could have
importance for an analysis of increasing-block tariffs.

equivalently, they could have increased the price of good 2 or *reduced* the price of the bundle. The latter case is interesting for us because it means that such bundling results in an increase in total surplus (and a Pareto improvement). Had we started at welfare-optimal (Ramsey) prices we would have achieved a welfare improvement from bundling. This means that (5.50) is also a sufficient condition for welfare-optimal mixed bundling to dominate welfare-optimal nonbundling prices.

In the bundling cases analyzed in the literature the assumption that consumers desire at most one unit of each of the goods is applicable to choices between discrete services, such as call forwarding and call waiting. However, the assumption precludes other application to telecommunications where quantities for many services vary continuously. The question is therefore how far the above results extend to the case of services supplied in varying quantities. It is only here that the difference between bundling and tying would matter. We would then want to use the bundling property for outlay schedules defined above.

5.7.3 Tying and bundling in oligopoly

McAfee, McMillan, and Whinston (1989) show that (5.50) extends to the case of *heterogeneous* Bertrand competition.[29] This is not surprising given that heterogeneous Bertrand competition is closely related to monopoly behavior.

More interesting is the analysis by Carbajo, De Meza, and Seidman (1990) who show that, under *homogeneous* Bertrand and Cournot competition, bundling can be profit maximizing even if consumers' willingness to pay for the two goods is perfectly correlated. In their analysis bundling is not a means of price discrimination but rather an additional strategic tool, one that is particularly important under Bertrand competition. Here the standard solution without bundling, under constant returns to scale, is pricing at marginal cost combined with zero profits for all firms which share the market symmetrically.

Now consider the case of two markets. In the market for good 1 firm A has a monopoly; in the market for good 2 firm A competes with firm B. Marginal and average costs are $c_i < 1$ with $i = 1, 2$. Consumers desire

---

[29]Heterogeneous Bertrand competition is defined for a set of firms, each being the sole supplier of a service that is an imperfect substitute for the services of all the other suppliers. A heterogeneous Bertrand equilibrium is a set of prices, one for each service, such that no firm can increase its profit by changing its price given the prices of all the other firms.

at most one unit of each of the products. Willingness to pay for each good is uniformly distributed in the interval $[0,1]$ and $v_1 = v_2 = v$ for each consumer. Under Bertrand competition both firms earn nothing in market 2 while firm A earns the monopoly profit in market 1.

Now, assume firm A resorts to pure bundling and that this decision is made before the pricing decision. Then anyone wanting to buy good 1 also has to buy good 2 from firm A. That leaves firm B with only those customers who do not have a strong willingness to pay for either good. In other words, firm B is stuck with customers with valuation $v_1 + v_1 = 2v < p_b$ and $v_2 > c_2$. Without bundling, firm A is earning monopoly profits in market 1 and nothing in market 2, and optimal prices and quantities are $p_1^* > p_2^*$ and $q_1^* < q_2^*$. Therefore, firm A can only gain through bundling if $p_b > p_1^* + c_2$. Hence, firm B is left with a discrete interval of reservation values of customers with $v_2 > c_2$. Any sale in this interval is profitable, and firm B will set its price of good 2, p_{2B}, such that $p_{2B} > p_2^*$. Thus, with bundling we get $p_b > p_{2B} > p_b - v > c$. In a bundling equilibrium the effect of (pure) bundling is therefore that the Bertrand competition becomes less fierce and consumers are worse off.

Under Cournot competition, bundling does not emerge that easily because prices in both markets are initially above marginal cost. A necessary condition for bundling is $q_1^* > q_{2A}^*$ and a sufficient condition $p_1^* > p_2^*$. As a result of bundling in the Cournot case, A's profit rises and q_{2A} increases, while B's profit falls, q_{2B} falls and so does total consumer surplus.[30]

Clearly, bundling is not part of a welfare-maximizing strategy for firm A in the Bertrand case, because the welfare optimum in market 1 can be implemented by firm A through marginal-cost pricing, while performance in market 2 is already welfare optimal. Neither is bundling welfare maximizing under Cournot because, in this case (with constant cost), the regulated firm can always implement the Harris–Wiens solution in market 2.[31] These statements are also in line with Schmalensee's result

[30] Carbajo, De Meza, and Seidman (1990) note that social surplus could also rise under bundling but they do not show that this is compatible with a bundling equilibrium.

[31] Harris and Wiens (1980) show that a welfare-maximizing firm in an oligopolistic market can always implement the efficient market outcome by committing itself to producing the difference between the efficient market output and the aggregate output of the other firms. If this commitment is credible, all the other firms will take the market price as given and extend their outputs such that $p = MC$. The commitment

on two indivisible products that are unrelated in production and in demand. Schmalensee shows that a monopolist cannot through bundling extend part of its monopoly power in one of these products to a competitive industry supplying the other.

5.7.4 Total-revenue discounts

Multiproduct total-volume discounts are common for airlines (in the form of frequent-flier discounts), and total-revenue discounts are quickly gaining importance for telecommunications. Total-volume discounts are applied to the sum of services generated by a customer while total-revenue discounts are applied to the revenues generated by a customer for the various services she purchases from the same supplier. One reason for the preference for total-revenue discounts over total-volume discounts in telecommunications lies in the inherent heterogeneity of telecommunications services. Quantity discounts do not easily aggregate over different qualities or services.

Both revenue and quantity discounts require that larger demands are more elastic than smaller demands. It is good to know that at least in a competitive setting the larger customers have the more elastic (firm-specific) demand. This is at least partly due to information costs and the costs of switching suppliers, both of which depend on the total communications needs of a customer.

Total-revenue discounts can be seen as a function $\theta(R)$ of consumer outlays, where $R = pq$ in the case of linear prices, but R can be as complicated as any invertible nonlinear outlay schedule. In the case of multiple goods p and q would be vectors. Now, by properly varying the function θ one can generate a wide range of nonlinear outlay schedules. In particular, we can create any desired schedule $R^*(q)$ from an invertible schedule $R(q)$.[32] Therefore, assume $R(q)$ to be invertible. Then, in the case of linear pricing, $\theta^*(pq) = R^*(q)/pq$ generates outlays $R^*(q) = \theta^*(pq)pq$. In the case of nonlinear pricing, $\theta^*(R) = R^*(q)/R$ generates outlays $R^*(q) = \theta^*\big(R(q)\big)/R(q)$.

The optimal function $\theta(R)$ thus depends on the original function $R(q)$.

---

is credible only if the welfare-maximizing firm has constant average cost or unlimited funds. Thus, the Harris–Wiens solution is rarely applicable. In those cases, where it is not, bundling by a welfare-maximizing firm may be welfare improving in a Cournot oligopoly.

[32] If $R(q)$ is not invertible we cannot assign a unique q to R. Assume that $q_1 \neq q_2$ lead to the same R value. Then they cannot lead to different R^* values.

In particular, $\theta(R)$ can involve revenue premia as well as revenue discounts. For example, if $R(q) = E + pq$, then a declining function θ will associate larger consumers with lower fixed fees. To avoid those, θ may have to be a function of the form:

$$\theta(R) = \begin{cases} R, & \text{for } R < \overline{R} \\ \hat{b}R + B, & \text{for } R \geq \overline{R} \end{cases} \tag{5.51}$$

with $\hat{b} < 1$ and $B > 0$. This means that consumers have to pay an additional fixed fee to be able to benefit from the total-revenue discounts for larger purchases. In practice, the additional fixed fee is often avoided by restricting the discount to additional revenues, just as in a declining block tariff. This would result in:

$$\theta(R) = \begin{cases} R, & \text{for } R < \overline{R} \\ \hat{b}(R - \overline{R}), & \text{for } R \geq \overline{R}. \end{cases} \tag{5.52}$$

For full optimization the firm may want to set $R(q)$ and $\theta(R)$ simultaneously. This procedure would actually make quantity discounts superfluous if the shape of the outlay schedule is unrestricted. The problem at hand, therefore, is to superimpose quantity discounts on a preexisting nonoptimal outlay schedule and to optimize only with respect to the total-revenue discounts. In practice, total-revenue discounts appear to be an imperfect way to generate nonlinear outlay schedules across various services. It appears that such discounts are attractive means of increasing profits and maintaining customers in the face of competition.[33] However, the welfare properties of such discounts have yet to be derived.

5.8   Nonlinear tariffs in oligopoly

The theoretical literature on nonlinear tariffs in markets other than monopoly is exceedingly small. It contains the work on bundling referred to in the last section and an article by Oren, Smith, and Wilson (1983). This gap is surprising, considering the widespread popularity of quantity discounts.

Oren, Smith, and Wilson investigate smooth nonlinear tariffs in a symmetric Cournot oligopoly. They assume that intensities of customer

---

[33] Quantity discounts have sometimes been criticized as predatory, for example, when AT&T introduced its Telpak tariff with large discounts for private line service, seeking to reduce the impact of private provision of microwave connections.

demands are ranked by a continuous type parameter τ uniformly distributed on the interval $[0, 1]$. Price schedules $p(q) = R'(q)$ are assumed to cross demand functions only once, from below. The authors discuss the possibility of analyzing six different kinds of Cournot models. The reason for this variety of options lies in the availability of different strategic variables. Cournot *quantity* is replaced under nonlinear pricing by a *function* using purchase size q, total outlay R, or buyer index τ as three possible market descriptors. The function itself could be measured in terms of number N of purchases of sizes q, or in terms of total quantity Q purchased.

The authors provide a detailed analysis of only two of the six models. The first one combines purchase size q and number of purchases N. This corresponds fully to the approach of the demand profile. Each firm assumes that the numbers of customers for each q increment of demand are given. The firm maximizes profit with respect to the residual demand profile. The result is similar to (5.36) above, that is:

$$\frac{p(q) - MC}{p(q)} = -\frac{1}{n \, \epsilon_{Np}}, \qquad (5.53)$$

where n is the number of oligopolists.

The second model combines buyer index τ with quantity purchased q. The Cournot assumption here means that each firm takes the quantity purchased from its competitors by each buyer type τ as given and maximizes profit with respect to the residual demands of all buyer types. In this case the authors derive:

$$\frac{p(q) - MC}{p(q)} = -\frac{1}{n\epsilon_{Np}}$$
$$+ \frac{K}{p(q)q} - (1 - \frac{1}{n}) \left[\frac{R(q) - C(q)}{p(q)q} - 1 + \frac{MC}{p(q)} \right]. \qquad (5.54)$$

This differs from the condition in the previous model by the terms in the second row. The net effect of these terms is impossible to sign a priori. K is a constant of integration that is determined from the transversality conditions of this problem. Since $R(q) - C(q) > 0$ and $MC/p(q) < 1$ by profit maximization the term in brackets cannot be signed. In a numerical illustration with constant marginal and average cost the authors find that the price schedule under the first model lies above that of the second model for all $0 < n < \infty$.

Wilson (1989b) uses (5.53), and its generalization in (5.36), as the typical case for the oligopolistic equilibrium under nonlinear pricing. While this conjecture has obvious appeal given the complication apparent from formulations such as (5.54), it is still quite likely that the oligopolists' world is not as simple as (5.53) would make it appear. Very often individual oligopolists will specialize on different size consumers. This has, for example, happened in the United Kingdom in the 1980s under the duopoly between British Telecom and its first licensed network competitor Mercury, where Mercury has specialized in supplying large telecommunications users.

5.9   Second-best piecemeal policy

The analysis and implementation of nonlinear tariffs substantially increases the informational, computational, and conceptual requirements for the tariff-setting firm or regulator. In particular, market demand as the basis for tariff setting loses much of its usefulness. Instead, either individual consumer demands are ranked by consumer types or the different purchase quantities of individual consumers are aggregated as separate markets. It is surprising to see then that the inverse elasticity rule as the main result of the previous chapter carries over to nonlinear pricing. Under nonlinear pricing there is some presumption that larger consumers receive lower marginal and average prices than smaller consumers. This is certainly true if nonlinear tariffs take the form of sets of optional two-part tariffs.

In this chapter it has become increasingly clear that improved and innovative pricing techniques become progressively more complex. In particular, multiproduct and competitive interactions lead to complications on the firm level that one otherwise encounters only at the general equilibrium level. AT&T, for example, offers thousands of differently priced services to its customers. In particular, one would then like to learn about the compatibility and optimality of such a multitude of simultaneous tariffs.

We know of only two attempts at solving such a general pricing problem for the multiproduct firm. Wilson (1989b, Chapter 13) formulates the problem with fairly general functional forms, based on demand profile analysis and allowing for multiple type parameters. Stolleman (1988) formulates the problem as one of open network architecture (ONA) pricing. However, his model is one of nonlinear pricing of separate services in general. It may be linked to, but is certainly not restricted to, ONA pricing.

Simplified functional forms. Stolleman's particular innovation is that he approaches the complexity of the issue of multiproduct nonlinear pricing by simplifying the functional forms and using approximations to general functional forms. Stolleman's approach can be viewed as the end point of a particular strategy toward a manageable *second-best piecemeal policy*. The strategy imposes simplified functional forms on demands, costs and prices:

- Demand-side simplifications refer to absence of income effects, the independence of demands for various services, and linear or constant-elasticity demand curves.

- Cost-side simplifications refer to affine linear cost functions and the separability of costs of various outputs. If demands and costs are separable, then the pricing problems for the various services can also be treated separately.

- Pricing simplifications start with linear (Ramsey) prices and independent demands. More complicated functional forms on prices can subsequently be introduced through two-part tariffs, block tariffs, and, ultimately, simple functional forms of smooth nonlinear tariffs.

The simplest such smooth tariff is a quantity discount of the form:

$$p = p_0 - \phi q, \tag{5.55}$$

leading to an outlay function:

$$R(q) = p_0 q - \frac{1}{2}\phi q^2. \tag{5.56}$$

In our view, the welfare and profit properties of such a two-parameter tariff should be theoretically investigated, because such tariffs are simple and closely resemble the quantity discounts in actual tariffs.

Stolleman (1988) chooses a welfare-optimization problem in which he allows for interdependence on the demand and cost side and in the non-linear price terms. He generalizes the two-parameter smooth outlay function (5.56) to include interactive terms for the various services. His m-product outlay function has the form:

$$R(q) = p'q + \frac{1}{2}q'P(q), \qquad (5.57)$$

where p' and q' are row vectors of dimension m, and $P(q)$ is a symmetric $m \times m$ matrix with elements P_{ij}. To see that this is a generalization of (5.56), assume that $m = 1$. Then (5.57) becomes $R(q) = p'q + \frac{1}{2}q'P_{11}(q)$ which equals (5.56) for $p' = p_0$ and $P_{11}(q) = -\phi q$.

Stepwise improvement. A second type of second-best piecemeal strategy starts with existing tariffs and seeks ways to improve them in a stepwise fashion. This approach is taken under optional tariffs that can lead to Pareto improvements. Since a move from the current tariff to the optimal tariff may actually make some consumers worse off, it may be impossible to reach the optimal tariff via a sequence of Pareto improvements. Hence, this approach may have to stop at a suboptimal point.

Other stepwise improvements include Bös' suggestion to reduce pro-portionally all Lerner indices for the firm's products. Bös (1985b) ar-gues that such a reduction is always welfare (surplus)improving, while the reduction of an individual Lerner index in isolation may be welfare reducing. However, the policy suggested by Bös may be infeasible if the firm is already at the budget constraint.

Restrictive assumptions. A third strategy is the one chosen by Wil-son (1989b). He starts out with an analytical model using general func-tional forms for individual relationships but makes restrictive assump-tions about these relationships and their interaction. In particular, he assumes differentiable multiproduct demand profiles and differentiable and concave outlay functions. Costs are assumed to be additively sep-arable among customers and to depend only on the bundle q supplied to each customer. $C(q)$ is assumed to be differentiable and convex. Wilson's assumption on separability of cost by consumers appears to be unrealistic and unusual in this literature. Wilson recognizes that individual consumers will only buy a small subset of the firm's products. Consequently, commodity bundles will contain many zeros. The resulting pricing formula appears to be some kind of generalization of the inverse elasticity rule, but with a much less transparent interpretation. Recognizing the mathematical problems incurred under this general approach, Wilson suggests calculating simulated numerical solutions in addition to, or instead of, deriving analytical results.

6

Cost-based tariffs

The tariffs discussed in Chapters 4 and 5 are the result of (weighted) surplus maximization. Costs enter this maximization procedure as a major argument, along with consumer willingness-to-pay. In contrast, the tariffs to be discussed in the current chapter are derived in a different way. Here we look for tariffs that at least (or at most) cover some notion of costs related to the provision of the various services, to serving various consumer groups, or to serving various consumption patterns (individually and in the aggregate). The yardstick against which *cost-based tariffs* are measured is some concept of costs. The feasibility of such tariffs, rather than their optimality, is the starting point for our analysis. This will not, of course, preclude us from criticizing cost-based tariffs for failing to be optimal.

6.1 Subsidy-free pricing

The concepts of subsidy-free prices and sustainable prices are central to the analysis of cost-based tariffs. The rationale for these concepts is twofold. The first rationale links fairness to presumed cost causation, giving precision to the notion that a consumer should pay neither more nor less than the cost that she causes. The second rationale links economic freedom of opportunity to the presumed efficiency of (potential) competition. In its pricing policy an incumbent firm should be put on equal footing with potential entrants, where these entrants could be either competitors or consumers who supply themselves and thus bypass the network.

6.1.1 Alternative concepts of subsidy-free linear prices

There are a number of concepts that relate pricing to cost causation and competition, concepts that are sometimes complex and hard to sort out. To assist the reader we will repeat definitions using different wordings and compare and summarize the concepts later.

The first fundamental concept is that of subsidy-free prices, introduced rigorously by Faulhaber (1975):

> A set of prices by a multiproduct monopolist is *subsidy free* (or free of cross subsidies) if revenues at these prices cover total costs and if no subset of services produced by the firm at these prices could be produced at costs lower than the revenues generated for this subset by these prices.

Hence, subsidy-free prices prevent one *service* from subsidizing or from being subsidized by any other services. The conditions for subsidy-free pricing can be stated in terms of two tests:

1 Revenues from a service (or set of services) cannot exceed the *stand-alone cost* of this service (or set of services). This is known as the stand-alone cost test.

2 Furthermore, if there are no diseconomies of scope, then subsidy-free prices also have the property that revenues for any subset of services are never below the *incremental costs* of producing this subset. This is known as the incremental-cost test. Incremental costs here are defined as the difference in the total costs of producing *versus* not producing this subset.

The presence of cross subsidies is illustrated in Figure 6.1. Here AC indicates the average cost curve for total output as well as average stand-alone cost for each subset of output measured from the origin. MC indicates marginal cost of total output as well as average incremental cost of an additional subset of output given that some output is already produced. Total output is Q_{A+B}, sold at prices p_A and p_B, respectively, to consumer groups A and B.[1] The stand-alone cost test is violated because group A pays more than its average stand-alone cost SAC_A. The incremental cost test is violated because group B pays less than its average incremental cost MC.

---

[1] For illustrative purposes we have assumed that demands by these two groups can be aggregated into demand curve D. In order for this to be consistent it is best to assume that each consumer demands at most 1 unit of the service and that the willingness-to-pay of all members of group A is above the willingness-to-pay of all members of group B.

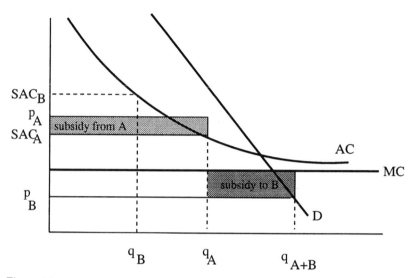

Figure 6.1
Internal subsidization

Thus, in the absence of *dis*economies of scope (itself an inefficiency!)
there are two alternative tests for determining whether prices are subsidy free. Both cost tests require the observation of stand-alone costs.
Stand-alone costs are empirically very hard to calculate because, given
economies of scope and cross subsidies, no separate subset of commodities is ever likely to be produced. However, Palmer (1989) shows that
in the absence of diseconomies of scope an upper bound for the stand-
alone cost of a service i at q_i is given by $C(q) - q_i \partial C(q)/\partial q_i$, where
$q = (q_1, .., q_i, .., q_m)$. Thus, if all that can be observed is total cost *in
the neighborhood of current outputs*, then prices that exceed this upper
bound (for the stand-alone cost test) or are below marginal cost (for
the incremental cost test) definitely contain cross subsidies, while other
prices may or may not. In the presence of profits arising from one of the
services (e.g., because the firm is not regulated) both tests may have to
be conducted.

There are two additional complications arising under the incremental
cost test. First, individual outputs may fulfill the test while at the same
time combinations of such outputs may not. The reason is that joint

costs of several outputs are not incremental costs of each individual output but they are part of the incremental costs of combinations of the outputs viewed together.

The second complication derives from interdependencies in demand between services. The revenue gained from an additional service may, due to substitutability, reduce the revenue of another service. This leads to the *burden test* (or *net revenue test*) as defined in Baumol (1986, p.117):

> A price p_i for product i constitutes no *burden* upon the consumers of other products supplied by the same firm if at that price the product's incremental cost is equaled or exceeded by its net incremental revenue (i.e., its [net] revenue after subtraction of [net] revenue losses on other products j resulting from the cross elasticity of demand between i and j).

Baumol argues that the incremental cost test should be used as a criterion to judge fairness of prices between competitors, while the burden test should be used to judge the fairness between different consumer groups. By including the interrelation between outputs, the burden test considers Pareto improvements from adding a new product. The incremental cost test considers subsets of outputs one by one, and that is how competition occurs. Also, competition usually does not, and should not necessarily, lead to Pareto improvements among firms.

Faulhaber's (1975) definition of subsidy-free prices is entirely in terms of services, not in terms of customers consuming these services. Due to cost complementarities, a customer buying more than one service could still be subsidizing other customers. Therefore, a stronger notion involving consumption *bundles* rather than individual services is needed. As a first step in this direction Sharkey and Telser (1978) introduce the notion of support prices:

> *Support prices* p for a quantity vector q are defined by the property that no consumption bundle $q^* \leq q$ can be produced at costs $C(q^*) < p'q$. A cost function $C(q)$ is *supportable* at q if such support prices exist.

Even if no subsidy-free price structure in terms of services exists, there may still exist subsidy-free prices in terms of the bundles demanded by consumers. Such prices are called consumer subsidy free:

> *Consumer subsidy-free prices* are defined by the property that total revenues at demanded quantities cover total cost and that no coalition of consumers could produce their demanded quantities at lower costs than what they pay under these prices.

Faulhaber and Levinson (1981) show that any cost-covering price structure is consumer subsidy free if all consumers have the same demand patterns (except for a common scale factor). Thus, if all telephone customers consume long-distance and local services in the same proportions, then there would be no consumer cross subsidies in spite of service cross subsidies. Testing for consumer subsidy-free prices requires knowledge of individual demand functions.

Clearly, a supportable price structure is subsidy free, and no customer (group) will subsidize any other customer (group). However, we also want the quantity q to be compatible with market demand:

> *Anonymously equitable prices* are support prices that satisfy $q = D(p)$ (Faulhaber and Levinson, 1981).

A support price is not necessarily anonymously equitable. To see this, consider the example in Figure 6.2. The price p_{min} is not anonymously equitable, because the demanded quantity $q(p_{min})$ cannot be produced profitably and the cost function is not supportable beyond the minimum of the average cost curve. Ten Raa (1983) shows that an (upper hemi-) continuous market demand (correspondence) and a supportable cost function are sufficient to guarantee the existence of an anonymously equitable price vector.

Anonymous equity is the strongest concept so far, since anonymous equity implies that prices are subsidy free, are consumer subsidy free and are support prices. As Palmer (1989) notes, the stand-alone cost test and the incremental cost test are each sufficient conditions for testing anonymous equity if services are substitutes and are necessary conditions if services are complements.

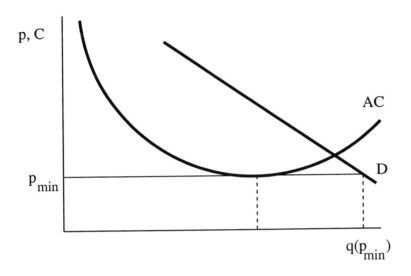

Figure 6.2
Anonymous equity and support prices

6.1.2 Sustainable prices and the second-best core

Sustainable prices. The concepts discussed so far characterize a single firm and are defined in terms of consumer coalitions. Panzar and Willig (1977) extend Faulhaber's (1975) notion of cross subsidization to a world of outside competitors and introduce sustainable prices. The question, phrased by Rosse (1978), is "Under what circumstances can a socially desirable monopoly be expected to survive without the protection of legal entry barriers?"

To this end, *sustainable prices* p^* are defined by the following two properties:

(1) Revenues at quantities demanded at these prices cover costs:

$$p^* \prime q(p^*) - C(q(p^*)) \geq 0, \quad \text{and} \tag{6.1}$$

(2) There exist no prices and quantities, p^e and q^e, such that:

$$p^e \prime q^e - C(q^e) \geq 0 \text{ and } p_i^e < p_i^* \text{ for some } i \text{ and } q^e \leq D^e(p^*, p^e). \tag{6.2}$$

That is, no potential entrant can undercut the incumbent monopolist's prices, serve all or only part of the quantities demanded at these prices, and make a profit. Note that sustainability is not an equilibrium concept.[2] Nevertheless, it is a very useful property for regulators who have to set or approve tariffs for incumbent regulated firms that face (entry) competition. A tariff may be unsustainable because it has been set inefficiently or because the firm (or monopoly market) is not sustainable. Thus, we say that a firm (or monopoly market) is unsustainable if no sustainable tariff exists.[3]

In order to be sustainable, a monopoly has to fulfill several interesting (necessary) conditions:

1 It earns zero economic profits.

2 The industry output is produced at minimum cost. This implies natural monopoly and production on the (minimum) cost function.

3 All subsets of the monopoly's outputs fulfill the incremental cost test. This also implies that prices cover marginal costs.

4 If the potential entrant and the incumbent firm have the same cost function, then sustainable prices are anonymously equitable.

A set of sufficient conditions for sustainability is contained in the "weak invisible hand theorem" by Baumol, Bailey, and Willig (1977). In the formulation by Rosse (1978):

> If the monopolist's cost function exhibits decreasing ray average costs and trans-ray convexity at the equilibrium point, [if the outputs are weak gross substitutes] and if the price-quantity equilibrium satisfies the conditions of Ramsey optimality, then the monopoly is sustainable there.[4]

---

[2] For attempts to embody sustainability in Bertrand equilibria see Knieps and Vogelsang (1982), Mirman, Tauman, and Zang (1985b), and Tirole (1988), p. 310.

[3] Outputs produced at different points in time can be regarded as different services. This property allows Baumol, Panzar, and Willig (1982) to extend the definition of sustainability to the sequence of outputs over time. The authors show that intertemporal unsustainability may occur if the production capacity of the incumbent firm requires lumpy investments (economies of scale in investment) and if both demand and the required investment increase over time.

[4] Decreasing ray average costs are defined by the property that, for any output vector $\mathbf{q}$ and for any number $r > 1, C(r\mathbf{q}) < rC(\mathbf{q})$. Decreasing ray average costs correspond to increasing returns to scale. A cost function is said to be transray convex if the cost of producing an output vector $\mathbf{q}$ is lower than the the linear combinations of costs of producing any outputs $\mathbf{q}^a$ and $\mathbf{q}^b$ such that $\mathbf{q}$ is a linear combination of $\mathbf{q}^a$ and $\mathbf{q}^b$: $C(\mathbf{q}) = C(k\mathbf{q}^a + (1-k)\mathbf{q}^b) \leq kC(\mathbf{q}^a) + (1-k)C(\mathbf{q}^b)$ for any number k with $0 < k < 1$.
Transray convexity means that in the multiproduct context product-specific economies of scale are outweighed by economies of scope.

Baumol, Bailey, and Willig (1977) further argue that Ramsey prices are the only sustainable prices that the monopolist can find using only local information on costs and demands. This suggests that the monopolist might want to implement Ramsey prices, simply in order to safeguard against inefficient entry. However, this does not necessarily prevent entry if some of the services are complements and could therefore have prices below marginal costs.

The second-best core.   Spulber (1986, 1989b) develops the concept of the *second-best core* of the cost-sharing game. The cost-sharing game is played by a set of consumers $N = 1, \ldots, n$ who jointly wish to produce a vector q of outputs. Any subgroup of consumers has freely available to it the same subadditive cost function $C(\cdot)$. Each coalition must choose a price to allocate the jointly produced goods among its members. Members of a coalition can buy as much as they want from the coalition but nothing from outside.

A price vector p is feasible for a coalition $S \subseteq N$ if at the resulting demands the profits of S are nonnegative and the demands by members of S are fully met. A price vector p is in the second-best core if it is feasible for the grand coalition N of all players and if there is no price vector p^S such that for a subset $S \subseteq N$ profits are nonnegative and members in S unanimously prefer p^S to p. The second-best core is thus the set of prices that allow a firm to cover at least its costs if it satisfies all demand at those prices and that are undominated by any other set of cost covering prices which could lure away at least some subset of customers.

Spulber (1989a) shows that the second-best core has a number of interesting properties. In particular, the second-best core is a subset of the set of Ramsey prices. Ramsey prices exist under very general conditions, and very often they are unique.[5] In contrast, second-best core prices require more restrictive conditions. Thus, they need not exist whenever there are Ramsey prices. Clearly, second-best core prices are cost covering and Pareto optimal.[6] However, the second-best core prop-

---

[5]Dierker (1991), however, shows that only under restrictive conditions are the first-order conditions used to characterize Ramsey prices sufficient for a second-best optimum.

[6]Ramsey prices are usually unique when they are defined as those that maximize constrained social surplus. However, if Ramsey prices are defined as constrained Pareto-optimal prices, then there may be many such prices.

erty is stronger than conventional Pareto optimality, which is defined over individuals rather than over sets of coalitions. The existence of a second-best core then means that there are Ramsey prices that are not vulnerable to entry (as defined by the second-best core, that is, by linear prices and no nonprice rationing).

A second interesting property is that any price vector in the second-best core is consumer subsidy free. However, the reverse need not be true.

Sustainable prices need not be in the second-best core. Conversely, second-best core prices need not be sustainable. Both statements are easily verified by the example of Ramsey prices for two independently produced outputs with different demand elasticities purchased by identical consumers. In this case, sustainable prices are equal to average costs for both products while Ramsey prices will deviate from average costs. These Ramsey prices are second-best core prices because all consumers buy the same bundle of outputs. The reason that these second-best core prices are unsustainable lies in two properties. First, under the rules for construction of sustainable prices, individual consumers can buy from the incumbent and from the potential entrant at the same time. In contrast, by definition of the second-best core, individual consumers can buy from only one supplier.[7] When it is preferable for a consumer to split up his purchases, then sustainable prices need not exist, whereas the second-best core may. Second, sustainable price vectors are defined as being no larger than those of potential entrants $(p^* \leq p^e)$, while the second-best core is defined in terms of utilities of consumers over consumption bundles. Thus a price vector p^* that is preferred by a consumer i, $(V_i(p^*) \geq V_i(p^e))$, may still be unsustainable because an element k of the price vector is higher $(p_k^* > p_k^e)$.[8]

In economic terms we may characterize the difference between the concepts of a sustainable monopoly and the second-best core by the type of competition. Under the sustainability concept the incumbent firm (or the regulator) is behaving as a Stackelberg leader and sets prices for unlimited quantities while the potential entrants are Stackelberg followers that have the possibility of setting quantities below the amounts de-

---

[7] In the technical terms of the cost-sharing game (used for construction of the second-best core), consumers can be members of only a single coalition.

[8] Due to the independence in production, the cost conditions of the "weak invisible hand theorem" are also not satisfied in this example.

manded. In other words, the incumbent firm offers fixed-price contracts with no quantity commitment by customers, while potential entrants offer fixed price/quantity contracts. In contrast, under the second-best core concept, incumbents and potential entrants (coalitions) would offer only fixed price/quantity contracts.[9] In this context, total-revenue discounts may be seen as an incentive-compatible mechanism to enforce quantity commitments by purchasers.

The lesson from these characterizations of competition is that different types of markets imply different types of constraints on the tariff optimization problem imposed by competition.

For example, Stackelberg leadership by a quantity-setting incumbent leads to the concept of *quantity sustainability*, the properties of which are characterized by Brock and Scheinkman (1983) and Knieps and Vogelsang (1982). A single-product natural monopoly is always quantity sustainable and it may earn positive profits under free entry.

These two properties are also obtained by Motty Perry (1984) for a price-setting natural monopoly, in which the incumbent offers its outputs under a price-discriminating upward-sloping supply schedule. Customers who are served first receive lower prices than customers who are served later. The incumbent firm is assumed to move first. Through price discrimination it can reduce the number of customers willing to buy from the potential entrant. Thus, the incumbent here restricts supply in a manner similar to the potential entrant under the Panzar and Willig (1977) definition of sustainability.

Using a Coasean argument, Zupan (1990) shows that unsustainability can be avoided if a carrier is allowed to reach bilateral pricing agreements with individual customers.

6.1.3 Sustainability and the second-best core with nonlinear prices

In order for a supplier to retain the whole vector of purchases in the face of potential competition from a customer and from competing firms, the cost function must have the subadditivity property (transray convexity). This raises the issue of sustainability and the second-best core property of nonlinear outlay schedules. While sustainability refers to vector dominance of linear prices (that is, $p^* \leq p^e$), the second-best core refers to

---

[9]Subsidy-free allocations are in the core of a different cost-sharing game defined by Faulhaber (1975).

the preference of consumers with respect to such price vectors (that is,
$V_i(\boldsymbol{p}^*) \geq V_i(\boldsymbol{p}^e)$).

The first to make the connection between nonlinear prices and the
sustainability of natural monopoly was Rosse (1978). His proposition is
that, under increasing returns to scale, linear prices by an incumbent are
unsustainable against a potential entrant using nonlinear prices. This
proposition extends to the second-best core and is most easily explained
and possibly generalized using Willig's 1978 result on Pareto-improving
nonlinear outlay schedules. As explained in Section 5.6.7, for at least n
consumer types there always exists an n-part tariff that Pareto dominates the optimal $(n-1)$-part tariff. Clearly, a Pareto dominating n-part
tariff makes the optimal $(n-1)$-part tariff unsustainable and destroys the
second-best core of $(n-1)$-part tariffs.

Both concepts, sustainability and second-best core, need to be generalized to allow for nonlinear outlay schedules.[10] Sharkey and Sibley
(1991) suggest such a definition for the sustainability of optional two-
part tariffs in terms of a cooperative game without side payments:

> Let $N = 1, \ldots, n$ represent the set of all customer types.
> Thus we will say that a set T^N of Pareto-optimal two-part
> tariffs is sustainable if no entrant can devise another set of
> tariffs T^S which will attract a subset $S \subseteq N$ of the incum-
> bent's customers while satisfying the incentive compatibility
> constraints, and allow the entrant to earn nonnegative profit,
> using the same technology as the incumbent firm.[11]

In our view, this definition is not an extension of vector sustainability.
Rather, it extends the concept of second-best core to optional two-part
tariffs.

Based on Spence's consumption outlay model, Panzar and Postlewaite
(1984) define subsidy-free outlay schedules (R, q) by the property that:

$$\sum_{i \in S} R_i \leq C\left(\sum_{i \in S} q_i\right) \quad \text{for all } S \subseteq N. \tag{6.3}$$

---

[10]Rosse (1978) suggests a definition that, in our view, fails to distinguish aggregate
output and the distribution of output among consumer types.
[11]The requirement of using the same technology as the incumbent firm makes this
definition differ from the bypass problem as dealt with in Einhorn (1987) and discussed in Section 6.1.4 below. Spulber (1989a) defines the second-best core for two-
part tariffs.

They then go on to define a *sustainable outlay schedule* (R, q) by the property that there exists no other outlay schedule (R^*, q^*) such that for any subset of customers $S \subset N$ there is a Pareto improvement and that the subset of consumers can supply itself without making losses.

Again, this is in fact an extension of the second-best core concept. The reason why this route is the most natural one to take may be the difficulty in constructing a straightforward extension of the sustainability concept. Let us consider such an extension. A nonlinear outlay schedule $R(q)$ offered by an incumbent would be sustainable if $\sum_i R(q_i) - C(\sum_i q_i) \geq 0$ and if there is no other schedule $R'(q)$ with $R'(q) < R(q)$ for all q and with $\sum_j R'(q_j) - C(\sum_j q_j) \geq 0$ purchased by a subset J of consumers whose individual demands need not be fully served under $R'(q)$. The problem is that when the set J is not fully served there must exist a rationing rule that is defined only in terms of purchased quantities. If the rule is announced in advance, it would ration consumers in a certain quantity band $[q_1, q_2]$. Then it has to be made incentive-compatible so that consumers who are no longer served have the correct incentive to choose other quantities or turn to the incumbent supplier.

Taking this problem into consideration we suggest that a nonlinear outlay schedule $R^*(q)$ with $R^{*\,\prime}(q) = p^*(q)$ be defined to be *sustainable in terms of the demand profile* if:

$$\int_0^\infty p^*(q) N(p^*, q)\, dq - C\left(\int_0^\infty N(p^*, q)\, dq\right) \geq 0, \tag{6.4}$$

and there exist no $p^e(q)$ and $N^e(q)$, such that:

(a) $\quad N^e \leq N(p^e, q),$ $\hspace{6cm}$ (6.5)

(b) $\quad N_i^e < N_j^e$ $\quad$ for all $q_i > q_j,$ $\hspace{4cm}$ (6.6)

(c) $\quad R^e(q_i) < R^*(q_i)$ and $p^e(q_i) < p^*(q_i)$ for some $i,$ $\hspace{1.5cm}$ (6.7)

and:

(d) $\quad \int_0^\infty p^e N^e\, dq - C(\int_0^\infty N^e\, dq) \geq 0.$ $\hspace{4cm}$ (6.8)

Condition (6.4) says that the incumbent firm can at least break even. Condition (6.5) states that not all customers may be served fully by the potential entrant. Condition (6.6) assures that N^e is downward sloping in q, meaning that the potential entrant cannot serve a customer's larger quantities if he has not served the smaller quantities as well. In this connection it is assumed, however, that the potential entrant can ration a customer based on the customer's total purchases from the entrant. Condition (6.8) requires the potential entrant at least to break even.

Admittedly, (6.5)–(6.8) are a cumbersome set of conditions, the presence of which is difficult to verify. In particular, note that sustainability in the context of nonlinear outlay schedules depends on the distribution of preferences as well as on the cost function.

The existence of sustainable tariff schedules has been raised in the context of the Spence (1977) consumption outlay model (Section 5.1) by Panzar and Postlewaite (1984) and in the context of optional two-part tariffs by Sharkey and Sibley (1991). These authors show sufficient conditions for existence and other properties of sustainable (second-best core) outlay schedules under their respective definitions of sustainability. In particular under nondecreasing marginal cost and nonincreasing average cost, the surplus-maximizing optional two-part tariffs or outlay consumption bundles are sustainable. In general, however, sustainable nonlinear outlay schedules need not exist. In particular, the surplus-maximizing nonlinear tariff may not be sustainable if marginal costs are *decreasing*. This could prevent Rosse's (1978) suggested extension of the "weak invisible hand theorem" to the sustainability of nonlinear tariffs.

In the context of constrained optimal discriminatory two-part tariffs, Brander and Spencer (1985) find the following:[12] If the budget constraint is not binding ($\lambda = 0$) and if for some group l, $\partial N^l / \partial E^l < 0$, then $E^l = 0$ and $p^l = \partial C / \partial Q^l$. Such a group would therefore be cross-subsidized if there are economies of scale.

Define the contribution of each group l above marginal cost as $K^l = (p^l - \partial C / Q)Q^l + EN^l$. Brander and Spencer then establish that $K^l > 0$ for all l with positive subscribership if the budget constraint is binding ($\lambda > 0$). This rules out cross subsidization for all (weakly) convex cost functions. This means that cross subsidization only occurs if marginal costs are decreasing. This insight parallels that of Panzar and Postle-

[12]See our discussion of the Brander–Spencer model in Section 5.4 above. Spulber (1989a) discusses properties of the second-best core under customer-class price discrimination, using linear prices.

waite (1984) and Sharkey and Sibley (1991) on the unsustainability of nonlinear outlay schedules.

Nonexistence of the second-best core for nonlinear tariffs can also be demonstrated by the example of the single-product case with natural monopoly and a U-shaped average cost curve. As first noted by Faulhaber (1975), no subsidy-free (sustainable) linear price exists in this case. Furthermore, neither does a (second-best core) sustainable nonlinear outlay schedule exist if there are no customer-specific fixed or variable costs (i.e., all costs only depend on market output) and if there are infinitely many consumers (and the usual assumptions about customer types and noncrossing of demands hold).

To see this, suppose the monopolist had found a sustainable schedule $R^*(q)$ such that:

$$\sum_i R^*(q_i) - C(\sum_i q_i) \geq 0. \tag{6.9}$$

By sustainability, equality would have to hold in (6.9). Now assume a potential entrant who offers an outlay schedule $R(q) = \alpha R^*(q)$ with $\alpha = 1 - \epsilon$ for all purchase sizes q_i except for those with the smallest average price $R(q_i)/q_i$ (which, by subadditivity of R, are either the largest or nearly the largest consumers).[13] To the latter purchasers he offers $R(q_i) > R^*(q_i)$ for some purchase sizes q_i. If the interval of these q_i is chosen large enough, then some customers will prefer $R^*(q)$. As a result, the entrant's overall demand shrinks and his average price goes up. At the same time, due to an overall output decrease, his average cost will decrease relative to that of the incumbent firm. Therefore, no sustainable outlay schedule exists.

6.1.4 Bypass

In recent years regulated telecommunications carriers have been losing customers to new suppliers who are not common carriers. This phenomenon has been termed *bypass*. In this wide definition bypass is indistinguishable from entry under unsustainability. In a narrower definition to be used in most of this section, bypass of a service offered by a regulated carrier means self-supply of a customer with that service. The

---

[13] In the case of optional two-part tariffs the outlay schedule is concave by incentive compatibility. In this case it is always the largest customers who pay the lowest average price.

distinguishing feature here is that the consumer supplying itself has an assured outlet for the bypass service and in that sense bears less risk and is better informed.

Bypass is efficient or economic (inefficient or uneconomic) if the regulated carrier's incremental cost from providing the service of the customer is higher (lower) than the incremental cost of bypass to the consumer. Inefficient bypass can occur if the regulated carrier charges more than incremental cost of supplying the customer. And efficient bypass can be prevented if the carrier charges less than the incremental cost of bypass to the customer.[14]

Self-supply. The relationship between rate design and efficient bypass has been modeled by Einhorn (1987). His main result is that a nonlinear tariff designed to avoid inefficient bypass may require a marginal price for usage by the largest customer (who would otherwise bypass) to be below marginal cost. This contrasts with the very general result in nonlinear pricing that the marginal price for the largest customer equals (or exceeds) marginal cost. Einhorn's result, however, is totally unsurprising when given its proper interpretation and background.

Einhorn assumes the availability of a bypass technology for a consumer with cost of setup Z^* and cost of usage $C^*(q)$. The incumbent telecommunications carrier facing the prospect of bypass has its own cost for supplying the customer of $Z + C(q)$, but it is assumed to have no access to the bypass technology.[15] Prices are set by a fully informed planner or firm (who must therefore know the incumbent firm's cost and the cost of bypass). The carrier also has common or fixed cost K to cover. To make the problem interesting, $Z^* > Z$ and $\frac{\partial C^*}{\partial q} < \frac{\partial C}{\partial q}$ have to hold.

Bypass in this case is efficient if the total cost of bypass is lower than the incremental cost of providing the same level of service to the customer through the carrier's network. As illustrated in Figure 6.3, this will hold for all usage levels $q > q^*$ where q^* satisfies $Z^* + C^*(q^*) = Z + C(q^*)$.

Now, if customers are characterized by a single type parameter τ with density $f(\tau)$ and if the noncrossing assumption holds, then there will

---

[14]Sharkey (1988, 1990) analyzes the sustainability of monopoly production under cost structures of networks with fixed costs and shared facilities.
[15]There may be regulatory constraints or diseconomies associated with the use of the bypass technology by the regulated incumbent.

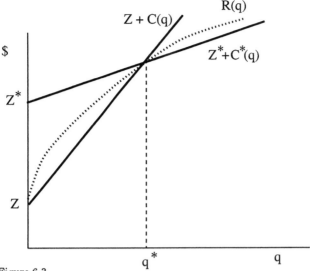

Figure 6.3
Nonlinear tariff to avoid inefficient bypass

be two types of marginal consumers. There is the small margin, for the consumer who is indifferent between consuming and not; consumer surplus for this consumer is zero. At the other end there is the large margin, for the consumer who is indifferent between purchase and by-pass; this consumer's incremental consumer surplus from purchasing (as opposed to engaging in self-supply) is zero. That means that the carrier will have to offer this consumer an outlay at q^* that equals the cost of q^* when supplied by bypass and also equals the incremental cost of q^* to the carrier. In order for the tariff schedule $R(q)$ to have this property at q^* and simultaneously to be below $Z^* + C^*(q)$ and above $Z + C(q)$ for all $q < q^*$ the slope of the schedule at q^* has to be between $\partial C^*/\partial q$ and $\partial C/\partial q$. In fact, as drawn in Figure 6.3, the nonlinear outlay schedule $R(q)$ at q^* will have the property:

$$\frac{\partial C^*}{\partial q} \leq \frac{\partial R}{\partial q} < \frac{\partial C}{\partial q} \quad \text{if} \quad \frac{\partial C^*}{\partial q} < \frac{\partial C}{\partial q}.^{16} \tag{6.10}$$

---

[16] This statement contradicts Einhorn's statement on p. 556 "that some customers must be indifferent .... and that $P(q_i) = C^* < C$ for these customers." Einhorn

This property is actually very similar to the price schedule chosen by a carrier with access to the bypass technology whose largest customer is just consuming at point q^*. At this point the carrier's total cost curve would have a kink and marginal cost of increasing output would be $\partial C^*/\partial q$.

Competitive supply. Woroch (1987) models bypass using the broader definition provided at the beginning of this section. He finds that "bypass occurs when facilities, erected alongside a public network, provide close substitutes for a selected set of services." Woroch analyzes the relationship between an efficient hub-and-spoke network under natural monopoly conditions and the equilibrium of an entry game played by a local exchange carrier (LEC) and potential entrants (bypassers). Woroch develops his own definition of sustainability against bypass. The distinguishing features compared to our earlier definitions are that the potential entrant supplies all demand at its prices. Due to legal entry restrictions in favor of the LEC, however, the bypasser restricts its supply to a subset of the LEC's services. This means that the LEC could resort to cross subsidization. Also, the potential bypassers are assumed to offer a two-part tariff (or two tied products, connection and transmission). Woroch finds that:

- Bypass could be efficient even though service between any two points is a natural monopoly.

- The LEC may be vulnerable to inefficient bypass.

- Conversely, the LEC may be able to prevent efficient bypass.

6.2   Cost-axiomatic pricing

Cost-axiomatic pricing is derived from postulates about the relationship between prices and costs. These axioms are simple and plausible, but have not been well-motivated in the literature.[17] A distinguishing property of axioms is that they are a consistent set of assumptions. However,

---

fails to recognize that $Z + C(q) \leq R(q) \leq Z^* + C^*(q)$ for $q < q^*$ and $Z^* + C^*(q) \leq R(q) < Z + R(q)$ must hold.

[17]A lack of motivation is also a feature of the axiomatic approach to concentration measurement, as brought out in the discussion, for example, in Curry and George (1983).

they have to be economically motivated if they are to serve a normative purpose. (As a source of explanation they may also serve poorly.) Axioms include:

1 *Cost sharing.* Total revenue equals total cost: $pq = C(q)$.

2 *Rescaling.* Changes in units of measurement have no effects on revenues.

3 *Consistency.* Services with the same effect on cost have the same price.

4 *Positivity.* A service that affects costs must have a positive price.

5 *Additivity.* If a service can be split up in the cost function into separate services, then the sum of prices for the individual services has to equal price for the combined service.

6 *Common cost correlation.* Assignment of common cost to services has to correlate with relative variable cost.

There are three economic motivations that could be used to defend axioms: efficiency, fairness, and competition. Not all the axioms are consistent with economic efficiency and competition. For example, Axioms 3 and 6 may be inconsistent with the efficiency requirement in that consumers may value services that have the same effect on costs differently and that any assignment of common cost may lead to inefficient choices. For the same reason Axiom 6 may also be inconsistent with competition.

While all the axioms are consistent with *some* notion of fairness, the four alternative notions of fairness discussed in Section 3.2.3 are served quite differently by the different axioms. All six axioms seem to be compatible with fairness defined by due process and equal opportunity. In our view, fairness defined by cost causality is not served well by Axiom 6, because common costs simply cannot be causally assigned.[18] Fairness defined by the status quo may or may not be compatible with the axioms; this compatibility actually depends on the specific status quo. Finally, fairness defined as an economic right to a service potentially

---

[18] As explained in our discussion of Ramsey prices in Section 4.2, cost causality may be a very one-sided concept of fairness, because it leaves out of consideration the different amounts of consumer surplus that the different buyers receive.

conflicts with most of the axioms, in particular with Axioms 1, 3, 4, and 6.[19]

The first five axioms uniquely define *Aumann–Shapley prices* for services $i = 1, \ldots, m$. These prices are characterized by:

$$p_i(C, q) = \int_0^1 \frac{\partial C(kq)}{\partial q_i} \, dk, \tag{6.11}$$

where q is the output vector and $0 \leq k \leq 1$ is a scalar.

Aumann–Shapley prices are fair in the sense that they distribute total costs among consumers as an average of the cost contributions of all possible consumer coalitions along a ray through the origin. They are average-cost prices if the cost function $C(q)$ can be separated into $C(q) = \sum_i C_i(q_i)$, with $i = 1, \ldots, m$. They are marginal-cost prices if $C(q)$ is homogeneous of degree one.

Bös and Tillmann (1983) show that Aumann–Shapley prices derived without the correlation axiom are demand compatible but may involve cross subsidization. Mirman, Tauman, and Zang (1985a) show that the modified Aumann–Shapley prices implied by the inclusion of Axiom 6 are sustainable and subsidy free.

The cost-axiomatic approach can be criticized from the efficiency and equity perspectives. The main weakness from an efficiency perspective is that the prices are not responsive to demand. This would be less of a disadvantage if information on demand were hard to come by and information on cost were readily available.[20] In fact, information on cost required to calculate Aumann–Shapley prices is highly detailed. The equity and fairness perspective appears to provide more fruitful interpretations of the cost-axiomatic approach. Since cost-axiomatic pricing can be viewed as a specific technique of fully distributed-cost pricing, we deal with this issue in the following section.

---

[19] Axiom 4 is not necessarily compatible with Rawlsian fairness.

[20] When no demand information is available, assuming equal price elasticities of demand is likely to lead to a more efficient result than using the cost-axiomatic approach to pricing. Ramsey prices with equal elasticities of demand would have markups proportional to marginal costs. The properties of prices proportional to marginal costs are discussed by von Weizsäcker (1986).

6.3 Fully distributed-cost pricing

6.3.1 Characterization

Cost-based pricing is straightforward as far as attributable costs of outputs are concerned. However, typically there exist costs that are shared
between different outputs (or shared by all quantities produced by a
single-product firm). Allocating such common or joint costs to the individual outputs (or quantities) on the basis of some formula is known as
fully distributed-cost pricing (FDC pricing). More formally, if we denote
directly attributable costs of output i by $VC_i(q_i)$ and the shared costs
of all outputs by $SC(q)$, and if total cost can be expressed as:

$$TC(q) = \sum_i VC_i(q_i) + SC(q), \tag{6.12}$$

then FDC prices have the property:

$$(a) \quad p_i = f[VC_i(q_i)] + g[q_i, SC(q)]. \tag{6.13}$$

This property means the price is the sum of a function of variable costs
and a function of quantity of output i and shared costs:

$$(b) \quad f[VC_i(q_i)]q_i = VC_i(q_i), \quad \text{and} \tag{6.14}$$

$$(c) \quad \sum_i g[q_i, SC(q)]q_i = SC(q). \tag{6.15}$$

Hence, by properties (b) and (c) the f-part of the price exhausts the
attributable costs of output i individually, while the g-part exhausts the
shared costs of all outputs taken together. Also, total revenues equal
total costs.

The function $g[\cdot, \cdot]$ is customarily a ratio between individual and total
revenues, or between directly attributable and shared costs, or between
individual and total output levels. The main feature of these methods
is their simplicity rather than their correctness. In fact, by definition
common or joint costs cannot be causally assigned to individual outputs.

However, cost assignment can serve as a proxy for cost measurement
in cases where the unmeasured costs are not actually joint or shared
and data are unavailable. For example, cost assignment proportional to
output quantities could be such a proxy.

FDC prices by revenue shares are:

$$p_i^r = f[VC_i(q_i)] + \frac{p_i}{\sum_i p_i q_i} SC(q)$$

$$= f[VC_i(q_i)] \frac{\sum_i p_i q_i}{\sum_i p_i q_i - SC(q)}. \tag{6.16}$$

FDC pricing by revenue shares involves a simultaneity problem in that revenue shares can only be calculated *after* prices are known, while here they are needed to determine such prices. One way to cope with this problem is to use lagged revenue shares. Note that the second equation in (6.16) assumes that the simultaneity problem in revenue shares is simply solved algebraicly by formula.

FDC prices by cost ratios are:

$$p_i^c = f[VC_i(q_i)] + \frac{VC_i(q_i)}{\sum_i VC_i(q_i)} SC(q)$$

$$= f[VC_i(q_i)][1 + \frac{SC(q)}{\sum_i VC_i(q_i)}]$$

$$= p_i^r, \tag{6.17}$$

so that FDC pricing by revenue shares and by cost ratios leads to the same prices.

FDC prices by output ratios are:

$$p_i^o = f[VC_i(q_i)] + \frac{SC(q)}{Q}, \tag{6.18}$$

where $Q = \sum_i q_i$ is the sum of outputs, assumed to be measured along the same quantity scale.

6.3.2 Subsidy-free FDC prices

FDC pricing has been viewed as fair by courts and regulators, and may thus have to be seen as an equity issue. Then the question arises whether FDC prices are subsidy free.

Spulber (1989a) constructs FDC prices that are subsidy free. He assumes that: $TC(q) = F + V(q)$ for $q > 0$, where $F > 0, V(0) = 0, V$ is continuous for $q \geq 0$, and $V(q) \geq 0$ for $q > 0$. $TC(q)$ is assumed to exhibit weak cost complementarities, meaning that $\partial^2 TC/\partial q_i \partial q_j \leq 0$

for all outputs i, j. Spulber then chooses subsidy-free prices f_i for the variable cost parts. Such prices exist by the assumption of weak cost complementarity. He then defines prices g_i for the fixed part such that FDC prices are:

$$p_i = g_i \frac{F}{q_i} + f_i \quad \text{with} \quad \sum_i p_i q_i = TC(q). \tag{6.19}$$

Spulber proves that these prices are subsidy free for all choices of $f_i \geq 0$ such that $\sum_i f_i = 1$. This result is quite straightforward if $V(q)$ is additively separable in the outputs q_i. In this case $V(q)$ actually represents the attributable costs, and the g_i are equal to output i's average incremental costs. Problems arise if $V(q)$ is not separable because then there can be joint or common costs of outputs contained in $V(q)$. In this case the choice of g_i already contains a nontrivial cost assignment problem that would ordinarily be solved by the FDC pricing formula rather than before applying such a formula.

Spulber also shows that under the above assumptions there exist FDC prices that are anonymously equitable, that is, subsidy free and demand compatible.

Spulber's results are quite in line with the observation that FDC pricing in the past has proven to be quite viable in a regulated environment of firms with legal entry barriers. FDC pricing is challenged, however, once entry becomes feasible and once efficiency of pricing becomes a major issue.[21]

6.3.3 Inefficiencies of FDC prices

FDC pricing has been the common practice under US public utility regulation. A systematic analysis of the efficiency properties of FDC pricing was first provided by Braeutigam (1980; see also Cole, 1981, and Braeutigam and Panzar, 1989). He finds that, compared to Ramsey prices, FDC pricing tends to sacrifice efficiency and can invite inefficient entry. We know that under efficient Ramsey prices the Lerner indices are systematically related to (super)elasticities of demand. FDC prices are ordinarily derived without any demand feedback. Hence, they would be

---

[21] Kelley (personal communications) notes that, in the United States, FDC pricing was a response to entry. The FCC adopted FDC pricing because it allegedly provided more carrier accountability. One can also argue that a regulator who wants to invite entry may use FDC pricing as a tool to disadvantage the regulated carrier.

efficient only by chance. This is borne out by Cabe's result (1988) that
essentially any arbitrary price vector can be generated through some
method of FDC pricing.

In this connection it may be noted that with independent demands
and cost functions of the form:

$$TC(q) = F + \sum_i v_i q_i, \qquad\qquad (6.20)$$

even Ramsey pricing can be generated as a type of FDC pricing. In this
case Ramsey pricing will be sustainable against potential entry. Under
the cost function (6.20) cost-axiomatic pricing also corresponds to FDC
pricing by the cost ratio method given in (6.17).[22]

Inefficient entry under FDC pricing can occur if FDC prices exceed
marginal costs of an output while a competing firm offers the output
with a constant-returns-to-scale technology at higher costs.

FDC prices are generally viewed as fair because every consumer pays
her attributable costs and a share of the unattributable costs. The
different methods of FDC pricing differ by the method in which this
latter share is derived. The methods (6.16)–(6.18) can be seen as simple
proxies for determining elusive cost causality.[23] Only the cost-axiomatic
method, however, is explicit in making this connection. The problem is
that this is done anonymously – all possible cost causalities are given
the same ex ante probability.

6.4   Special issues of carrier rates

6.4.1   Carrier rates and retail rates

In principle, the tariffs discussed so far can be applied to the sale of
telecommunications services as final goods and as intermediate goods.
There is nothing intrinsically peculiar about telephone rates charged by
one telecommunications carrier to another. However, some difference
in emphasis arises. Once we consider carrier rates we definitely leave
the realm of pure monopoly. Hence, some issues of horizontal and vertical competition and vertical integration naturally come up. We are
thus interested in the influence of carrier rates on the boundary of a

---

[22]Brown and Sibley (1986), p. 59.
[23]Baumol, Koehn, and Willig (1987) use the title "How Arbitrary is Arbitrary?" to
characterize FDC pricing.

telecommunications carrier. The issue of bypass was already considered in Section 6.1.4. The related issue of resale is taken up below.

As explained in Chapter 5, we do not consider the current theory of open network architecture (ONA) pricing (Stolleman, 1988) to be separable from general multiproduct nonlinear pricing. However, we believe that there are problems in ONA pricing that make it worth extending the theory. The particular issue appears to be that under ONA pricing vertically integrated networks are competing downstream with firms that buy their inputs from the networks. The main question here is one of efficient internal transfer pricing versus ONA pricing. Internal transfer pricing can always be at least as efficient as ONA pricing. On the other hand, networks may face diseconomies of scale or scope that could give the nonintegrated firms a cost advantage. If the tradeoff between pricing efficiency and production efficiency were played out on a level field, then ONA pricing would just be complex. In addition, however, there is the fear that integrated networks might want to use predatory pricing techniques to prevent the nonintegrated firms from expanding.[24]

6.4.2 Nonlinear tariffs, resale, and transactions costs

Resale at zero transaction cost constrains the sustainable outlay schedule with self-selection to be linear. More generally, the concavity of the outlay schedule is constrained by the transaction cost of resale. If transaction cost of resale per customer is $C_T = F_T + v_T q$ and if the reseller incurs a fixed cost of resale F then a sufficient condition on the outlay schedule for preventing resale is:

$$R(\sum_{i=1}^{m} q_i) + \sum_{i=1}^{m} v_T q_i + m F_T + F > \sum_{i=1}^{m} R(q_i) \qquad (6.21)$$

for all $m \geq 1$ and for all $\sum q_i \leq D(p_{min})$, where p_{min} is the lowest price on the outlay function $R(q)$. Otherwise, resale could be profitable for some combination of outputs. Condition (6.21) is empirically

---

[24] The vertical price squeeze is treated by Panzar (1980) who shows that the opposite problem of unsustainability may arise. This could occur if the incumbent firm faces entry by an inefficient rival who buys one of the incumbent firm's outputs as an intermediate input and competes with the incumbent firm on the final goods market. Optimal pricing rules in vertically related industries are developed in Spencer and Brander (1983) and Ebrill and Slutsky (1990). The latter paper reveals that the pricing rules themselves may be quite untractable even though the resulting quantity effects may follow the simple Ramsey rule of proportional deviations of all quantities from those corresponding to marginal costs.

hard to verify, not only because transaction costs of resellers have to be known but also because a large number of quantity combinations must be tested. If there were only variable costs associated with resale, then resale would concentrate on small final consumers. The presence of F_T limits the size of the smallest final consumer making use of resale. The presence of fixed cost F introduces economies of scale for the size of the reseller. In this sense reselling would have the property of natural monopoly, and the costs of resale would be minimized if the reseller were to capture the entire consumer population.

The transaction cost problems of resale closely resemble the transaction cost problems for customers of switching to other suppliers or switching to bypass. In each case there is a one-time transaction cost that has to be overcome. The comparison is then between the total outlay by the customer before switching and the outlay after switching plus the switching cost, resulting in a formula similar to (6.21).

Resale has an interesting connection to sustainability. A tariff that allows resale may itself be unsustainable due to the fact that resale restricts its curvature. However, there is an additional sustainability issue created by resale. Usually, unsustainability is defined with respect to a potential entrant who is able to supply a subset of the quantities demanded at the entrant's quoted prices. Thus, the entrant is under no obligation to serve. Should the entrant have an obligation to serve, then unsustainability of incumbent firms (as opposed to unsustainability of tariffs) would hardly be an issue. With resale, however, this may be different. A potential entrant could then fulfill its obligation to serve by purchasing from the incumbent any quantities demanded beyond what the entrant himself is willing to produce. This is particularly important at the time the entrant is building his own capacity. It is also important for securing spare capacity that the entrant could fall back on in case of demand surges or capacity failures. While backup tariffs for such reserve capacity may be socially efficient because they help avoid unecessary duplication of capacity, their availability may also be a precondition for successful entry and bypass.[25] The ability of AT&T's competitors to provide "universal service" via leased AT&T lines or even via AT&T's WATS tariffs may have been critical for their market success.

[25]Default-capacity tariffs (backup tariffs) are treated in Weismann (1988).

6.5   Second-best piecemeal policy revisited

Cost-related pricing. In this chapter we have introduced and discussed a large number of cost-related pricing concepts.

Subsidy-free prices, support prices, consumer subsidy-free prices, and anonymously equitable prices are all concepts that refer to requirements governing the relationship between costs and prices for different subsets of the telecommunications supplier's outputs. These subsets refer to the firm's different types of services, to different consumption bundles, or to different consumers. Thus, this first set of pricing concepts primarily concerns the relationship between the supplier and its customers.

The concepts of sustainaility and second-best core refer to the robustness of a firm's set of tariffs in the face of various types of entry behavior by other firms. These concepts are related to costs because both the incumbent firm and potential entrants must cover their costs under the prices they charge. This second set of concepts concerns primarily the relationship between an incumbent supplier and competitive entrants. However, since consumers can potentially supply themselves individually or as a group, the second set of concepts is intimately related to the first. In this sense, bypass is both a specific kind of sustainability problem and also a problem of cross subsidization.

Both cost-axiomatic pricing and FDC pricing may be viewed as pricing based on accounting, rather than on economic, principles. Under accounting principles it is very important that rules are established that always lead to a feasible outcome and that can be applied mechanically. In contrast, under economic principles efficiency outcomes and equitable outcomes are viewed as paramount. Thus the accounting approach subordinates the outcome to the process, and in doing so may neglect efficiency.

Efficient versus inefficient entry. In this chapter we have considered requirements other than efficiency (surplus maximization) that we might want to impose on tariffs for reasons of equity or competition. How do the restrictions generated by the requirement of, for example, anonymous equity or sustainability interfere with our ability to construct an overall system of second-best tariffs? In other words, how is second-best piecemeal policy affected by these requirements? One might believe that such a policy might become even more difficult than sketched in

Chapter 5 if we add these fairly complicated concepts. On the other hand, these requirements may take the form of constraints that reduce the set of feasible options. Also, sustainable prices are linked to potential competition, and potential competition may supplant the regulator in the task of finding optimal tariffs.

A large literature has evolved, seeking conditions under which sustainable and subsidy-free prices can be found and deriving the shape of subsidy-free price structures. Such conditions have become immensely important for telephone services with network competition and bypass options for large customers. The main problem is the tradeoff between type I errors – welfare losses coming from biases in competition or from inefficient bypass (if prices are not subsidy free) – and type II errors – welfare losses from barriers to competition or barriers to efficient bypass.

Assume that an industry is characterized by a certain cost function $C(\cdot)$ that is freely available to an incumbent and to potential entrants. Prices could be either regulated or set by the (profit-maximizing) incumbent. What, then, is the tradeoff in terms of the likely type I and type II errors to be made if one adopts a *general* type of pricing and entry policy with respect to the problem of sustainability?

Let us consider an extreme alternative: Allow completely free entry and completely free pricing by any potential entrant. Permit the incumbent to make the first price move, and impose on him an obligation to serve at these prices. This is the model implicit in the sustainability and contestability literature. The following are three possible outcomes:

1 If the market is sustainable and contestable the outcome will be efficient.[26]

2 If the market is sustainable but not contestable, then the incumbent will price above Ramsey prices.

3 If the market is not sustainable, then there will be no equilibrium.

The first of these three cases is probably restricted to some niches in the telecommunications market such as long-distance microwave transmission.

In the past the second case has been the most likely one in telecommunications. It would hold for all independent outputs where there are

---

[26] A market is contestable when costless "hit-and-run" entry and exit is possible before the incumbent firm can react to change its price or quantity.

no diseconomies of scale or for interrelated outputs where economies of scope are not outweighed by product-specific economies of scale. The presence of sunk costs substantially increases the cost and demand range for the second case (Knieps and Vogelsang, 1982). For the time being the second case appears to be empirically valid at least for local telephone calls. The outcome here may lie between efficient pricing and unconstrained monopoly pricing.

The third case is hard to evaluate, because we have no disequilibrium story. The worst we could expect here is nonexistence of the market. More likely are temporary market breakdowns. Also, there may be new market eqilibria with more than one firm.

The sustainability concept has added the third disequilibrium case to the older discussion about the effect of potential entry on market outcomes. The older discussion (started by Bain, 1956) emphasized entry barriers. The size of these barriers is still relevant for the second case. Hence efficiency through entry competition has become a knife-edge problem between entry barriers and unsustainability. If unsustainability is seen as the more likely problem, then additional legal entry barriers and price regulation appear to be the best solution. If entry barriers are seen as the more likely problem, additional legal entry barriers are not needed while price regulation may or may not be needed. In other words, the decisionmaker must have either Bayesian priors on the state of the market or have specific information on economies of scale and scope, market size, and market growth.

Thus, the extreme policy of free entry and no price regulation appears to be a second-best piecemeal optimal policy only for a natural monopoly close to the knife edge between barriers to entry and unsustainability. Otherwise, price regulation may be needed, with or without legal entry barriers. If legal entry barriers are established we are back to the problem posed at the end of Chapter 5 (possibly enlarged by the requirement of fulfilling the net revenue test). Our own view is that the policy errors made by the presence of legal entry barriers tend to be more detrimental than the errors made by their absence.[27] Without entry barriers the optimal pricing problems resemble those discussed in competitive sections of Chapters 4 and 5. The "invisible hand theorem"

[27]Entry barriers are preferable only if unsustainability is an issue. However, the conditions for unsustainability are very hard to establish in the absence of competition.

may be invoked. However, care has to be taken regarding its validity
under nonlinear pricing. In addition, it has to be noted that regulated
carriers are not necessarily viewed as benevolent by potential competitors. Thus, safeguards against predatory pricing, such as the net revenue
test, may become an issue.

Constrained market pricing. A specific suggestion for solving the
problems of fairness and efficiency (competition and predation), called
"constrained market pricing," has been made by Baumol and Willig.[28]
It is to allow the firm freedom to set its price structure within the range
provided by incremental cost of a service as a lower bound and stand-
alone cost (SAC) of a service as an upper bound. The difficulty with this
approach is that the bounds are not easily measured. Incremental costs
are only roughly approximated by average variable cost. SAC is characterized by Willig (Testimony, p. 40) as the price that would rule for
the service if the market were contestable, and by Baumol (Testimony,
p. 25) as the price that would induce entry by an efficient entrant in
the absence of entry barriers. Finding such a price requires substantial
counterfactual calculations.

For these reasons Baumol and Willig suggest that the regulated utility
would have to apply the constrained market pricing test only if challenged by a customer (or group) and after a demonstration that competition for the service in question is inadequate.

---

[28]Both in Testimony in Buckeye Pipeline Co. case before the Federal Energy Regulatory Commision (FERC), Docket No. IS87-14-000.

III

TELEPHONE RATE STRUCTURES IN THE UNITED STATES

7

Regulation and US retail rates

In Part II of this book we have reviewed and synthesized the theory of optimal pricing to the extent that we believe it is applicable to telecommunications services. In Part III we will survey innovative US practice in setting telecommunications tariffs.

This chapter links theory and practice. First, in Section 7.1 we establish linkages between theoreticaly optimal prices and their implementation in the regulatory process. Next, in Section 7.2 we survey the basic retail rate structures in effect for local and long-distance telephone services. (Optional rates at the retail level are covered in detail in the following chapter, and rate structures for bulk purchase are taken up in Chapter 9.) Finally, in Section 7.3, we describe price caps as a recent regulatory innovation that will move regulated rates away from fully distributed-cost (FDC) pricing rules and possibly toward efficient rate structures.

7.1 The impact of regulation on rate setting

7.1.1 The implementation problem

As indicated in Chapter 1, pricing theory and practice may influence each other in various ways. In particular, there are several reasons why practical solutions may differ from theoretically prescribed tariffs. Three such reasons appear to be particularly relevant:

- The real world is much more complex than the economist's models. The implications of such complexity for pricing were outlined in Sections 5.9 and 6.5.

- Policymakers may have objectives and constraints that differ from those assumed by economic theorists. Since this book is about

optimal tariffs in a normative sense, we really have little to say
about this second reason. Convincing objectives and constraints
should, in principle, be open to economic modeling.[1] In a positive
sense, regulators may be found to have selfish or inconsistent objectives, partly in response to competing interest groups. Besides
constraints imposed by a lack of power to subsidize or tax the
firm, regulators may be constrained by procedural rules (exclusion
of franchise bidding), by court decisions (inability to make longrun
commitments to bind future regulators), and by regulatory agency
budgets (limitations on information gathering).

- Even if policymakers agree with the objectives of normative economic models they may be unable to implement the resulting optimal tariffs against the interests and the information advantages
  of other concerned parties. This third reason – imperfect implementation – has been the subject of economic analysis for some
  time.

The starting point for economic modelling of imperfect implementation has been US rate-of-return regulation, under which regulated prices
are set so that they recover a utility's variable costs plus an allowed rate
of return on its rate base (the firm's assets). Averch and Johnson had
shown already in 1962 that rate-of-return regulation with an allowed
rate of return above the cost of capital could lead a regulated, profit-
maximizing monopolist to make inefficient input choices. Based on the
Averch–Johnson model other writers suggested that rate-of-return regulation also led to output price distortions. In particular, a rate-of-return
regulated firm would refrain from pricing in the inelastic portion of the
demand curve (Westfield, 1965), would use less than the optimal amount
of peak-load pricing (Wellicz, 1963), and would deviate from the Ramsey
pricing formula (Sherman and Visscher, 1979).

These conjectured inefficiencies led to attempts at empirical verification and to theoretical models for the implementation of optimal pricing.
The main problem appeared to be that regulated firms would have an
objective function different from that of the regulator and would possess
superior information about the underlying cost and demand parameters. For example, regulators typically must base prices on cost data

---

[1] See, for example, Bös (1985b), who discusses optimal pricing under the objective
of vote maximization in a median-voter model.

supplied by the regulated firm. The firm may then want to report, or
even actually incur, higher costs in order to be allowed higher prices.
How then can the regulator be sure that prices suggested by the firm (or
calculated by the regulator) are maximizing the regulator's objective?
Two strands of the theoretical literature – Bayesian and non-Bayesian
regulatory mechanisms – have tried to cope with the resulting incentive
problem.[2]

7.1.2 Bayesian regulatory mechanisms

The Bayesian mechanism design literature is based on the principal-
agent model of an informed agent (the regulated firm) who is employed
by an uninformed principal (the regulator). The first major paper in this
tradition of modeling the regulatory process was by Baron and Myerson
(1982). The literature is Bayesian in the sense that regulators start
out with prior probabilities about the relevant parameters. However,
regulators usually cannot correctly observe parameter realizations, even
ex post. The regulated firm, which does observe these parameters, then
has to be induced to report its observations so that the regulators can
implement optimal prices. It turns out that truthtelling is a dominant
strategy (revelation principle) and that firms have to be bribed to tell
the truth. These bribes take the form of price distortions which help the
firm to make positive economic profits (informational rents).

Typically, the regulator is assumed to maximize the expected value
of its objective function under an incentive-compatibility constraint and
a participation constraint. The incentive-compatibility constraint takes
care of the regulated firm's profit-maximization incentive; the participation constraint takes care of the firm's incentive not to participate if it
cannot break even. Since the regulated firm will be able to break even
under the worst state of the world, it will necessarily be profitable under
all other states.

The resulting informational and incentive rents could, in principle,
be financed through outside subsidies or, more likely, through two-part
tariffs. Hence, two-part tariffs may emerge as a regulatory tool that
helps extract information from, or set incentives for, the regulated firm.
However, in most of this literature the fixed part of two-part tariffs

---

[2]They are both reviewed in Besanko and Sappington (1987), Baron (1989), and,
with special reference to pricing, Laffont and Tirole (1990a, 1990b).

is assumed to have no effect on the number of consumers, removing the tradeoff between the allocative efficiency of price setting and the incentives for productivity and information revelation. The tradeoff was first addressed by Sappington (1983) and extensively analyzed by Laffont and Tirole(1990a, 1990b). The latter authors develop Bayesian Ramsey prices, peak-load prices, two-part tariffs, and general nonlinear tariffs. Their main insight is that an incentive correction may have to be added to the pricing formulas derived in Part II of this book. One of the key results of this literature is then that under asymmetric information optimal regulatory implementation may require prices to deviate from marginal costs even under constant returns to scale.

It is fair to say that Bayesian regulatory mechanisms dominate the theoretical discussion. There are several reasons, however, why this literature has so far had little normative effect on tariffs in practice, although it has been quite successful in explaining actual regulatory behavior and institutional procedures:

- Bayesian priors are different for different people. Hence, regulators would have to adjudicate such priors, something that does not necessarily go well with the US regulatory process. As Baron (1989) puts it, "the designer of a regulatory institution might prefer a regulatory mechanism that is invariant to the subjective assessments of whoever occupies the position of the regulator."

- Bayesian mechanisms work best if the information of regulators is fairly precise. Otherwise, the rents required to obtain the optimal outcome may be quite high.

- Bayesian mechanisms are hard to derive and to understand if demand and cost functions are not very simple.

7.1.3 Non-Bayesian regulatory mechanisms

The alternative, non-Bayesian approach to the regulatory implementation of optimal tariffs delegates much of the pricing decision to the regulated firm. This approach takes asymmetry of information to its extreme by assuming that the firm is fully informed (no uncertainty) while the regulator only has some very basic information about the market. In particular, the regulator knows no parameter values of either the cost or the demand function (even in a probabilistic sense).

How then can the firm be induced to act in the regulator's interest? For the case in which the regulator knows the firm's demand function, Loeb and Magat (1979) solve this problem through a generous bribe – a subsidy that is equal to the consumer surplus realized by the firm's customers. This way the firm's objective function (profit plus consumer surplus) equals that of the welfare maximizer, and the firm will implement marginal-cost prices. Funding the subsidy will induce distortions in the economy. Loeb and Magat suggest that such distortions can be avoided under a franchise-bidding scheme in which the winning bidder pays for the right to supply this market. Such a scheme would work if there are many well-informed bidders and if the firm's assets are readily transferable. However, these conditions are rarely met in a regulated industry.

Adjustment mechanisms. Vogelsang and Finsinger (1979, in the following abbreviated as V–F) suggest a regulatory adjustment process that avoids subsidies and does not require demand information by the regulator. The regulator does, however, have to observe the firm's total costs (expenses) in the last period. Regulation here takes the form of a constraint on prices that gets tighter from period to period. The constraint simply takes the form $p'_t q_{t-1} - C(q_{t-1}) \leq 0$, where prices and quantities are vectors. Thus, the firm is allowed to charge prices in the current period that would not result in any positive profit if they were applied to last period's outputs and costs. If the firm operates in a stationary environment, if its cost function exhibits no decreasing returns to scale, and if it maximizes profits, then prices will converge to Ramsey prices. In each period the firm will, on average, lower its prices and move closer to the Ramsey price structure.

Although the V–F mechanism ultimately converges to a Ramsey optimum, it is not optimal from a Bayesian point of view. The main reason is that the information on costs and demands revealed by the firm's choice in each period is never used by the regulator. Also, Sappington (1980) showed that the firm may have weak incentives to reduce its costs on the way to the optimum. Lastly, changes in the cost and demand functions may interfere with the convergence process (Brennan, 1989; Neu, 1988).

These difficulties have led to a number of refinements of the Loeb–Magat and V–F mechanisms. First, Finsinger and Vogelsang (1982) suggested that Loeb–Magat be implemented by giving the firm a subsidy

S_t, based on observable data, that would allow the firm to earn a first-order approximation of the social surplus change in each period, $S_t = -\pi_{t-1} + q_{t-1}(p_{t-1} - p_t)$. This approach would lead to a converging process that reaches marginal-cost prices in the limit. Subsidies would only be incurred on the way to the optimum and would likely be small anyhow. Vogelsang (1989) showed that these subsidies could be replaced by the fixed part of a two-part tariff such that $E_t = [-\pi_{t-1} + q_{t-1}(p_{t-1} - p_t)]/N_{t-1}$, where N_{t-1} is the number of customers of the firm in the last period. If the fixed fee acts as a lump-sum tax, then Coase two-part tariffs would result in the limit. If the fixed fee discourages some customers, then the process would converge to constrained optimal two-part tariffs.[3]

These refinements are closely related to the V–F mechanism and thus subject to weak cost-reducing incentives for the firm and to the stationarity of the environment. One way of coping with these two problems is to construct mechanisms that incorporate changes in the firm's environment and in the firm's opportunities. The other is to reduce the effect of environmental changes by constructing mechanisms that converge in one period.

Price caps. The prime example of the first type of mechanism is known as price caps. Price caps can be defined by the following four properties (Acton and Vogelsang, 1989):

1 The regulator directly sets a ceiling for prices to be charged by the regulated firm. The firm may choose prices below the ceiling.

2 Price ceilings are defined for baskets of services offered by the regulated firm. They can be expressed as price indexes for these baskets, and different ceilings may apply for each basket.

3 The price indexes are adjusted periodically by a preannounced adjustment factor that is exogenous to the regulated firm.

4 In longer intervals of several years, the adjustment factors, baskets, and weighting schemes for the indexes are reviewed and possibly changed.[4]

---

[3] See Hagerman (1990) for other refinements.
[4] While price caps as defined by these four properties were developed by Littlechild (1983), major parts of the concept can be traced to Baumol (1968, 1982).

Property 2 enables the firm to change its relative prices, as in the V–F adjustment process, and property 3 links price caps with changes in the firm's economic environment. There are three such changes of particular importance:

- The price level in the economy may change. This affects consumers' willingness and ability to pay for the firm's services. The adjustment factor therefore should include an economy-wide price index.[5]

- The firm's input prices may change. Some of these changes are already captured in the economy-wide price index change. Another part may be captured in adjustment terms for specific inputs and taxes, under the assumption that the firm cannot influence these price changes.

- The firm's technical opportunities may change through exogenous technical progress or the firm's own innovation. This factor is usually captured by an annual percentage adjustment (X) based on expectations of the firm's capability to reduce its input requirements. The crucial role of this expectations factor links price caps with the Bayesian approach.

Since price caps adjust periodically, they can be expected to adapt well to a changing environment. Since the adjustment factors are independent of the firm's behavior, they do not interfere with the firm's incentive to minimize costs and to introduce cost-reducing innovations.[6]

On the other hand, exogenous adjustment factors are always imperfect. This leads to excessive or insufficient profits of the firm over time and potentially to allocative inefficiencies (Schmalensee, 1989). Hence, property 4 is needed.

Incremental surplus schemes. An example of the second mechanism for coping with changes in the firm's environment is Sappington and Sibley's (1988) incremental surplus subsidy (ISS). These authors let the regulator give the firm a subsidy ISS_t such that it earns the exact change in social surplus, $ISS_t = -\pi_{t-1} + CS_t - CS_{t-1}$, where CS is

[5]RPI in the United Kingdom or GNP-PI in the United States.
[6]Kahn and Shew (1987) extensively deal with the problem of how to set prices optimally if the firm does not minimize costs. There is no straightforward solution to this problem.

consumer surplus. This mechanism will make the firm charge marginal-cost prices and minimize costs immediately after its introduction. So, both the problems of convergence in a changing environment and of perpetual subsidies are eliminated. One-time subsidies in the first period may have to be high, though.

Again, these subsidies can be avoided by two-part tariffs. Assuming that there is only one consumer, Sibley (1989) suggests that the firm be confronted with a mandatory two-part tariff having last period's price p_{t-1} as the variable fee and $-\pi_{t-1}$ as a fixed fee. In addition the firm can offer the consumer any optional two-part tariff as long as the consumer has the choice of the mandatory tariff. It turns out that the firm has the same incentives to offer a variable price equal to marginal cost as under ISS. In a related approach Vogelsang (1990a) includes the ISS in a price-cap mechanism. He suggests that the price caps act as mandatory prices and that the firm may in addition offer any optional two-part tariffs to its customers. This again will lead to the ISS result. However, Vogelsang (1990b) allows for many customers and multiple services. The (fully informed) firm would use discriminating fixed fees to finance marginal cost prices. Customers would not be exploited because they can always revert to the capped prices. These capped prices are usually derived by imperfect methods that are, at best, based on the regulator's Bayesian priors about the market.

In practice, non-Bayesian and Bayesian mechanisms may have to be combined, and this is what has actually happened when price caps were introduced in the United States. However, before we examine the details of the US price cap innovations we first present the basic US retail rates to which these price caps apply. An understanding of US retail rates is also essential background for the pricing innovations to be discussed in subsequent chapters.

7.2   Basic US retail rates

US telephone calls are priced according to broad calling area categories that correspond roughly to increasing distances (Figure 7.1). Within the local access and transport area (LATA), local calls include calls to telephones served by the same local switching office and usually the immediately neighboring offices, out to a distance of perhaps twenty miles. In some communities subscribers can purchase extended-area

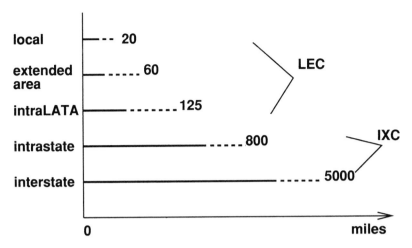

Figure 7.1
Rate structures and distance

service which enables them to call into the designated areas at local
rates. Otherwise, other calls within the LATA are trunk calls billed
under the local exchange carrier's (LEC's) intraLATA toll rates.

Calls between two LATAs are transported by interexchange carriers
(IXCs). Within a single state, interLATA calls come under state regulation, and different tariffs and market conditions prevail in each state.
Calls between two states are subject to federal regulatory policies and are
sold under uniform national tariffs. The rate structures for intrastate
and interstate long-distance calls are generally similar. However, intrastate rate levels vary a good deal and often exceed interstate prices.

The overlapping criteria that define the calling areas in which different rate structures apply result in a mixed pattern of prices in some
instances. For example, a subscriber who lives in a city near a state and
LATA border could make a series of calls of ten miles distance under
each type of rate.

7.2.1 Local rates

Rates for access to the telephone network and for local calling are set
out in tariffs filed by local exchange carriers with state regulatory commissions. The structures of these rates and the average rate levels vary
considerably from one state to the next. In most states, price levels also

vary according to the number of subscribers in the community served
and the average cost of the local company that serves it.

Residence and business rates.   Local-service pricing is the principal
instance of customer-class pricing in US telecommunications (Section
4.6). Local rates classify subscribers into residential and business groups,
and businesses pay substantially higher rates for essentially equivalent
services. For residential subscribers, the most common rate structure is
a *flat rate*, which has a fixed monthly charge for an unlimited number of
calls within the local calling area. The size of this area varies widely, but
always includes other subscribers served from the same central office, and
most commonly encompasses the immediately adjacent offices as well.

A few metropolitan areas, including New York and Chicago, have
mandatory measured service rate structures. In addition to a monthly
charge, there is a price for every local call. In some areas, or in daytime
periods, a per-minute price also applies. In many other communities one
or more measured-service rates are available as options to the residential
flat rate.

In some cities, per-message or per-minute rates are charged for calls
covering more than a specified distance or traversing two local zones. In
a few cities, residences can select an optional plan that permits them to
make calls over an extended area at local rates.[7]

One-time connection charges apply for establishing a telephone subscription. Additional charges apply if a drop wire or connection block
must be installed at the customer's location. Wiring on the consumer's
premises is not included.

Terminal equipment is not included in local tariffs. Main and extension telephone sets, answering machines, and other equipment are widely
available in retail stores.

In most communities, business subscribers are billed under a mandatory measured-service rate that has a higher fixed monthly price than
that charged to residential subscribers.

Average rates, calculated from a sample of ninety-five cities in late
1990, are shown in Tables 7.1 and 7.2. Residential flat rates range from

---

[7]In some instances a LEC has included a non-adjacent community within the
extended-area rate structure. More frequently, extended-area service has been offered in the form of measured-service rates to specific additional exchanges. Some of
the issues raised by expansion of a local rate area have been examined theoretically
by Dansby (1983) and Larson and Lehman (1987).

Table 7.1
Average monthly local rates

| | Residential | Business, per line | |
		One line	Threeline[1]
flat-rate[2]	$12.40	$33.20	$45.80
subscriber line charges	3.55	3.69	5.72
touchtone	1.31	2.18	2.27
taxes	1.83	4.94	6.92
total	19.09	44.01	60.71
range w/o touchtone	8.14–27.11		
measured service	8.46	16.22	20.96
usage	(includes	16.09	15.99
	50 calls)	(for 200 calls)	(for 200 calls)
subscriber line charges	3.55	3.55	4.91
touchtone	1.31	2.43	2.69
taxes	1.48	4.46	5.05
total	14.80	42.75	49.60
marginal price, 5-min call	.090	.093	.093
lowest monthly rate[3]	5.66		
subscriber line charges	3.55		
taxes	1.14		
total	10.35		

Notes: 95 City Sample, October 1990.
[1] Three access lines with a common telephone number.
[2] Unlimited calling in local area.
[3] Usually shared (multiparty) flat-rate service.
Source: FCC *Telephone Rates Update*, January 30, 1991.

$8.14 to $27.11. The lowest generally available residential rate, which may be a shared line or measured-service rate, averages $10.35.

In most states some residential subscribers are eligible for subsidized lifeline rates. These social tariffs are described in Chapter 11.

A number of optional "vertical" services can be added to basic telephone service, including call-waiting, call-forwarding, abbreviated dialing, and voice mail. Customers requiring several lines may subscribe to Centrex service and have a choice of a wide variety of optional office-communications features. LECs offer many of the optional services in mixed bundles (see Section 5.7).

Cellular telephone rates. Cellular telephones provide an alternative form of access to the telephone network. Each metropolitan area is

Table 7.2
Average connection charges

	Residential	Business one line
minimum connection[1]	$43.02	$71.73
touchtone		1.60
taxes	2.37	4.16
total one-time charge	45.39	77.49
range	12.00–67.45	

Note: [1] Additional charges apply if drop line and connection block needed.
Source: FCC *Telephone Rates Update*, January 30, 1991.

limited by the FCC to two suppliers, one wireline carrier (such as the regional Bell operating company that provides local wireline service in the city) and one non-wireline carrier (for example, McCaw or a telephone operating company from a different region).

Cellular penetration has grown very rapidly, and particularly in cities where commuting by automobile is prevalent. Mobile telephone sets, initially priced at some $2500, can now be purchased for as little as $300-$400, and equipment discounts are sometimes tied to subscribing to service from a particular carrier.

In California, two optional two-part rate structures have emerged in the major urban markets (Table 7.3). Subscribers are billed for all minutes of air time, including incoming calls, at peak or off-peak rates. In addition, ringing time for busy and no-answer cellular phones is charged at one-half the per-minute rate.

Resellers can purchase service from one of the two metropolitan carriers at wholesale rates that constitute some 74-9 percent of a retailer's costs.[8] In California in 1988, duopoly carriers held 70 percent of the market, independent resellers 16 percent, and affiliates of duopoly carriers 14 percent.

Large organizations can purchase bulk-rate service at large-user rates. They then incur the costs of billing and collecting from their members. California regulates this rate to be at least 5 percent above the wholesale rate for resellers.

[8] California PUC, Decision 90-06-025, June 6, 1990, p. 72.

Table 7.3
Retail rates for cellular service in California

City	Plan name	Access per mo.	Usage per minute Peak	Off-peak
Los Angeles	basic	$45.00	$.45	$.27
	personal	25.00	.90	.20
San Francisco/	basic	45.00	.45	.20
San Jose	personal	25.00	.90	.20
San Diego	basic	35.00	.40	.24
	personal	19.95	.75	.19
Sacramento	basic	20.00	.25	.15
Fresno	1-5 numbers	31.00	.35	.20
	6+ numbers	28.00	.35	.20

Note: Peak hours are 0700–1900 Monday-Friday. Rates are the
same for both carriers in each metropolitan area. In some cases,
reseller rates vary slightly.
Source: Comments of Division of Ratepayer Advocates, California
Public Utilities Commission, OII No. I.88-11-040, June 1989.

The cellular systems' switches are interconnected with local exchange
carriers in their metropolitan areas. Cellular systems both originate and
terminate calls and the cellular carriers pay switched-access charges to
the LECs for interconnection (see Chapter 10). In California, however,
cellular firms do not pay an access charge to support the nontraffic sensitive costs of the local exchange.

7.2.2 Long-distance rates

Most long-distance telephone calls in the United States are purchased
from AT&T under its Message Telephone Service (MTS) tariff or from
other interexchange carriers under similar rate structures. In the case of
AT&T's interstate services, these rates are regulated by an overall price
cap that applies to residential and small business services – basket #1
(see Section 7.3).

Intrastate rates. The structure of intrastate toll rates is similar to
AT&T's interstate rate structure, which is described below. Rates
are differentiated by distance, time-of-day/weekend periods, and first-
minute/additional minutes of duration. However, the *levels* of intrastate

Table 7.4
Average intrastate toll rates (5-minute daytime calls)

Distance (miles)	IntraLATA (1986) Total entry restricted		InterLATA (1987)	
	Yes	No	ROR regulation	Price flexibility
0-10	$0.59	$0.66	$0.77	$0.70
11-16	0.78	0.89	0.91	0.89
17-22	0.96	1.02	1.09	0.99
23-30	1.16	1.32	1.27	1.22
31-40	1.35	1.46	1.43	1.32
41-55	1.52	1.56	1.59	1.39
56-70	1.68	1.71	1.71	1.59
71-124	1.82	1.81	1.85	1.66
125-196			1.95	1.80
197-292			2.04	1.84

Source: Mathios and Rogers (1988), Table VI:1 and Table VII:1.

toll rates vary widely across the United States. For example, in 1986 the price for the first minute of a twenty-three to thirty mile daytime intraLATA call ranged from $0.21 (Oregon) to $0.62 (West Virginia). InterLATA intrastate calls of the same distance varied in price from $0.15 (Texas) to $0.46 (Mississippi).[9]

Table 7.4 reports average state rates for intraLATA and interLATA five-minute daytime calls by distance bands, as estimated by Mathios and Rogers (1988). Their study distinguishes intraLATA markets according to whether entry was totally restricted, limited to resellers only, or unrestricted. In states in which entry was totally restricted the average price increased in all distance bands between 1983 and 1986; in states that permitted entry there were smaller rate increases at short distances and decreases at longer distances. In the interLATA markets, states that allowed carriers some pricing flexibility had lower average rates in all distance bands, and somewhat greater rate decreases over the 1983-7 period.

AT&T's interstate rates. AT&T's rates for interstate calls are uniform within most of the United States (all intramainland, mainland–Alaska and Mainland–Hawaii calls). The MTS rate structure consists of

[9]Mathios and Rogers (1988), Appendix D.

three basic *rate elements* that apply to customer-dialed calls – distance, duration, and time-of-day/day-of-week period.

The same rate is charged for all routes that are within a distance band (measured as airline distance between urban centers of the originating and terminating calling areas). Thus, high-cost and low-cost routes of a given distance are priced the same, and this form of geographic *rate averaging* has been a long-standing practice encouraged by the FCC.

MTS rates. The 1990 AT&T interstate rate structure (Table 7.5) has eleven distance bands. However, rates increase only moderately with distance, and even transcontinental-distance calls (up to 3000 miles) cost less than 40 percent more per minute than the shortest-distance toll calls, which can be as short as one mile. This relatively small distance gradient in the rate structure reflects the compression in distance-sensitive charges that has occurred over time. Similarly, the number of separate distance bands has been reduced.

Charging by distance in the rate structure is consistent with the higher marginal costs that result from additional intermediate switching in the long-distance network and the increased use of scarce transmission capacity over greater distances. The reduction in rates that has occurred over time, particularly at longer distances (see Section 4.5.1), reflects lower marginal costs achieved with fiber-optic and other high-capacity transmission systems. It is also consistent with higher price elasticities of demand observed at longer distances, and the emergence of the most vigorous competition in those longer-haul markets.

The MTS rate structure has historically had one rate for the first period of each call and a lower rate for additional minutes. Thus any call, however short its duration, incurs a minimum price. In earlier years, this first period was three minutes, but it is now just one minute. Furthermore, the discrepancy between the first-minute and additional minute price had, by 1990, been reduced to 1 cent or less in AT&T's tariffs, so that charges are virtually proportional to call duration.

In addition to the opportunity costs of occupying network transmission and switching facilities during conversation time, each call incurs some duration-independent costs. These costs result from the time and equipment required to "set up" a call (including calls not completed when subscribers are busy or do not answer) and the costs associated with billing. A differential initial-period charge is consistent with these

Table 7.5
AT&T interstate MTS rate structure

	Day		Evening		Night/Weekend	
	1st	add'l	1st	add'l	1st	add'l
Distance	min.	min.	min.	min.	min.	min.
1 - 10	$ .1800	$ .1700	$ .1206	$ .1139	$ .1000	$ .0975
11 - 22	.1975	.1975	.1340	.1340	.1130	.1100
23 - 55	.1975	.1975	.1454	.1454	.1200	.1200
56 - 124	.2160	.2150	.1454	.1454	.1200	.1200
125 - 292	.2160	.2150	.1457	.1457	.1215	.1215
293 - 430	.2300	.2300	.1457	.1457	.1250	.1225
431 - 925	.2390	.2390	.1495	.1495	.1300	.1260
926 -1910	.2490	.2490	.1496	.1496	.1325	.1300
1911 -3000	.2490	.2490	.1496	.1496	.1350	.1325
3001-4250	.3100	.3000	.2077	.2010	.1650	.1600
4251-5750	.3300	.3200	.2211	.2144	.1750	.1700

Call category	Surcharge per call
dial station	–
customer-dialed calling card station	$ .80
operator station	1.75
person-to-person	3.50

Notes: July 1990. Rates per minute vary somewhat for some mileage bands for calling-card, operator station, and person-to-person calls. For US–mainland to Hawaii, Puerto Rico, and Virgin Islands calls higher rates apply with distance based on 4 bands of geographically proximate states.
Day: 8 a.m.–5 p.m. Monday-Friday
Evening:5 p.m.–11 p.m. Monday-Friday, Sunday
Night/Weekend: other hours.
Source: AT&T Tariff No. 1, FCC Tariff Division.

incremental per-call costs. However, common-channel signalling has substantially reduced the costs of setting up calls. Furthermore, competing carriers have successfully promoted simplified rate structures that have the same per-minute price for all minutes.

The third rate element is the time of day and day of week during which the call is made. For many years, interstate rates have distinguished three periods on weekdays – day, evening, and night – with reduced rates in effect on weekends and holidays. These periods broadly reflect the occurrence of peak traffic volumes in most sections of the interstate network during the day period (8 a.m.–5 p.m.), with volumes that are nearly as high during the evening (5 p.m.–11 p.m.) in many areas.

AT&T's rate differential between peak and off-peak rates has declined over time. Initially, AT&T established the evening and night rates as

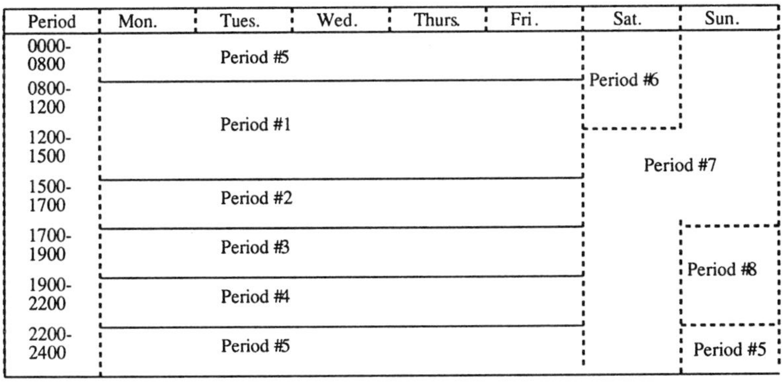

Period	Mon.	Tues.	Wed.	Thurs.	Fri.	Sat.	Sun.
0000-0800		Period #5				Period #6	
0800-1200		Period #1					
1200-1500						Period #7	
1500-1700		Period #2					
1700-1900		Period #3				Period #8	
1900-2200		Period #4					
2200-2400		Period #5					Period #5

Figure 7.2
Rate periods for AT&T area code calling plan

a uniform percentage discount from the day rates. However, the introduction in 1984 of carrier access charges at a constant per-minute rate at all hours established a minimum variable cost per minute for the interexchange carriers, and the rates in evening and night/weekend periods have subsequently been set according to distance band. In the July, 1990 rate structure the evening period rates are 60 to 73 percent of the day rate, and the night/weekend rates range from 53 to 60 percent (Table 7.5).

Peak-load pricing. AT&T's time-of-day rate structure reflects the feasibility constraint of a small number of distinct prices and pricing periods that is required for acceptance by retail consumers. In a given distance-band market the same price structure applies every weekday. Also, the peak rate hours are the same in all distance bands.

AT&T has maintained the hours of the three rate periods for many years, with one significant modification. In the face of rapidly increasing Sunday evening traffic, the previous night rate, which had applied to all weekend hours, was eliminated and replaced by the evening rate for Sunday 5 p.m.-11 p.m. In a limited, further modification the optional calling plan rates have begun the night period one hour earlier, so that it is 10 p.m.-8 a.m. instead of 11 p.m.-8 a.m.

It is of interest, however, that in 1990 AT&T filed an optional calling plan rate structure that provides for as many as eight separate time-of-day/day-of-week pricing periods (Figure 7.2). This new rate plan applies to calls placed to a single, customer-selected national area code. As currently implemented, only two different time-of-day rates apply to the calls in any distance band, but the structure gives the carrier the flexibility to use more time-differentiated pricing, calibrated to demand and competition in individual distance-band markets.

The day/evening/night rate structure may also be considered in terms of customer-class pricing. With limited exceptions, business users' demand is concentrated almost entirely in the regular weekday hours 8 a.m.-5 p.m., and much of the opportunity for residential long-distance calling occurs after working hours and on weekends. Pricing day and evening calls at separate rates allows the supplier to exploit the relatively inelastic demand of business subscribers.

Service charges. AT&T and other carriers levy additional charges for calls that are not directly dialed and automatically billed to the calling telephone. AT&T's earlier tariffs had separate rate structures for operator-handled and person-to-person calls. These services incurred higher charges for both the initial period and for all additional minutes. Today, this structure has been replaced by levying a separate charge per call for operator and credit-card calls and billing minutes at essentially the direct-dial rate (Table 7.5).[10] This set of fixed surcharges is in line with the incremental cost of manually handling a call and of additional billing expenses for credit card use.

Rates of other carriers. MCI, as AT&T's first competitor in switched long-distance service, initially priced its Execunet service at a substantial discount below AT&T's retail rates. These prices reflected both promotional pricing and a real difference in service quality. MCI and other market entrants were handicapped by technical limitations on access to local exchange switches that required their subscribers to first dial a local telephone number, and then an authorization code, before placing each call.

As part of the divestiture of AT&T, LECs were required to upgrade local switches to provide "equal access" capability to every interexchange

---

[10] AT&T's 1990 per minute rates for credit card and operator-handled calls differ slightly from the direct-dial rates in some distance bands and day periods.

carrier that established a point of presence in the LATA. As a result, today almost all consumers can "presubscribe" to any interexchange carrier and their long-distance calls are automatically routed to that carrier without extra dialing.[11]

The 1990 retail rates charged by MCI, US Sprint, and other IXCs closely resemble AT&T's. All of the major competing carriers have rate structures incorporating rate elements for distance, duration, and time-of-day. Differences in rate levels have narrowed substantially.

The vigorous competition for retail customers, which has developed most intensely in the form of optional rate structures described in the next chapter, suggests that the cost structure of interexchange service has at most only weak elements of natural monopoly. In this setting, the FCC's requirement that AT&T continue to average rates geographically makes the sustainability of AT&T's uniform rates for distance bands uncertain. Competitors have made inroads into the retail market by bundling usage and offering volume discounts.

7.3   Price caps

Since divestiture in 1984, the FCC has continued to regulate AT&T as a dominant interstate carrier in the market for long-distance telephone services. In the spring of 1989, price cap regulation of AT&T replaced traditional rate-of-return regulation.[12] The change was designed to provide AT&T with improved incentives and greater pricing flexibility in increasingly competitive long-distance markets, while protecting against cross-subsidization, monopoly and/or predatory pricing.

Before price cap regulation, AT&T had to submit tariffs under service-specific proceedings that could drag on for years. Voluminous cost and revenue support data were required to demonstrate that the new rates for the service would cover fully distributed costs. A simple rate rebalancing could be held up for several months. These delays hampered AT&T's ability to respond rapidly to increasingly aggressive competition from the other interexchange carriers. Commercial customers were demanding a host of new digital and other advanced telecommunication and data services. AT&T's incentives to efficiently invest in new technology were

---

[11] Consumers can also select a different carrier for any particular call by prefixing the telephone number with "10" plus the desired carrier's three-digit access code.
[12] See the Federal Communications Commission (1989).

muted by rate-of-return regulation. Thus, in 1987, the FCC began to investigate new incentive-based regulatory approaches.

Under price cap regulation, AT&T is subject to a greatly streamlined tariff review process so long as its new rates and service offerings do not violate price cap pricing formulas. These formulas consist of separate price indexes, with upper and lower component pricing bands, for each of three service "baskets." Services are grouped into baskets by major customer classes. The use of separate indexes for each basket protects against cross-subsidization. Upper and lower pricing bands restrict excessive movements in individual components that might signal either predatory or excessive monopoly pricing for a particular service.

Price cap regulation substituted a greatly simplified tariff review period. Under the expedited review procedures, AT&T no longer has to cost-justify service-specific tariff revisions. So long as AT&T's rates do not violate the pricing formulas specified in the regulation, the new rates become effective in fourteen days. The price cap indexes are designed to adjust automatically to account for inflation, exogenous cost shifts (beyond AT&T's control), and for projected increases in productivity. Any incremental cost savings in excess of those projected by the price cap formulas increase AT&T's profits. This provides the improved incentives which were desired. Furthermore, price cap regulation lessens the administrative costs of regulatory oversight, and increased competition in long-distance markets makes a lessening of oversight feasible.

7.3.1 Service baskets and indexes

Under price cap regulation, AT&T's services were divided into four categories: the first three were subject to service-basket price caps while the fourth category included all of the specialty services which would continue to be regulated as they were before price cap regulation became effective.[13] The three service baskets are:

1 Residential and small business services, including domestic and international residential and business MTS service.

2 "Toll-free" 800 Services.

---

[13] See Appendix (A.3) for a list of the formulas and additional details.

3 Business Services, including WATS, private line and various switched commercial services such as AT&T's Software Defined Network (SDN).[14]

The prices of each basket were capped at their existing rates and the Price Cap Index (PCI) was set to 100.0 for December 31, 1988. The PCI is adjusted up or down to account for general inflation, as measured by movements in the overall GNP price index (GNP-PI) and exogenous shifts in total costs beyond AT&T's control. These exogenous shifts include changes in carrier access charges (fees paid by interexchange carriers to local telephone companies for circuit connections to originate and terminate long-distance calls), taxes, regulatory adjustments, etc. In addition, the PCI is reduced by 3 percent per year to account for projected productivity increases due to technical innovation.[15] If we ignore exogenous cost adjustments, the productivity factor guarantees that the PCI will rise less slowly than inflation, and so, on average, real rates will decrease over time.[16]

At least once a year, as well as each time AT&T files a new tariff revision, AT&T must calculate the Actual Price Index (API) for each basket and show that the API does not exceed the PCI. The new API is computed by recalculating the index formula with the new rates. Since each basket is composed of numerous services, each of which is priced according to a schedule of rate elements (e.g., first and additional minutes, time-of-day, mileage bands, etc.), the differing rate elements are weighted by their contribution to total basket revenues.

The rate element weights are based on the revenue share of base period demand (in minutes or messages) evaluated at current rates (which might have changed since the base period). Base period demand is the actual demand for the year which ended six months before the current reporting period. This procedure ensures that the weights will change over time to reflect demand shifts induced by prior rate changes.

---

[14]Business services are described in Chapter 9.

[15]The 3 percent number is based on estimated historical productivity growth of 2.5 percent plus a "consumer dividend" of 0.5 percent. The dividend is designed to assure that AT&T passes on cost savings to consumers via lower average rates.

[16]Since the PCI is adjusted for general inflation, it may not accurately reflect cost changes affecting the telecommunications sectors of the economy. The FCC doubted the significance of potential discrepancies and felt that none of the available telephone-specific indexes which might have been used as an alternative provided adequate coverage of both investment and consumption goods.

Service bands. In addition to the basket price caps, there are Service Band Indexes (SBIs), which restrict rate changes for individual services to a 10 percent band (i.e., ±5 percent above and beyond the change in the PCI) centered around the June 30 price.[17] When new rates are approved, new SBIs are computed.

In its annual filings, AT&T reports the PCIs and APIs for each basket and the SBIs for each sub-element in the baskets. New values for these indexes are reported in subsequent filings only when tariff revisions require a change in the values. AT&T made its second annual filing as of July 1990.[18]

New services. The FCC distinguishes "new" and "restructured" services. The former represent an increase in customer options; while the latter reflect a change in the way existing services are provided and/or charged. Both sorts of changes must be submitted for forty-five day review. New services are included in the price cap in the first annual filing which follows the completion of the first base year in which the service becomes effective. Under this approach, new services are exempt from price caps for a period of up to eighteen months. After the new services are included, the demand weights will reflect their contribution to total revenue. In addition, new services must satisfy a revised "net revenue test."[19]

When existing services are restructured, base period demand is reallocated to the new tariff elements.[20] Restructured tariffs may require remapping demand between the three service baskets (see Table 7.6). The change in the API is estimated by comparing the revenue effect of

---

[17]Residential services are subject to tighter banding. AT&T cannot raise the rates of Domestic evening or Domestic night/weekend services by more than 4 percent; other service categories in the basket are subject to the standard 5 percent limit. In addition, one further limit applies to the residential basket: average residential rates cannot rise by more than 1 percent per year relative to the PCI (which guarantees real rates will fall by at least 2 percent per year). AT&T reports a "residential only" services SBI which excludes small business services in order to verify that this bound is not exceeded.

[18]See AT&T Revised Tariff Filings, Transmittal No. 1618 (May 17, 1989) and No. 2396 (June 28, 1990).

[19]Within the lesser of the following two periods, a new service must contribute to its basket's net revenue: (a) within twenty-four months following the effective date of the first annual price cap which includes the new service; or, (b) within 36 months of when the tariff which first offered the service became effective. See FCC Order (1989), p. 244.

[20]Only base demand is remapped. There is no attempt to estimate changes in the level of base demand due to the changes in average rates.

Table 7.6
AT&T tariff filings requiring remapping of base demand

Tariff filings (January–June 1989) that required reclassification:†	
8	subdivide a rate element
2	aggregate a rate element
2	remap within a band
2	remap within a basket across bands
3	remap across baskets
29	Total

Between August 1989 and May 1990, 28 of the tariffs filed implemented
rate structure changes. It is unclear how many of these required
rebalancing across baskets.‡

Sources: †Exhibit #2, AT&T Revised Tariff Filing, Transmittal #1618, May
17, 1989.
‡Exhibit #3, AT&T Revised Tariff Filing, Transmittal #2396, June 28,
1990.

the new proposed rates as calculated under the new proposed structure
with the revenues from the existing rates.

Rate revisions which do not violate service bands and are below the
PCI are approved in fourteen days. If AT&T exceeds the lower bound
for a service band, then it must submit additional cost and revenue
information to show that the service will cover its average variable costs
under the new rates.[21] In that case, the tariff will not be approved for
forty-five days (the typical statutory review period for tariff revisions
under pre-price cap regulation). If AT&T violates the upper service
band indexes and/or price caps, the tariff revision must be submitted
on ninety-day notice with substantive cost and revenue support.

The basic basket structure reflects concerns that, unless business and
residential services are separated, AT&T might raise rates to residential
customers in order to cross-subsidize services subject to more aggressive
competition in the commercial market. This led to the construction of
the Residential (#1) and Commercial (#3) services baskets. The third
basket for 800 Services (#2) was separated from Basket #3, since it was
felt that AT&T still possessed significant market power in these services.

[21] In its August 31, 1989 tariff submittal (see Transmittal No. 1762) AT&T filed lower
rates for SDN services (in Basket #3) which violated the lower SBI. It submitted
revenue and cost information which demonstrated that longrun incremental costs
would still be covered under the new rates.

Table 7.7
Tariffs excluded from AT&T price cap regulation

Tariff 5	Special construction services. These are nonrecurring expenses.
Tariff 11	Essentially a pass-through tariff of charges AT&T incurs to obtain special access circuits under LEC special access tariffs.
Tariff 12	Custom-designed services such as Special Routing Arrangement, Service Defense Telecommunications Network, Digital Tandem Switched Network and Arrangements, and Virtual Telecommunications Network Service.
Tariff 15	Customer-specific tariffs offered in response to specific offerings by AT&T competitors, e.g., the Holiday Inn Rate Plan.
Tariff 16	Government services such as Oahu Telephone Communications Service and FTS-2000.

Note: Tariff 12 and Tariff 16 are the most important (in revenue terms) of the services excluded from the AT&T Price Caps. US Sprint estimated that AT&T's Tariff 12 revenues were "in excess of $1 billion." (See: Reply Brief for Petitioner US Sprint in the US Court of Appeals proceeding between MCI Telecommunications and the FCC, Nos. 89-1382, July 13, 1990, p. 3.)

Opponents of the added pricing flexibility afforded AT&T by the new regulations argued that even more baskets should be required. They wanted to separate other special services from Baskets #1 and #3. If there are too many baskets, however, then the process would resemble the former service-specific approach and much of the proposed benefits of price cap regulation would disappear.

A number of increasingly important services, listed in Table 7.7, are exempt from price cap regulation and must follow the old regulatory process for tariff review. These include many of the most technically advanced services which have been created in order to keep large corporate customers from shifting their traffic from public to private networks. Services which are customer-specific, subject to separate accounting requirements, involve longterm contracts or significant one-time construction costs are not well-suited for price capping. The customers for these services are large, sophisticated commercial enterprises. These are the customers and services that are most subject to direct competition by the other carriers.

7.3.2 *Price changes under price caps*

To date, AT&T has filed two annual tariffs which provide a complete list of the relevant price cap indexes. These include the three sets of basket specific indexes: PCI, API, and SBIs.[22] The SBIs allow one to track service-specific rates, while the APIs allow one to track the trend in overall rates. The PCI data will facilitate tracking the changes in exogenous costs and access rates. Otherwise, the PCI is not interesting except in so far as it guarantees that price caps will decline on average 3 percent per year relative to the GNP-PI.[23]

These annual filings will allow one to track the interstate traffic for the services which account for the bulk of the dominant carrier's revenues. Table 7.8 shows the contribution of price cap services to AT&T's revenues by individual service in 1988 and by service basket in 1989. (Unfortunately, the two annual filings do not report data at the same level of detail.) Excluded services probably account for something less than 5 percent of total AT&T revenues. These services, however, account for many of the most innovative forms of pricing and many of the customers for whom competition is most agressive.

Table 7.9 summarizes available data on AT&T price caps by individual service band from the annual filings. Using the new pricing flexibility the carrier has made the largest percentage rate reductions in evening and optional residential rates, the high-volume Megacom 800 toll-free service, and selected business bulk-rate services.

---

[22]See Appendix Tables A.2-A.3 for summary data.
[23]It is possible, but unlikely, that real rates in any given year could actually increase if they had been sufficiently below the price cap in the previous year.

Table 7.8
Revenue shares for AT&T by price cap basket

	Revenue† (1988) $ Million	Revenue Shares of basket	of total	Change 1988 to 1989
Basket #1 (Residential and Small Business Services)				
Domestic Day MTS	$ 3,193.4	19.2%	12.2%	
Domestic Evening MTS	3,218.4	19.4%	12.3%	
Domestic Night/Wkend	1,842.9	11.1%	7.0%	
International MTS	4,448.3	26.8%	17.0%	
Operator and Card	3,020.5	18.2%	11.5%	
Reach Out America	895.5	5.4%	3.4%	
Residential (only)	12,096.6	72.8%	46.1%	
Total for 1988	$16,619.0	100.0%	63.4%	
(Total for 1989‡)	$16,105.1			-3.1%
Basket #2 (800 Services)				
Readyline 800	$ 270.7	7.9%	1.0%	
AT&T 800	2,544.9	74.2%	9.7%	
Megacom 800	561.3	16.4%	2.1%	
Other 800	51.9	1.5%	0.2%	
Total for 1988	$ 3,428.8	100.0%	13.1%	
(Total for 1989‡)	$ 3,361.1			-2.0%
Basket #3 (Business Services)				
PRO WATS	$ 1,622.3	26.2%	6.2%	
AT&T WATS	1,467.3	23.7%	5.6%	
Megacom	628.9	10.2%	2.4%	
SDN	138.8	2.2%	0.5%	
Other Switched	122.7	2.0%	0.5%	
Voice Grade Private Line	1,948.9	31.5%	7.4%	
Other Private Line	254.3	4.1%	1.0%	
Total for 1988	$ 6,183.2	100.0%	23.6%	
(Total for 1989‡)	$ 5,994.6			-3.1%
Total	$26,231.0		100.0%	
(Total for 1989‡)	$25,460.8			-2.9%

Notes: †1988 demand at June 30, 1989 prices.
‡1989 demand at June 30, 1990 prices.
Source: AT&T Revised Tariff Filing, Transmittal #1618, (5/17/89), Exhibit #5 and Transmittal #2396 (6/28/90), Exhibit #2 and #4. In 1989, new services added $6.3 million to base revenue. The 1989 data did not include service specific revenues.

Table 7.9
AT&T price cap and BLS index values

		Index value		Percent	Band Limits	
					lower	upper
		(7/1/89)	(7/1/90)	change	(for 7/1/90)	
Basket #1 : Residential and Small Business Services						
PCI		97.5	94.3	-3.3%		
API		97.5	94.3	-3.3%		
SBIs:	Domestic Day MTS	94.7	91.8	-3.1%	86.3	95.5
	Domestic Evening MTS	98.9	91.4	-7.6%	90.1	98.8
	Domestic Night/Wkend	99.1	99.9	0.8%	93.4	102.4
	International MTS	98.0	94.6	-3.5%	88.8	98.3
	Operator and Card	98.1	98.7	0.6%	90.9	100.6
	Reach Out America	95.3	88.5	-7.1%	85.5	94.6
	Residential (only)	98.1	94.5	-3.7%		95.5
Basket #2 : 800 Services						
PCI		97.7	94.0	-3.8%		
API		94.8	92.8	-2.1%		
SBIs:	Readyline 800	92.8	90.2	-2.8%	84.8	93.9
	AT&T 800	95.8	94.7	-1.1%	88.8	98.3
	Megacom 800	90.2	85.3	-5.4%	80.0	88.5
	Other 800	100.0	90.0	-10.0%	87.0	96.3
Basket #3 : Business Services						
PCI		99.5	96.7	-2.8%		
API		96.9	93.1	-3.9%		
SBIs:	PRO WATS	95.9	91.1	-5.0%	86.7	95.8
	AT&T WATS	94.8	94.7	-0.1%	89.8	99.2
	Megacom	92.7	88.6	-4.4%	84.0	92.9
	SDN	81.9	76.8	-6.2%	73.0	80.7
	Other Switched	100.2	99.0	-1.2%	94.3	104.2
	Voice Gr. Private Line	101.2	98.1	-3.1%	93.2	103.0
	Other Private Line	99.5	76.1	-23.5%	72.2	79.8
BLS Price Indexes						
CPI - overall				-4.5%		
CPI - telco				-0.3%		
CPI - interstate toll				-1.2%		
CPI - intrastate toll				-2.2%		
PPI - interstate MTS				-0.1%		
PPI - intrastate MTS				-4.8%		
PPI - international MTS				-0.5%		

Source: For 7/1/89 AT&T data, see AT&T Revised Tariff Submittal #1618 Exhibit #4; for 7/1/90 data, see Transmittal #2396, Exhibit #5. For CPI and PPI Price Index Data: Bureau of Labor Statistics data provided by James Lande, Common Carrier Bureau, FCC, August 1990. CPI/PPI growth rates are for June 1989 to June 1990.

8

Optional calling plans

In Chapter 5 we observed that suitably designed optional two-part tariffs are equivalent to nonlinear tariffs when both consumers and the supplier have full information and there are no transaction costs of changing tariffs. In fact, despite additional transactions costs, optional tariffs are in growing use in US telecommunications. In this chapter we examine the theory of optional multipart tariffs in greater detail, review an experiment with optional rate structures, and describe the optional calling plans that have been introduced in national markets.

8.1 Theory of optional tariffs reconsidered

8.1.1 Optional two-part tariffs

When consumers face a choice among optional tariffs Train, Ben-Akiva, and Atherton (1989) suggest that many of them do not correctly anticipate their individual demands. That is, viewed ex post, consumers have made choices under optional tariffs that do not minimize their expenditures for the quantities purchased.[1] This means that some consumers are actually worse off under optional tariffs than under the "equivalent" nonlinear tariffs. The question is whether the supplying firm is better off and, if so, by how much? Clearly, at the "incorrect" consumption levels chosen by these consumers the supplier is better off because he receives higher revenues for a given output. However, when consumers choose the "incorrect" optional tariff they also change their consumption levels and thus the firm's costs. In which direction does this effect go?

Assume that the two tariff choices are a linear tariff (p_0) and a two-part tariff (E, p_1), and that in offering the two-part tariff the supplier assumed that consumer demand curves do not cross. If this assump-

---

[1] A very simple test for this proposition would be to look at the number of consumers consuming quantities in the neighborhood of kinks in the induced nonlinear outlay schedules. There should be no consumers in some neighborhood of these kinks.

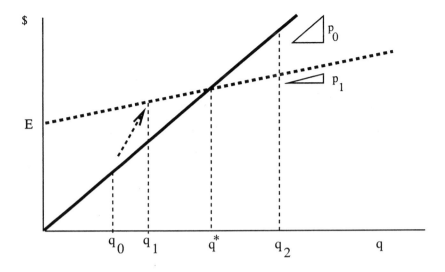

Figure 8.1
Linear and two-part tariffs

tion is justified (as suggested by Train, Ben-Akiva, and Atherton), then larger anticipated purchases will go along with lower marginal prices. Figure 8.1 illustrates for a consumer at q_0 who initially consumes on a linear tariff and switches to the two-part tariff. If the consumer has mistakenly choosen the tariff with the lower marginal price he will consume less than the correct consumption range (q^* or more) for that tariff but more (q_1) than he would with the correct tariff (q_0). This effect makes the consumer compensate part of the mistake of choosing the incorrect tariff. But the consumer is nevertheless worse off than under the correct choice of tariff.[2]

It remains to be shown whether the difference in quantities decreases the supplier's net revenues at all and, if so, by enough to make him refrain from offering optional tariffs that would make some consumers worse off (than under the "equivalent" nonlinear tariff). For the firm to be better off than under the original schedule it is sufficient that marginal prices for both the original schedule and the optional tariff are

---

[2]However, a consumer who mistakenly does not switch to the new optional tariff is still as well off as before.

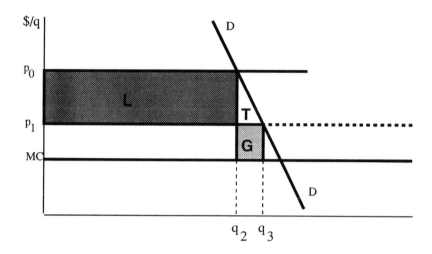

Figure 8.2
Optional and ex-post tariffs

above marginal cost and that the "equivalent" nonlinear outlay schedule
is concave. In this case a consumer at q_0 who mistakenly chooses the
new schedule consumes too much but pays more than the additional cost
of this additional consumption. And a consumer at q_2 who mistakenly
stays on the original schedule consumes and contributes as much as
before.

However, it may well be that the firm could be still better off under the
"equivalent" nonlinear schedule (the ex post tariff) because consumers
who mistakenly stay on the original schedule may have contributed more
under the new schedule. This is because under the new nonlinear schedule with the lower marginal price they would have consumed more.
Specifically (see Figure 8.2), if the corresponding fixed fee E plus the
profit from the additional consumption, $G = (p_1 - MC)(q_3 - q_2)$, out-
weigh the higher per unit profit under the original tariff, $L = (p_0 - p_1)q_2$,
the firm will be worse off under the incorrectly chosen optional tariff than
under the ex post tariff. A sufficient condition for this to happen is that
the fixed fee E be larger than the loss in profit L on the consumption

under the original tariff.[3]

Consumer choice under optional tariffs. The question is, Why would consumers choose an optional tariff that is nonoptimal for them? One answer is that consumers simply over- or under-estimate their demand for the good, for example, due to producer advertising. These errors of commission or omission would vanish over time through learning, and consumers would therefore eventually switch from the incorrect tariff to the correct one (provided switching costs are negligible). A second possibility is that a consumer's *tariff* choice depends on an expected state of the world, while the *consumption* choice depends on the realized state. Under uncertainty about states of the world the two choices are likely to differ for many consumers, and such discrepencies are likely to persist as long as states of the world are uncorrelated over time.

In this context, the question that arises is: Do consumers use optional prices as an insurance against certain states of the world? There are at least two arguments against this proposition. First, the potential losses of consumers from choosing the incorrect tariff are likely to be small relative to a consumer's total income and relative to the "cost of insurance" due to incorrect choice ex post. As a result the risk involved appears to be too small to warrant insurance. Second, under the "equivalent" non-linear tariff the consumer will always be better off (unless, in a second round, the tariff levels are adjusted to bring the supplier's profit down to its level prior to introduction of the optional tariff).

In spite of these problems consumers may receive positive net benefits from optional tariffs:

- Choice may provide satisfaction associated with the exercise of sovereignty.

- The choice of an optional tariff may increase awareness among consumers about the price schedule. That is, consumers may make the incorrect tariff choice in the first place because they do not know either the price or the quantity they consume. In the United States they will usually know their total payment; in countries where itemized billing is not customary consumers may know only their aggregate monthly bill. If they mistakenly move to the new

---

[3] At the same time the fixed fee has to be smaller than the total consumer surplus gain, $L + T$, from moving from the original to the new price.

option, then it means that they implicitly thought that they were
consuming more and that price was lower than it is. (Or, they
thought that their elasticity was higher.)

- Requiring the firm to offer optional tariffs may restrict the firm's
  choice to a concave outlay schedule. The same result, however,
  would be achieved if consumers could exercise their option ex post.
  This is what Mitchell (1980) has called the *ex post tariff*.[4]

It is also safe to assume that the supplier is not fully informed about
consumer demands. The question therefore arises: To what extent do optional tariffs provide better information for the supplier than the equivalent nonlinear tariff? The distinguishing feature here is that under
the optional tariff the consumer reveals some information about her demand before the purchase decision. Consequently, the critical point is,
to what extent this advance information can be used by the supplier to
improve his production decision (or subsequent pricing decisions). This
information would be potentially valuable when the supplier has to commit capacity before the consumer makes her actual purchasing decision.
Since it would be inappropriate to bind a consumer to a tariff for too
long, this kind of information is much more valuable for the dispatch
of existing capacity than for the construction of new capacity. The dispatch of existing capacity appears to play an important role for electric
utilities or airlines but it is not clear that it does for telephone carriers.

Optional tariffs under competition. Optional tariffs resemble
some aspects of longterm contracts, characteristics that may play a role
in competitive markets. If the option under the tariff has to be exer-
cised early and if it cannot be revised for a long time, then the optional
tariff could be viewed as equivalent to a longterm contract with price
commitment but with no quantity commitment. In fact, under compe-

---

[4]He notes that there may be additional metering costs associated with the ex post
tariff when the standard tariff has low metering cost. Hence, the ex post tariff may
be a Pareto improvement only in the ex ante sense. Such a Pareto improvement
can be guaranteed (under full information of the firm about its cost function and of
consumers about their preferences) if either the consumer who chooses the optional
tariff or the firm voluntarily pays the cost of metering. Nevertheless, it is hard to
guarantee Pareto improvements over time if cost changes trigger price changes. See
Mitchell (1980, 1988) for an equilibrium treatment of this issue.

tition suppliers may use an optional tariff as a substitute for longterm contracts in the sense of consumer inertia.[5]

If consumer inertia and quantity consumed are negatively correlated, then quantity discounts have a second rationale (besides the one that they are consistent with rational self-selection of consumers). In this case larger customers would need a higher discount than smaller customers in order to be induced to stay with their current supplier. What if there is no such correlation? Then the firm may want to offer discounts for smaller quantities as well but at some transaction cost, such as making customers also fill out a form (which is less effort than the transaction cost of switching suppliers). In this case, consumers with low inertia (low switching cost) or large quantities would opt for the discount tariff while consumers with high switching cost or low quantities would stay under the original tariff (on the assumption that switching cost to new supplier and switching cost to new tariff have to be highly correlated). The competitive and welfare aspects of this have not been worked out.

Another likely possibility is that the original tariff is regulated and essentially unchangeable, while the optional tariff can be changed at short notice (however, this does not exclude the use of the ex post option!). Then the optional tariff can be improved gradually as information about consumer response is collected. This type of firm learning appears to have been relevant for the Reach-Out America tariff experience, discussed in Section 8.2.

8.1.2 Optional three-part tariffs

The strategic pricing problem for the firm is: How can the supplier use an optional tariff to increase profits, given that it must continue to offer an existing tariff?

Assume a single product with constant marginal cost MC offered under a linear tariff with price p_0. If the firm offers an optional two-part tariff (Figure 8.1) it should set a high fixed fee E and lower usage price p_1 designed to attract only the largest users. A Pareto-dominating optional tariff of this type can always be constructed. But it will make only a limited contribution to increasing profits (or surplus), because only the largest customers find it worthwhile to choose the two-part tariff.

---

[5] Consumer inertia may be defined as the transaction cost a consumer incurs to switch to a different tariff or to a different carrier.

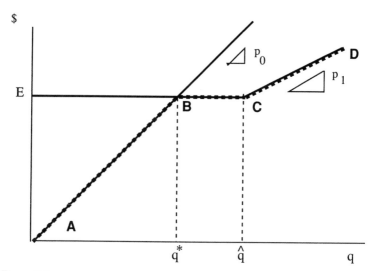

Figure 8.3
Block-of-time tariff

A potentially more profitable strategy is to design an optional tariff that would be selected by customers with *intermediate* volumes. With the skewed usage distributions that characterize telephone markets such consumers are much more numerous. Moreover, they may be more price-elastic as well. Finally, it may be possible for the firm to arrange the tariff so that any errors that consumers make in choosing a tariff work to the advantage of the firm.

Figure 8.3 shows a particular type of three-part "block-of-time" tariff, with outlay function:

$$E + p_1 \max(q - \hat{q}, 0) \tag{8.1}$$

where E is the fixed fee per month. Up to the level of $\hat{q}$, there is no charge for usage; thereafter, additional quantity is charged p_1 per unit. For quantities up to the "break-even" level q^* the linear tariff is less costly; thereafter, the three-part tariff has a lower outlay.

The equivalent block tariff, the path $ABCD$, is the lower, non-concave envelope of the linear tariff (p_0) and the three-part tariff (8.1).[6]

---

[6]Note the difference to optional two-part tariffs where the equivalent block tariff would have to be concave. See Section 5.6.4.

Because the three-part tariff is optional, consumers may actually select that tariff when, ex post, they would have had higher surplus from remaining on the linear tariff. We analyze the effect of choosing the three-part tariff for customers in three different usage segments. In each case, the change in profits can be decomposed into the change in revenue at the original volume, plus the incremental net revenue resulting from the increase in volume.

Figure 8.4(a) shows a small consumer with consumption under the linear tariff q_{S0}, where $q_S < q^*$. When consumption has increased to q the change in profits is:

$$
\begin{array}{ccc}
R_{S0} & -C_{S1} & +R_{S1} \\
= E - p_0 q_{S0} & -(q - q_{S0})MC & +p_1 \max(q - \hat{q}, 0).
\end{array}
\tag{8.2}
$$

This type of customer is quite profitable; the minimum monthly fee increases revenues at the initial usage level. There is some increase in cost from the stimulated demand, but its marginal cost is low. Up to the quantity $\hat{q}$ this additional demand returns no revenue, but if demand is strongly stimulated, the last units (beyond $\hat{q}$) earn incremental profits of $(p_1 - MC)$ per unit.

For a medium consumer $(q^* < q_{M0} < \hat{q})$ in Figure 8.4(b) the change in profits is:

$$
\begin{array}{ccc}
-R_{M0} & -C_{M1} & +R_{M1} \\
= -(p_0 q_{M0} - E) & -(q - q_{M0}) & +p_1 \max(q - \hat{q}, 0).
\end{array}
\tag{8.3}
$$

This type of consumer tends to reduce profit, because revenues at the initial usage are lower. Moreover, if the consumer has full information about usage and the marginal price, demand may be stimulated to at least $\hat{q}$ (because over this range the marginal price is 0), increasing costs somewhat. However, if demand is very elastic, the incremental profit on the final units could make this type profitable.

And for a large consumer $(\hat{q} < q_{L0})$ in Figure 8.4(c) the change in profits is:

$$
\begin{array}{ccc}
-R_{L0} & -C_{L1} & +R_{L1} \\
= E + p_1(q_{L0} - \hat{q}) - p_0 q_{L0} & -(q - q_{L0})MC & +p_1(q - q_{L0}).
\end{array}
\tag{8.4}
$$

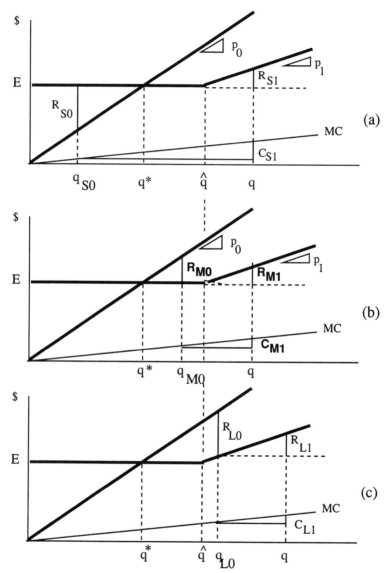

Figure 8.4
Customer sizes under block-of-time tariff

This type of consumer is also more likely to reduce profits, but in this case because the revenue loss on initial usage is greater. This is offset to a degree by incremental profits on stimulated demand.

Thus, the block-of-time tariff can increase profits if it succeeds in attracting small customers and those with high demand elasticities. It does so by targeting, not the largest consumers, but those with intermediate demands. To do so it must accept reduced profits from the largest consumers.

8.1.3 Arbitrage

Under the three-part tariff with an initial block of usage for a flat monthly fee, the marginal price is zero for low quantities and then jumps to a positive level, so that the marginal outlay increases at one point $(\hat{q})$. Nevertheless, when the tariff has a marginal price for additional consumption that is no greater than the average price at that point there is no opportunity for the consumer to engage in arbitrage by splitting his total quantity into several smaller quantities. Thus, subadditivity of the outlay function is sufficient to avoid arbitrage (see Section 5.5.2) and it is not necessary to require a nonincreasing marginal outlay, as assumed by Wilson (1989b).

8.1.4 Demand variation over periods

The minimum fixed fee for the block-of-time tariff must be paid every (monthly) billing period. However, users tend to subscribe to the tariff for several months, because of inertia and decisionmaking costs, as well as explicit costs of switching tariffs. Such multiperiod choices are often based on average monthly consumption.

When the same optional tariff applies for several months, shifts in the consumer's demand curve between months can lead to higher payments than under the minimum outlay schedule for each quantity purchased. For some months the consumer is on the "incorrect" tariff, in the sense that, if she could costlessly select a tariff in those months, a different tariff would yield a lower bill.

Assume the consumer has demands q_1 and q_2 in two months (billing periods), with average demand $\bar{q} = (q_1 + q_2)/2$. Under three types of tariffs the average bill $\overline{R}$ is:

linear: $\qquad \dfrac{pq_1 + pq_2}{2} = p\bar{q}$

two-part:
$$\frac{2E_1 + p_1(q_1 + q_2)}{2} = E_1 + p_1\overline{q}, \text{ if part 1}$$

$$\frac{2E_2 + p_2(q_1 + q_2)}{2} = E_2 + p_2\overline{q}, \text{ if part 2}$$

three-part:
$$\frac{2E + p\left[\max(q_1 - \hat{q}, 0) + \max(q_2 - \hat{q}, 0)\right]}{2},$$

which is $> E + p\max(\overline{q} - \hat{q}, 0)$,

if $q_1 > \hat{q}$, or $q_2 > \hat{q}$, but not both.

If a single two-part tariff is to be selected for both months, the mean $\overline{q}$ can be used without bias to compute the mean bill and select the less costly of two two-part tariffs (or to choose between a linear and a two-part tariff). In contrast, the average bill under the three-part tariff can be higher than the outlay function calculated at the mean consumption. Relying on mean consumption to select a tariff will bias the consumer's choice toward a three-part tariff when a linear rate would be less costly. Also, under the three-part tariff, variance in consumption increases revenues and tends to increase profits.

8.1.5 Tariff selection

When fully informed consumers choose between a linear and a multi-part tariff for a single period they may separate into two clearly distinct groups. Assuming a single consumer type parameter and noncrossing demands, the separation into linear tariff and optional tariff subgroups occurs at a unique quantity. All consumers (types) with small consumption quantities choose the linear tariff; all larger ones prefer the optional tariff (Figure 8.5a). In practice, however, a number of factors lead to a range of output in which both tariffs are chosen by differing proportions of consumers, with the proportion of optional-tariff consumers rising with increasing output (Figure 8.5b):

- When consumers are heterogeneous in their degree of price responsiveness, those with high elasticities will select the optional rate at a lower output than less elastic users.

- In the AT&T optional calling plan, the three-part tariff provides a single per-minute rate as the alternative to the standard rates

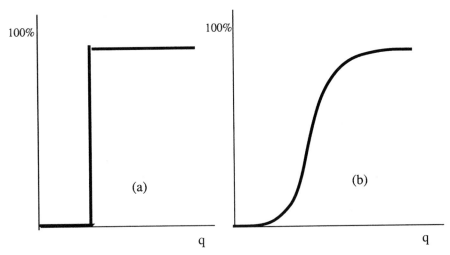

Figure 8.5
Take rates for optional tariff

that increase with the distance called. For a given number of minutes consumers who call the farthest distances will face a higher
standard bill and therefore select the optional plan at a lower total
number of monthly minutes than consumers who make predominantly shorthaul calls.

- Given costs of switching tariffs, consumers will select one tariff for
  a several-month period. At a given average monthly rate of usage
  those with high month-to-month variation in usage will prefer the
  standard rate.

- Several of the optional calling plans include discounts on calls made
  at standard prices in other time-of-day periods (e.g., a 5 percent
  discount on evening calls), foreign, or credit-card calls. Consumers
  who have high demands for these calls will select an optional calling
  plan at a low rate of (night/weekend) usage, to which the three-
  part tariff applies.

- Consumers must select the tariff in advance of consumption. Uncertainty about demand for calling during the month makes total
  outlay a random variable. The consumer can reduce the risk of a
  large bill by selecting the three-part tariff, to ensure a lower out-

lay at high volumes. If consumers choose to avoid such risks, then those with greater uncertainty (larger variance) will select the optional calling plan at a lower average usage level than those with more nearly constant demand. This behavior has been described as purchasing "insurance" against a high bill. However, as noted in Section 8.1.1, it is not adequately explained by risk aversion, since the amounts at risk are quite small fractions of wealth.

- The theoretical analysis is based on consumers who know their own demands. But under the multipart tariffs the marginal price of the next call is a function of the accumulated volume of usage during the month (billing period) to date. Without keeping a telephone diary, consumers have no exact measure of the number and length of night/weekend calls thay have made.

  Moreover, a fully informed consumer who knew his future demands with certainty would know his total monthly demand for calling, and therefore the marginal price of his last minute of calling. It is this final price, rather than the price that applies to calls as they accumulate during the month, that is (neglecting time discounting) the cost to the consumer of increasing the minutes of calling on *any* day during the month (Ellis, 1986).

8.2   Development of AT&T's optional calling plan

In 1983 AT&T obtained FCC permission to test a new rate concept for its residential customers – optional calling plans (OCPs). For an additional monthly charge an OCP provides reduced per-minute prices for many interstate long-distance calls during off-peak periods. Following a six month period of experimentation AT&T reported quantitative results and filed for two nationwide optional rate plans whose parameters were based on experimental findings.

These new tariffs were approved by the FCC and went into effect in June, 1984 under the name "Reach-Out America." The following year the FCC issued its "Optional Calling Plan Guidelines Order" setting forth general standards for options to the standard (residential and business) tariffs for switched message services. AT&T has filed periodic tracking reports summarizing experience with the tariffs.

Our analysis of the AT&T optional calling plans is based on filings by AT&T that describe the experiment, proposed rates, and subsequent tracking reports; comments filed by other parties; and the FCC's order. In several instances AT&T has reported data only in summary or projected form.

The Reach-Out America plans have proved to be popular. AT&T has subsequently introduced additional optional calling plans, and other interexchange carriers now also offer optional discounted rates for a monthly fee.

In the following sections, we first describe the experiment and AT&T's analysis of the data that were obtained from it. Next, we review the experience with the nationwide optional tariffs that were introduced following the experiment. This leads to a discussion of the currently available plans and some general findings.

8.2.1 The optional calling plan experiment

AT&T, authorized by its regulator, conducted a six-month experiment with optional residential rates during July–December 1983.[7] At that time the standard direct-dial rate structure included rate elements for the first minute and additional one-minute increments of usage; three time-of-day periods (day, evening, and night/weekend); and eleven distance bands. The experiment tested three rate structures that a customer might purchase for his night/weekend (and possibly evening) direct-dial interstate calls. They were:

1. *Two-Part Plan.*[8] Monthly fee E_1 to obtain a uniform percentage discount on night/weekend calls.

2. *Tapered Plan.* Monthly fee E_2 to obtain a per-minute price p_1 for the first hour of night/weekend usage, and a lower per minute price p_2 for additional usage. The same price applies for all distances.

3. *Block-of-Time Plan.* Monthly fee E_3 to obtain a one- (or two-)hour allowance for night/weekend usage, and a (lower pro-rata) price p_3 per minute for additional usage. Again, the same price applies for all distances. (Monthly fees ranged from $8 to $16; the rates for additional minutes ranged between $5 and $7 per hour).

---

[7] Systematic experimentation with rate structures is not commonly used in US telecommunications. But in 1975–8 GTE conducted a significant experiment with measured-service rates for local calling in three Illinois communities. See Park, Wetzel, and Mitchell (1983) for analysis and further references.

[8] AT&T referred to this rate structure as the "Linear Plan."

Table 8.1
AT&T experimental plans, 1983

Type of plan	Number of customers
Block-of-Time	1603
Two-part	1572
Tapered	1232
Total	4407

Each of the three rate structures was tested at five rate levels, for a total of fifteen experimental treatments. The rates were offered to all residential customers in twenty-four central office numbering codes in three states – California, New York, and Iowa – encompassing 151,000 customers. An additional twelve exchanges, encompassing 60,000 customers in the same states, were used as statistical controls.

AT&T promoted the optional plans by direct mail and by telemarketing. Some 1.6 percent of the 151,000 customers who received the initial mailing responded by subscribing to an experimental plan. A follow-up telemarketing campaign to a random 20 percent sample of the customers was more successful and achieved an 8.2 percent take rate. Overall, some 2.9 percent of the eligible customers subscribed to an experimental plan, distributed as shown in Table 8.1.

8.2.2   Analysis of plan choice and demand

Choice of rate plan (take rate).   AT&T analyzed consumer choice of OCPs by constructing an equation of consumer willingness to pay for a rate plan and estimated the equation from the first four months of experimental data.

For a consumer having full information, his willingness to pay for a two-part tariff, instead of a uniform tariff, is the increase in surplus from consuming at a marginal price p_1 rather than at a uniform price p_0 (the sum of areas L and T in Figure 8.2 on page 178). All consumers for whom this gain in surplus exceeds the fixed monthly charge for the two-part tariff would choose the two-part tariff; all others would continue to consume under the uniform tariff.

For a multipart tariff such as the experimental block-of-time tariff – a three-part tariff with an expenditure allowance and hence a zero marginal price for the initial units of consumption, plus a positive marginal price for usage exceeding the allowance – the willingness to pay is calculated separately for each marginal price.

However, results from the experiment show that consumers do not divide sharply into two groups as predicted by this full-information model. Instead, some consumers who in fact have zero consumption are observed to choose the optional tariff, and the proportion of consumers who do so increases with the total quantity of consumption.

As noted earlier, there may be a number of explanations for such systematically observed choices. They include uncertainty about future consumption and standard telephone rates, month-to-month variation in consumption, consumer preference for making telephone calls at a zero marginal price, and persistent misperception of actual consumption. In addition, in place of the distance-sensitive set of first-minute/additional-minute rates, the OCP substitutes a uniform per-minute price for all night/weekend calls. As a result the "break-even" number of minutes will vary among customers according to the lengths and distance patterns of their calls.

AT&T's analysis postulates that the proportion of customers who take an OCP can be represented by a logit choice model in which the proportion is a function of the total bill savings that would be realized at a consumer's pre-experimental level of consumption. AT&T estimated the plan choice model using data for the experimental customers who were offered the block-of-time rate plans. Because each of those plans itself involved two choices – Plan A, the night/weekend tariff, and Plan B, the night/weekend tariff plus a discount on evening-period calls – the logit choice model was extended to trinary choice.

AT&T's forecast using this model underestimated the relative attractiveness of Plan B, which included a 15 percent discount on evening-period calls.[9] AT&T had projected customers would choose Plans A and B in about equal numbers; in fact about 68 percent selected Plan B in the first year.[10] Moreover, the proportion subscribing to Plan B has increased each quarter, reaching 84.6 percent at the end of the third year.[11]

[9] Discounting of evening calls was apparently experimentally tested to only a limited degree in one state (Iowa).
[10] Roscitt (1985b), p. 12.
[11] AT&T (September 30, 1987).

OCPs have proved attractive to customers, and other interexchange carriers have also introduced optional residential tariffs. The experimental results may thus have some continuing proprietary value to AT&T. In any case, detailed empirical results from this analysis have not been made public. However, some summary statistics have been reported for the first year of the nationwide rate, which was introduced in the year following conclusion of the six-month experiment.

Demand stimulation. AT&T postulated a demand-stimulation model that explains the change in minutes of use as a linear function of the change in the marginal price of use. Change in use is measured as the difference between experimental usage and pre-experimental usage, after adjusting for usage changes during the same period observed in the control group. The sample is cross-classified into sixteen cells: four usage segments (0, 1-60, 61-120 , >120 minutes) and the time in months since choice of the optional plan (1, 2, 3, and 4 months). The sixteen price-response coefficients are estimated by weighted least squares (without, however, accounting for between-equation correlation).

Further details and results of the demand stimulation analysis have not been made public. It is unclear, for example, exactly how marginal prices were calculated. Under the standard tariff the marginal price facing a consumer would depend on call distance and duration, so that the change in the marginal price for an OCP subscriber depends on the distribution of his calls. Nor have the estimates of the price effects themselves been reported.

Projected effects. AT&T used the estimated price-response coefficients to project the demand stimulation expected under the proposed nationwide tariff. For this purpose, night/weekend usage was classified into seven segments (0, 1-15, 15-30, 30-45, 45-60, 60-120, >120 minutes). For each usage segment and for each distance rate step in the standard tariff, the marginal price change under the optional plan was calculated and the change in minutes projected. These changes were then aggregated to obtain the projected average change in usage for each usage segment.

Next, the plan choice model was used to estimate the take rate at each given level of usage; this rate was multiplied by the projected demand stimulation for that usage segment and summed to obtain the total

Table 8.2
Changes in usage and revenues under experimental rate plans

Customers and long-distance statistics	Up to 120 min./mo.	More than 120 min./mo.
customers	69.3%	30.7%
calls	+ 74.3%	+26.7%
length of conversation	+ 22.7%	+ 5.5%
minutes	+117.6%	+27.4%
revenues	+116.9%	+17.5%

projected increase in usage. This estimate of potential stimulation was then scaled down to account for the planned advertising and promotion effort.

To account for demand stimulation under Plan B, with its 15 percent discount on evening calling, similar evening-period price-response coefficients were estimated from the experimental plans with this feature. These estimates were then used to adjust the national projections for consumers projected to select Plan B.

Offering optional night/weekend and evening discount rate plans was expected to have some effects on the demands for daytime and operator-handled calls. AT&T extended its standard Rate Evaluation System (RES) model (which is used to project the effects of changes in standard residental tariffs) to account for these cross elasticities. However, those estimates have not been reported, and it is unclear whether they anticipated the effect observed during the first year – a small increase in daytime calling by customers who selected an OCP.

Observed effects. AT&T has not reported estimates of individual price effects or disaggregated demand changes. Instead, some summary measures are available, representing the stimulation observed after adjusting for usage changes observed in the control sample. These estimates are shown in Table 8.2.

About 70 percent of the experimental customers make fewer than two hours of long-distance calls per month. On the experimental plans, these users faced a zero marginal price for the first hour of calling. They made 74 percent more night/weekend calls and increased the average length of their conversations, so that total minutes increased 118 percent.

Table 8.3
Growth in optional calling plans

Period	Customers (million)	Plan A (%)	Plan B (%)	Δ minutes (million)	Δ revenue ($ million)
1st year†	1.10	32.1	67.9	262.3	80.7
Q5 (July-Sept.,85)	1.48	30.2	69.8	148.4	36.0
Q6	1.84	29.4	70.6	198.4	46.6
Q7	1.87	28.4	71.6	181.7	39.0
Q8	2.10	25.2	74.8	272.5	64.6
Q9	2.20	18.6	81.4	225.9	57.3
Q10	2.40	17.3	82.7	273.3	60.3
Q11	2.50	15.6	84.4	297.7	57.8
Q12	2.68	15.4	84.6	264.2	54.5

Note: †(6/7/84–6/30/85)

The remaining 30 percent of the customers, who already make more than two hours of calls per month, faced a positive and generally lower marginal price. They also increased their minutes of calling, but by only 27 percent, almost all of which was accounted for by additional calls.

8.3   Nationwide optional calling plans

After experimenting with the three types of optional plans, AT&T decided to offer the block-of-time plan as its basic plan, and to provide the added, largely untested option of a uniform discount on evening-period calls. Of the types of OCPs tested, Plans A and B which were finally selected guaranteed the company the greatest minimum monthly revenue from every subscriber choosing a plan and strongly encouraged additional night/weekend calling by low-volume users.

The new rate structures proved popular (Table 8.3). Plan B, which included the discount on evening calls, initially attracted two-thirds of the market, and by the end of the third year 85 percent of OCP customers chose Plan B.

The actual prices charged under the OCPs have been revised several times to reflect nationwide reductions in the carrier access charge AT&T pays to local exchange carriers for each minute of calling. Since 1989, the OCPs have been subject to the overall price cap on AT&T's residential and small business services, thus requiring some reductions over time to account for imputed productivity gains (see Section 7.3).

Table 8.4
Customer distribution by night/weekend usage, 1984-5

Night/weekend minutes	Cumulative Percentage of Customers			
	Plan A	Plan B	Plan A + Plan B	Standard rate plan
> 20			70.1	
> 40			55.1	
> 60	49.7	37.2	41.4	6.4
> 80			30.2	
>100			22.1	
>120			15.9	1.9

Note: Post-choice usage, year 1.
Source: Roscitt (1985a), p. 7

8.3.1 Choice of plan

OCPs are chosen by subscribers with high levels of night and weekend telephone usage. Nearly 50 percent of the Plan A subscribers call more than sixty minutes a month during the night/weekend period, compared to just 6.4 percent of all AT&T residential subscribers (Table 8.4). Customers who chose Plan B and benefit from the discount on evening calls also make large use of night and weekend calling.

On the other hand, a sizeable number of customers who choose an OCP have low monthly calling volumes even after switching to the plan and incur a somewhat higher average monthly bill than they would pay for the same use under the standard rate. It is likely that many of the 45 percent of OCP subscribers who use fewer than forty minutes a month during night/weekend period have in this sense selected the "incorrect" tariff.

8.3.2 Competitive optional calling plans

AT&T has subsequently increased the number of optional plans that it offers and has developed a broader variety of pricing structures. Its major interexchange competitors have responded to AT&T's success with OCPs by offering plans of their own. The optional plans available from AT&T, MCI, and US Sprint in mid-1990 are shown in Table 8.5–8.7.

The popularity of rate discounts has led all three carriers to broaden the use of discount rates during the evening calling period. MCI's block-

Table 8.5
AT&T Reach-Out America plans

Plan number	Monthly charge	Unbilled usage night/weekend only	Added Usage billed at	Discounts
1	$8.70	1 hr	$0.11/min	10% days 25% evenings 5% intrastate 5% international
2	4.00	1/2 hr	0.12/min	10% evenings 5% intrastate 5% international
3	7.80	1 hr	0.11/min	15% evenings 5% intrastate 5% international
4	7.15	1 hr	0.11/min	none
area code plan	1.90	as below		5% other calls
miles 1–55 56–1910 1911+		0800–1700 M-F .19/min .20 .21		Other hours .11/min .12 .13

Note: (1990). Optional Calling Plan rates apply during night-weekend hours: 10 p.m.-8 a.m. Sunday-Friday, all day Saturday and holidays; Sunday until 5 p.m. There is a $5 service order to begin service.

of-time rate begins at 5 p.m. and two of US Sprint's plans begin discounted rates at the same hour. Furthermore, some optional plans now offer rate discounts on daytime calling as well. Interestingly, AT&T has added a plan to appeal to lower-volume customers. That plan has a lower monthly fee and a one-half hour allowance of night/evening calling.

In March 1991, MCI introduced a new type of OCP. Under this rate structure a subscriber receives a 20 percent discount on calls to twelve pre-selected numbers. The novelty of the plan is that the designated numbers must also be MCI customers. In this way the carrier creates an incentive for subscribers to promote MCI service and limits the rate discount to bundles of consumer groups.

Optional plans are used as marketing tools in national advertising campaigns. Sign-up fees are often waived and additional shortterm discounts have frequently been offered.

Since the first OCPs were introduced in 1984 the standard intercity

Table 8.6
MCI optional calling plans

Plan Number	Applies to	Monthly Charge	Unbilled Usage Night/Weekend	Added usage Billed at	Discounts
1	interstate, evening, night	$8.00	1 hr	$.1083/min	10% other hours
2	state+interstate evening, night	8.75	1 hr	.1083/min	10% other hours
3	9 a.m.–5.p.m.	12.00	1 hr	.20/min	none
3a	9 a.m.–5.p.m.	14.00	1 hr	.20/min	10% other hours
4	interstate Saturday	5.00	1 hr	.0833/min	none

Note: (1990). Night-weekend hours are 10 p.m.-8 a.m. Sunday-Friday, all day Saturday and holidays; Sunday until 5 p.m.

Table 8.7
US Sprint optional calling plans

Plan Number	Applies to	Monthly Charge	Unbilled Usage	Added Usage Billed at	Discounts
1	interstate, evening, night	$8.10	1 hr	$.11/min	10% interstate day 5% interstate card
2	interstate, 5 p.m.-11 p.m.	8.00	—	billed at night rate	10% when mo. bill ≥ $25
3	interstate day	1.95	—	-15% day rate	

Note: (1990). Night-weekend hours are 10 p.m.-8 a.m. Sunday-Friday, all day Saturday and holidays; Sunday until 5 p.m.

rate structure has changed. Today, the standard price of a long-distance call is virtually proportional to its duration, with only a minimal difference between the price of the first minute and an additional minute of calling. Also, the difference between standard day and night rates has narrowed. In contrast, the OCP tariffs offer an especially low off-peak rate.

8.3.3 Area code plan

In mid-1990 AT&T introduced a somewhat different type of optional calling plan which enables a subscriber to obtain reduced rates in one selected market. Under this plan, all directly dialed calls to one area code are billed under uniform per-minute rates based on time-of-day and day-of-week.[12] Compared with the standard rate structure, rates offer discounts of up to 30-50 percent on evening calls, depending on area/distance, and smaller discounts at other times for most areas. In addition, calls placed to other area codes receive a 5 percent discount from the standard rates.

The Area Code rate plan is unusual in another way. It has been filed with eight separate time-of-day/weekend rate periods, allowing AT&T to potentially graduate prices on weekdays by up to six different pricing periods (see Figure 7.2, page 165). The initially effective rate structure in a single market is far less complex, with just two different prices in effect during the full week. But, by filing the more finely divided rate structure, AT&T gains the flexibility under price cap regulation of fine-tuning the optional calling plan in response to demand, should large demand responses emerge in some markets.

8.3.4 Demand stimulation

OCPs markedly increase calling. During the first year, AT&T's OCPs increased the mean minutes of subscribers' night/weekend calling by 42 percent.[13] The overall price elasticity for night/weekend calling of the group of OCP subscribers is of the order of -2 or higher, considerably larger than AT&T estimates for all residential subscribers. The implied price elasticity for evening-period calls (for Plan B subscribers) is also large, and there is some stimulation of daytime calling also.

Because OCPs are optional, they will be selected systematically by, among others, customers with high price elasticities, who at any given level of demand benefit most from the lower marginal prices in the OCP. Moreover, under the block-of-time rate structure the greatest stimulus to demand occurs for usage levels below one hour per month, when the marginal price of additional minutes is zero. It is notable that customers

---

[12] One area code usually covers a region of a state, but large metropolitan areas may be split into several area codes.
[13] Roscitt (1985a), p. 5.

making fewer that two hours of calling increased both the number of calls and the lengths of their conversations much more than did heavier users (Table 8.4). Most of these customers use less than one hour of calling per month and experienced the largest price reduction.

8.4   FCC guidelines for optional calling plans

A year after authorizing AT&T to introduce nationwide optional rate plans the FCC set out its reasoning in what became known as the "OCP Guidelines Order" (FCC, 1986). The guidelines offer the regulated carrier a broad degree of flexibility in designing new optional rate structures, while establishing general standards that they must meet.

A regulated carrier has wide latitude to innovate in the structure of rates. It is free to develop new rate elements, to bundle or unbundle existing elements, to charge fixed monthly and usage rates, and to discount standard rates. Rates need not be related to distance (although the FCC stated that it would not accept geographical deaveraging of rates). Initiation and termination charges are permissible, but such fees must be related to cost. (This implies that level of the entry/exit fee cannot be used for nonlinear pricing; the carrier must rely on a recurring fixed fee for that.)

With its OCP Guidelines the FCC departed fundamentally from the long-standing practice of requiring regulated carriers to demonstrate that rates for a service were sufficient to cover some type of fully distributed costs. The FCC recognized basic defects of fully distributed-cost pricing: reliance on historical costs when business decisions depend on future demand and costs, and the tendency to set too high a price standard which then protects competitors from full price competition.

The FCC sought a standard that more closely approximates marginal or incremental cost. It noted, however, a difficulty involving the fixed costs of access which are recovered from interexchange carriers by a per-minute carrier access charge (Chapter 10). These fixed costs are unchanged with increased usage and therefore are not marginal. But if the pricing test for an OCP were simply that price exceed marginal cost it is possible that, with demand shifts, the total revenue available to cover the fixed access cost would decline and require higher prices for other services.

The carrier offering an OCP must demonstrate, with periodic reporting, that introduction of the OCP does not burden other services or subscribers. For this purpose the FCC established a Net Revenue Test (see Section 6.1.1). The OCP as a whole, and also any OCP element that is offered as a separate option, must have an increase in revenues that exceeds the increase in costs. This standard must be met within twelve months and the optional plan, calculating on a present-value basis, must be profitable within a three-year period. Calculation of the change in net revenues must take into account cross-elastic revenue and cost effects on other switched services.

To guard against discrimination, the carrier must continue to offer standard tariffs at the same rates. Resale, sharing, and interconnection of services purchased under optional rates cannot be restricted.

The institution of price cap regulation of AT&T in 1989 placed optional calling plans in the residential/small-business basket of services. Price caps place some additional limits on new rates or changes in existing optional plans. The average price under all optional calling plans is constrained to change by not more than $\pm$ 5 percent per year relative to productivity improvements (see Section 7.3.1).

9

Business bulk-rate tariffs

Consumers with more extensive telecommunications demands than a single household include commercial establishments, government offices, and other organizations housing several employees. They are conventionally referred to as the "business" customers of a telephone company. In this chapter we examine the rate structures for the major business telephone services.

9.1 Local rates

Network access and local calling is provided by local exchange companies (LECs) to business customers under tariffs separate from residential rates. Typically, the monthly business access rate is more than twice the charge to a residential consumer (see Section 7.2.1). And, in most localities, the business tariff includes a measured-service rate for each local call or minute of use, whereas most residential subscribers have either flat-rate service or measured service as an optional rate. Local service rates are the clearest example of customer-class pricing.

Businesses with sufficient calling to require more than a few access lines usually have a significant volume of intrabusiness communication. These calls may be supplied by the local exchange carrier (LEC) through a Centrex service, which uses the local central office switch to connect individual access lines. Centrex provides abbreviated dialing to reach users within a business, redirection of calls to an attendant, and a wide variety of other features.

Alternatively, the business customer may lease or purchase a private branch exchange (PBX) switch that is located on its premises to provide intrabusiness telephone services. The PBX is then connected to the public network by trunk access lines terminating at the local exchange.

9.2   WATS tariffs

The volume of long-distance calling generated by business customers
varies widely. Interexchange carriers offer switched service at bulk rates
under a variety of WATS (wide area telecommunications service) tariffs
for directly dialed calls. These and other high-volume services, customarily referred to as business services, are available to all network
subscribers on the same terms.

The original AT&T WATS tariffs were based on dividing the country
into a series of five roughly concentric bands of states radiating from the
customer's location. A separate WATS access line was required for calls
to each band. Two optional tariffs were available – a two-part tariff
consisting of a monthly charge and a price per hour of monthly line
use to that band, and a "full business day" tariff with a much higher
monthly charge and no charge for usage. AT&T subsequently revised
these rates and shifted to a tapered structure, with lower per hour rates
in effect after 25, 75, and 100 hours of use per month during the day
period, and, separately accumulated, during the evening hours. Higher
hourly rates applied to the more distant bands.

AT&T has recently replaced this banded set of rates with a WATS rate
structure that more directly resembles the standard message telephone
service (MTS) rates for directly dialed calls (Section 7.2.2), but which
has lower usage prices at higher volumes. A single WATS access line
can be used to make calls of all distances. Calls are billed for an initial
thirty-second increment and thereafter in six-second increments of usage
(*versus* one minute under MTS) and are differentiated by eight distance
steps (*versus* eleven steps in MTS).

AT&T and other IXCs currently offer interexchange service under
several optional WATS tariffs designed to appeal to a wide range of
customers. For the smallest-volume customers, AT&T first offered a
choice among three optional plans – PRO WATS I, II, and III – which
provided for progressively lower usage prices and higher fixed monthly
charge as usage increased (Table 9.1). AT&T has now replaced this
set of optional two-part tariffs with a single nonlinear PRO WATS tariff
(Table 9.2) that provides increasing discounts at higher total volumes. In
effect, the carrier has shifted from a set of optional tariffs to a roughly
equivalent multiblock tariff, a change that is consistent with "higher"
rationality in purchasing decisions by business customers. As a result,

Table 9.1
AT&T PRO WATS I, II, and III

PRO WATS plan	Monthly billing($) (usage hours)		Monthly charge	Discount on day dial usage (varies with mileage band)
I	$120–450	(7–35hrs)	$ 12	10%
II	$450–2400	(35–200hrs)	$ 80	23%–28%
III	$2400+	(200+ hrs)	$285	33%–38%
access line:	$ 33/month			
installation:	$176/line + $180/order			

subscribers are assured of the lowest total bill for a given month's usage.

By using separate WATS access lines, other moderate-volume users will select the mainstay AT&T WATS tariff, with somewhat higher monthly fees, lower usage rates, and similar total-revenue discounts. Rate elements again apply across eight distance bands and three time-of-day periods (Table 9.3)

Businesses with high volumes at one location (above 500-600 hours per month) find it worthwhile to order separate bulk access lines and subscribe to the Megacom WATS service to obtain the lowest marginal usage price, also shown in Table 9.3. This service is a take-or-pay form of contract in which the customer must commit to a minimum, seasonally averaged monthly usage, and discounts apply only when higher specified monthly volumes are realized.

The three WATS tariffs are distinguished by different access arrangements. PRO WATS customers obtain bulk rates over regular local access lines, which they also use for local calls and calls to other interexchange carriers. Access to AT&T WATS is via lines dedicated to interexchange calls. Megacom WATS customers have special high-volume (T-1) access. The monthly charges for access via dedicated and high-volume arrangements constitute higher fixed charges in the multipart tariffs than the $5 per month for PRO WATS access.

The declining-block tariffs that result from these rate structures are shown in Figure 9.1. Because of the differences in the costs of access, no single tariff is dominant over all volumes. For small users whose long-distance calling originates from different locations, PRO WATS, with

Table 9.2
AT&T PRO WATS tariff

Mileage band	Day Rates	
	First 30 secs.	Additional 6 secs.
0– 55	$.0980	$.0196
56– 292	.1100	.0220
293– 430	.1180	.0236
431– 925	.1220	.0244
926–1910	.1270	.0254
1911–3000	.1270	.0254
3001–4250	.1270	.0254
4251–5750	.1270	.0254

Monthly charge: $5 per main billed account

Total monthly billing	Volume discounts	
	Day	Evening
$0–$200	0%	0%
$200–$2000	8%	3%
above $2000	21%	5%

Other discounts apply to calling card
and international calls.

Note: Mainland US day rates shown;
evening and night usage rates are lower.

access over regular lines, provides some price reductions over standard dial rates. Other small- as well as medium-volume users can segregate their interexchange calling on separate access lines and obtain somewhat lower per-minute rates. Customers with the highest volumes benefit by special access arrangements that incur lower carrier access charges and the lowest per-minute rates.

The WATS market experiences vigorous competition, and AT&T's market share has declined to an estimated 44 percent. The major competing IXCs have their own WATS offerings positioned to compete at each volume level with AT&T. The broad features of the rate structures are generally similar, offering increasing percentage discounts at higher volume, shorter minimum-call requirements, and volume aggregation over several locations.

The FCC guidelines for volume discounting state that:

volume-discounted offerings should be integrated into a rate

Table 9.3
High-volume AT&T WATS tariffs

Mileage band	AT&T WATS		Megacom WATS	
	First 30 secs	Additional 6 secs	First 18 secs	Additional 6 secs
0- 55	$.0900	$.0180	$.0345	$.0115
56- 292	.1030	.0202	.0405	.0135
293- 430	.1085	.0217	.0441	.0147
431- 925	.1150	.0230	.0483	.0161
926-1910	.1195	.0239	.0519	.0173
1911-3000	.1260	.0252	.0549	.0183
3001-4250	.1335	.0267	.0594	.0198
4251-5750	.1370	.1010	.0615	.0205
discounts:	-10% @ $200/mo.		-5% @ $7500/mo.	
	-15% @ $2000/mo.		-10% @ $30000/mo.	
Monthly charge:	$63		$50	
installation:	$267+$99/order		$545 + $99/order	
access:	dedicated line		T1 trunk	

Note: Mainland US day rates shown; evening and night usage rates are
lower.
Source: AT&T Tariff No. 1, July 13, 1990.

structure of similar service offerings with no restrictions on customers or uses. This ... [and] resale, sharing, and ... interconnections, will limit ... ability to discriminate.[1]

And, indeed, attractive rates for long-distance services are also available from two other types of firms. *Resellers* purchase switched service in volume under Megacom or similar high-volume tariffs from a major IXC; they add billing features and resell it to smaller users. *Aggregators* offer similar rates, combining the monthly traffic of a number of smaller users, but relying on the primary IXC for billing service. The presence of these intermediate firms in the interexchange market limits the discrepancy between usage rates among the different WATS tariffs to the additional costs of resale, as explained in Section 6.4.2.

For AT&T, some degree of resale may be desirable. The dominant carrier is obligated to supply all demand at its tariff rates, whereas resellers may limit sales, as well as their promotional activities, to targeted markets. By establishing a relatively large spread between its standard

[1] FCC (1984), §35.

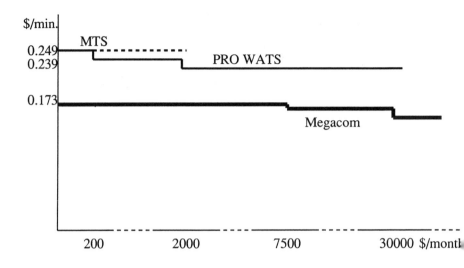

Figure 9.1
AT&T bulk rates (1000 mi.)

rates and bulk rates, AT&T increases profits from smaller customers while giving up the most price-sensitive customers to resellers. The obligation to offer any rate to the entire market makes it unattractive for AT&T to itself engage in "resale" to those customers at intermediate rates.

9.3 800-number services

A "toll-free" 800-number has come to be an important marketing tool in many service industries who wish to solicit customer inquires and orders. Such 800-number services can be purchased to terminate on regular business lines, on dedicated 800-number access lines, and via bulk (T-1) access lines. Each rate structure (Table 9.4) includes a monthly charge per line and a usage charge per hour. Usage is measured in billing increments of one or six seconds, with a minimum average call duration, and monthly volume discounts apply. Rates are distance sensitive over a series of geographic bands and three time-of-day periods.

Carriers offer a wide variety of options that add information, billing,

Table 9.4
AT&T 800-service rates

Service Area	Day Rates ($ per hour of use)	
	800 and Readyline	Megacom 800
1	$13.42	$9.19
2	13.88	9.69
3	14.11	9.95
4	14.55	10.46
5	14.79	10.71
6	16.15	12.25

Discounts		
	above $50/month	5%
	above $350	10%
	above $1350	15%
	(access line)	1%/min.

Note: Day rates shown; evening and night
usage rates are lower.

Monthly charges		
access line		
	Readyline	none
	800-Domestic	$36.70
	Megacom	customer-provided
per routing arrangement		
	Readyline	20.00
	800-Domestic	20.00
	Megacom	50.00
per PBX termination		27.40

and management features to their 800-services.

9.4 Virtual private networks

Customers with multiple locations frequently have significant requirements for communications among their sites in addition to their demand for calling on the public switched network. Private networks to
serve these needs have conventionally been assembled on a customized
basis by leasing private circuits between sites and connecting them to
customer PBXs.

The availability of common-channel signalling in IXC networks has
enabled carriers to offer a customer the functionality of a private network

using the facilities of the switched IXC network. In a virtual private network (VPN) customized software processes each call and routes it over the shared facilities. Customers can access such VPNs by using dedicated access lines, ordinary local exchange lines, or by dialing an 800-number. The software permits calls to both an on-net number (one of the subscriber's other telephones) and to public network (off-net) numbers.

The rate structures for usage on VPNs are similar to WATS. In AT&T's Software Defined Network (SDN), for example, usage is billed per initial eighteen seconds and then in six-second increments, using eight distance bands and three time-of-day periods. Separate rate tables apply to on-net and off-net calls, reflecting differences in the respective carrier access charges levied by the LECs. AT&T in addition offers customers the option, for an additional monthly fee, of specifying a "LATA-pair" and obtaining lower usage rates for on-net calls between these specified LATAs.

Optional features to control access, provide billing and announcements, and change call routing are available. They are priced using a combination of initial installation and monthly charges.

VPN service is designed for high-volume customers, and most carriers require a minimum volume or subscription period. AT&T offers discounts that increase with volume up to 12 percent in year one and reach 20 percent in year three, with higher discounts for custom feature subscribers. US Sprint and MCI's virtual network services have similar tapered volume discounts.

9.5 Discounts for bundling

Interexchange carriers have included volume discounts in their rate structures for WATS, virtual private network, and 800-services. Recently the carriers have extended discounts based on the *combined* volume of both outbound and inbound services.

For example, MCI has offered business customers who make a twelve-month commitment to its Corporate Account Service discounts that range from 14 percent to 23 percent of their charge for 800-service. US Sprint's virtual private network customers who also purchase an 800-service receive an additional 15 percent WATS discount.

Discounting across a range of services is a bonus for brand loyalty, a pricing arrangement that somewhat resembles "frequent-flyer" mileage plans used by competing airline carriers. It gives the customer an incentive to purchase the complete bundle of services from a single supplier.

In 1990 AT&T sought to provide similar bundled discounts to customers who purchased both SDN and 800-services under a one-year or longer commitment. It proposed to add 800-service usage to the SDN usage in computing the volume eligible for discounts. The maximum effective discount would be 27 to 29 percent.

Provision of 800-service within the interexchange network requires that a user-dialed 800-number be translated into the "real" telephone number of the 800-number subscriber. Under current technology for making this translation it is not possible for an 800-service subscriber to change to another interexchange carrier without also changing to a different 800-telephone number. The FCC found that this condition gives the incumbent AT&T, which first developed the 800-service market, advantages over other 800-service suppliers.

The FCC rejected AT&T's proposed combined-discount rate, finding that AT&T would be "leveraging its significant advantage in the 800-number market to gain a competitive advantage in the SDN market."[2]

AT&T provides a different type of bundling in its optional multi-location calling plan. Customers selecting this rate structure receive a discount on the combined usage aggregated over multiple locations throughout the United States. Using such geographic bundling of service enables a nationwide carrier to retain customers who might otherwise be lost to resellers who are predominantly local and regional.

MCI, followed by AT&T, extended bundling of services to small business customers in early 1991. MCI customers who spend between $50 and $1500 per month on long-distance services can consolidate interstate toll and 800-number usage at a distance-invariant, volume-discounted rate. Usage at up to five residential locations and on credit cards can be included. AT&T's competing plan permits bundling outbound (but not 800-number) usage across fifty business and five residential sites to obtain a 10 percent discount on total revenues above $200 per month.

[2]FCC (1990), §20.

Table 9.5
AT&T private line interoffice transport rates

miles	Analog		Digital (56Kbps)	
	fixed	per mile	fixed	per mile
1-50	$72.98	$2.84	$232	$7.74
51-100	149.28	1.31	435	3.68
101-500	229.28	0.51	571	2.32
501+	324.24	0.32	1081	1.30

9.6   Private lines

Private lines provide dedicated, unswitched circuits between two customer locations. Private lines are available in a wide spectrum of qualities, ranging from low-speed analog data lines for alarm sensing to high-capacity digital circuits for data and video transmission. They are supplied by local exchange carriers (for local and intra-LATA circuits), interexchange carriers, and also metropolitan area network operators.

Pricing for most private-line services is based on several rate elements: local access, central office connection, central office functions, interoffice transport, and channel options.

The interoffice transport charges consist of a fixed monthly rate plus a monthly per-mile rate. There is no usage charge, reflecting the dedicated nature of the capacity. AT&T's voice-grade private line tariffs are multiblock rates, with a declining marginal price of distance (Table 9.5). For digital service AT&T offers volume discounts, increasing with both volume and years of service.

Central office connections are typically priced per month, plus an installation fee. Analog channel options that provide conditioning and other quality attributes carry specific monthly charges. Other options include special routing to achieve diversity, and multiplexing to combine or split signals. The subscriber commits to a minimum period of private-line service, and a cancellation charge applies to early disconnection.

9.7   Custom tariffs

In 1989 AT&T obtained the FCC's approval to offer both private line and switched services to customers under a contract governed by a single integrated tariff. Under Tariff No. 12 AT&T publishes the basic pricing and network configuration information as a specified option to the generic tariff; a private section of the contract covers proprietary customer information.

Under Tariff 12 most or all of a customer's interexchange telecommunications requirements are provided for, including both voice and data services. Customers forecast their requirements and contract for service over a three- to five-year period at stable rates. For pricing purposes, the customer's virtual network is described in terms of hubs (a traffic concentration point), several types of ports (which originate or terminate traffic) and transmission capabilities (digital transmission links at various speeds).

For example, the Option I that AT&T originally proposed under Tariff 12 would supply service to a customer with four hubs (in four different LATAs), 2070 ports and 380 data transmission capabilities. The customer commits to nearly this many ports as a minimum, and also cannot exceed an upper limit without recontracting. For this option, approximately 60 percent of the revenue is recovered through fixed monthly charges for ports plus fixed and per-mile rates for data transmission. Usage charges apply to initial thirty-second period and additional six-second increments. For this customer no distance or time-of-day rate elements apply to on-net calls to telephones in the public network.

The packaged Tariff 12 offerings have proved attractive to large customers. By late 1990 AT&T had sixty-three options in effect.[3] Rates and accounting procedures can be tailored to customer preferences, allowing for various combinations of flat-rate, distance-sensitive, and time-related structures.

In a different type of custom tariff offering, AT&T obtained pricing flexibility in 1988 under Tariff No. 15. The initial rate plan of this type was designed for business customers with relatively small calling volumes that did not justify subscribing to WATS service. Under the "competitive necessity" doctrine (Larson, Monson and Nobles, 1989),

---

[3] However, as a result of a legal challenge, at the end of 1990 several of the Tariff 12 options were remanded to the FCC for further determination.

the FCC permits AT&T to offer an individual customer a price discount if it can establish that a competitor has made a prior offer at a lower price and that the proposed price would pass a net revenue test.

10

Pricing of carrier services

Telecommunications carriers purchase services from each other in several markets. Long distance carriers pay nationwide rates, established by US regulatory policies, to local exchange carriers for access to final customers. In addition, carriers lease private lines and other facilities from each other to fill gaps in their own networks, and to interconnect their networks. A second group of firms, value-added carriers and resellers, purchase interexchange transport and switching services in volume as large customers under interexchange carriers' regular bulk-rate tariffs, such as WATS, and sell calls and message services to final subscribers at retail rates.

In Chapter 9 we discussed bulk-rate and private line tariffs for regular business customers. In this chapter we examine the carrier access rate.

10.1   Carrier access rates

Prior to 1984, the long-distance and local rate structures of AT&T were designed to transfer revenues from interstate services to local services. The 1984 divestiture of the Bell local operating companies from AT&T ended these large internal transfers. To replace them the FCC established two new prices: a Subscriber Line Charge (SLC) that final subscribers pay monthly for each local exchange line, and a carrier access charge that AT&T and other interexchange carriers pay to local exchange carriers (LECs) for access to their originating and terminating facilities.

The carrier access charges are levied as rates per minute of interexchange calling. The charges fall into two categories: the carrier common line (CCL) charge that recovers nontraffic-sensitive (local loop) costs and the other access charges that recover traffic-sensitive (local network) costs.[1]

---

[1] In addition, a directory-assistance charge is levied on a per-message basis.

To calculate the CCL for a given year, industry accounting formulas assign an agreed-upon fraction of the local exchange carriers' local loop costs to a nationwide cost pool.[2] The total sales of interexchange minutes of all interexchange carriers are also calculated. Dividing the allocated local-cost figure by total minutes yields an average cost per minute, which is the carrier common line access rate that each interexchange carrier must pay the following year.

These fixed costs are largely costs that are common to the supply of local and interexchange services – the historic costs of constructing local loop facilities and the terminating equipment at local switches. Currently, some 27 percent of local loop costs are recovered from interstate rates (roughly 60 percent via the Subscriber Line Charge and 40 percent via interstate access charges paid by interexchange carriers). These costs amounted to some $8 billion in 1989.[3]

The Carrier Common Line charge is levied separately for originating and for terminating minutes. In addition to recovery of a portion of the fixed local loop costs, carrier access fees are also used to recover costs of dedicated access facilities that are needed to connect IXCs to local exchange networks and the traffic-sensitive costs of locally switching the interexchange calls.

At the end of 1984 only 3 percent of US telephone lines had "equal access" to interexchange carriers other than AT&T.[4] Modernization of local switches and installation of additional equipment enabled the local exchange companies to remove this impediment to competition, and by early 1991 more than 90 percent of all subscribers could dial the normal "1-plus-area-code" to obtain long-distance service from any pre-selected carrier. During the transition period, AT&T's competing interexchange carriers paid a reduced originating-minute access charge for calls placed from lines that had not yet been converted to equal-access. Their lower costs enabled them to charge lower rates for calling that required dialing additional digits.

Table 10.1 shows that average carrier access rates (for originating, terminating, and traffic-sensitive costs) have been reduced sharply, from

---

[2]For the largest LECs, costs are no longer pooled. Instead, the CCL is set within each state to recover the LEC's nontraffic-sensitive revenue requirement. Smaller independent telephone companies continue to receive revenues from some of the largest companies under complicated transition formulas.

[3]Federal-State Joint Board (January 1991), pp. 101, 105.

[4]FCC, Trends in Telephone Service, February 28, 1991

Table 10.1
Interstate carrier access charges (cents per minute)

Effective Date	#1 Orig.	#2 Term.	#3 Traf. Sens.	#4 Total per Conversation Minute
5/24/84	5.24	5.24	3.1	17.3
1/15/85	5.43	5.43	3.1	17.7
6/1/85	4.71	4.71	3.1	16.2
10/1/85	4.33	4.33	3.1	15.4
6/1/86	3.04	4.33	3.1	14.0
1/1/87	1.55	4.33	3.1	12.4
7/1/87	0.69	4.33	3.1	11.5
1/1/88	0	4.14	3.1	10.6
12/1/88	0	3.39	3.0	9.6
4/1/89	1.00	1.83	3.0	9.1
1/1/90	1.00	1.53	2.5	7.8
7/1/90	1.00	1.23	2.5	7.5
1/1/91	1.00	1.14	2.4	7.2

Notes: #1 Carrier Common Line Charge per originating access minute ("premium" access rate).
#2 Carrier Common Line per terminating access minute.
#3 Total traffic-sensitive charge per access minute (US average).
#4 Total per conversation minute (includes estimated 7 percent call setup time).
Source: Table 5.11, p. 383, Federal-State Joint Board *Monitoring Report*, January 1991.

$.173 per minute in 1984 to $.072 in 1991. Over the same period, the residential Subscriber Line Charge, paid by the final subscriber, has increased from its initial $1.00 per month in 1985 to $3.50 in 1991.[5] Despite this rebalancing of toll and local rates (see Appendix), access charges constitute the largest cost element of interexchange services. For example, $0.072 comprises 34 percent of the daytime per minute rate for a 100-mile AT&T call, and 62 percent of the night/weekend rate.

The use of a per-minute, usage-related price to recover fixed local exchange costs from interconnecting carriers is theoretically a distortion of the interexchange market, the size and importance of which we discuss below. We examine two areas of concern – diversion of traffic away from local exchange facilities, and restricting the expansion of interexchange calling.

[5] Business customers pay subscriber line charges of up to $6.00 per line.

10.2   Bypass of the local exchange

An IXC can avoid payment of one part of the access charge – the originating-minute access charge – if its customer is connected to the IXC network by facilities that avoid using the LEC's local switch for outgoing calls.[6] Such arrangements bypass the local exchange carrier's switched network, and the originating minutes of calling are then not subject to the carrier switched access rate.

In one arrangement, "service bypass," the LEC itself supplies access lines that connect the customer directly to the IXC without passing through the LEC's local switch. These access facilities are similar to local loops but, because they terminate at the IXC's point of presence, the customer can use them only for calls handled by the IXC. Directory assistance and local calls, for example, may not be provided by an IXC and must then be made on separate lines.

The alternative arrangement, "facility bypass," consists of physical access facilities supplied not by the LEC, but by another firm, such as a metropolitan area microwave or fiber-optic network. These lines connect the customer directly to the IXC. In this case, too, the customer must use separate lines for some of the calls.

Bypass of the local network has been of intense concern to local carriers and regulators. The LECs face the loss of access charge revenues, and regulators confront the prospect of authorizing higher local rates to make up such a shortfall. Local telephone companies' estimates of revenue reductions in 1990 due to switched traffic bypassing their networks are $2.1 billion for service bypass and $1.1 billion for facility bypass.[7] Lacking studies of the cost structures of the local companies, it is unclear whether sustainable rate structures exist.

10.3   Incentive effects

Effective January 1991 the carrier access pricing system described above is replaced by a price cap system for the carrier access rates of the seven Bell Operating Companies and GTE. The price cap scheme resembles that already in effect for AT&T (described in Section 7.3); it incorpo-

---

[6]For 800-number calls, direct-access facilities for incoming calls can similarly avoid the per-minute terminating-access charge.
[7]Federal–State Joint Board, Monitoring Report, January 1991, p. 390.

rates adjustment factors for productivity gains and inflation and provides for pricing flexibility within broad categories of access services.

It is nevertheless of interest to analyze both the immediate and longer-term incentive effects on carrier behavior of the access charge system that has governed the transactions between LECs and IXCs in the first years following the divestiture of AT&T. Under that system of pricing a change in the quantity of switched minutes affects the access costs incurred by an IXC.

10.3.1 Bypass and demand reduction

Consider an IXC that seeks to attract additional customers to its network. It would appear that it can reduce the total cost of supplying interexchange minutes to a customer by offering the customer an access arrangement that bypasses at least some of the facilities of the local exchange carrier. Bypass avoids the originating portion of the switched-access charge but incurs other fixed costs for the alternate facilities. At sufficiently high usage the saving on access charges will more than offset these added costs.[8]

Figure 10.1 shows both switched access and bypass arrangements. We assume that the usage-sensitive costs of switched access are a constant marginal cost c per minute. When the nontraffic-sensitive access fee p per minute is added, the total costs of switched access are proportional to usage, given by R_1. Alternatively, the IXC can provide a dedicated high-volume access link at a fixed cost B. It is economic to serve subscribers with usage greater than q_B under the bypass technology. But charging for switched access on a usage-sensitive basis lowers the apparent break-even usage level to q_A, and when subscribers with usage less that q_B shift to a bypass supplier the total costs of supply are increased.

If the IXC uses a bypass arrangement to avoid the originating-access charge, its total originating minutes in the year will be reduced and, given the carrier access rate in effect, its total payments to the central pool will decline. During the initial year the cost reduction is equal to the access rate times the number of minutes shifted to bypass facilities.

However, the reduction in originating minutes will result in less revenue being collected in the pool than is required to cover the allocated local costs. The next annual adjustment in the carrier access rate will

---

[8]See also Section 6.1.4.

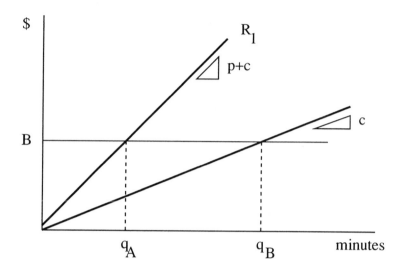

Figure 10.1
Switched access and bypass arrangements

therefore require an increase in the rate per minute in order to cover the
same amount of fixed local loop costs. In the second year the IXC thus
faces increased per-minute costs on all of its switched minutes. Its total
CCL access charge expense may show no longrun savings as a result of
having used bypass facilities.

10.3.2   Demand stimulation

Consider an increase in interexchange switched minutes, such as would
occur if the IXC successfully attracts new demand with a rate reduction
or the offering of an optional rate plan. The additional minutes will
require the carrier to increase payments to the pool fund by the prede-
termined per-minute access rate times the increased number of minutes.
In the first year the entire access rate is a variable cost to the carrier.

However, the total amount of nontraffic-sensitive local costs that is to
be recovered from all carriers under the access rate scheme is fixed. Any
increase in minutes above that projected for the year will over-collect the
assigned amount of local exchange costs. Therefore, in the second year
the observed change in the carrier's minutes will increase total industry

switched minutes and yield a reduced rate per minute for all carriers; it will also increase the carrier's share of the total minutes. The net effect will be to increase the carrier's total access payments, but by less than the per-minute price times the increase in minutes. If the increased demand for switched minutes is permanent, the additional costs to the carrier are the full per-minute price in year 1 plus smaller cost increases in subsequent years.

The magnitude of the second-year net cost effect depends on the carrier's market share of the total minutes. For a completely marginal carrier, with no perceptible share, additional minutes have no effect on its previous market share, and the second-year cost increase is effectively equal to the full per-minute access rate. For a very dominant carrier, on the other hand, who pays almost all of the industry's access fees, a larger number of minutes has almost no effect on total payments in the second year.

Thus, the effective marginal cost to an IXC of the access rate scheme depends on the market share of the IXC. For a small carrier, almost the entire access rate constitutes a marginal cost of increasing output; for the largest carrier, the cost in future years is only a fraction of the rate (Hatch and Stolleman, 1986). It is worth examining the effect of market share on the access rate in some detail.

Let C be the fixed cost that is to be recovered through access fees. In year t the fee p_t is the total cost divided by the total number of access minutes in the previous year:

$$p_t = \frac{C}{\sum_i Q_i^{t-1}}.$$

(10.1)

The ith interexchange carrier's cost in period t is:

$$C_i = s_i^t C,$$

(10.2)

where:

$$s_i^t = \frac{Q_i^t}{\sum_i Q_i^t}$$

(10.3)

is its cost share. If this share is permanent, the present value under interest rate r is:

$$TC_i = C_i \frac{1+r}{r}.$$

(10.4)

What is the effect of a change in the ith carrier's minutes of access (a decrease if an existing customer bypasses the local access network, an increase if a tariff innovation stimulates usage)? Assuming that the change is a permanent decrease (increase) in quantity, the present value of the change in cost is the sum of the change times the access fee in the current period, plus the discounted future cost share that reflects the change in the access fee:

$$\frac{\partial TC_i}{\partial q_i} = p \left(1 + \frac{1 - s_i}{r} \right). \tag{10.5}$$

For a firm with dominant market share ($s_i \to 1$), the cost effect is largely captured by the access fee p that is saved (or paid) in the current period. In the limit a monopoly firm pays the entire access pool costs. For a firm with a minor share of the pool the cost impact is larger; in the limit ($s_i \to 0$) a marginal firm's cost would increase by the present value of the access fee in every period.[9]

A firm's assumption about competitors' reactions to price changes will affect its anticipated market share. If the dominant firm expects its rivals to match any price reductions, a price decrease will leave its market and pool share unchanged (Simnett, 1989). But small rival firms are more likely to change prices independently and perceive their cost share as unaffected by rival responses.

In regulatory proceedings the interexchange carriers have taken positions with respect to the incentive effects of carrier access charges that are consistent with their market shares. AT&T, in proposing the first optional calling plans, argued that the (nontraffic-sensitive) exchange carrier revenue requirement would remain fixed, that the stimulated minutes of calling would reduce the access fee per minute, and that this adjustment would be made promptly. In projecting the effect of its optional calling plans (Section 8.2.2), AT&T therefore assumed that beginning in the second year the access fee reflected the addition of the stimulated demand.[10] MCI, with only a small share of the interexchange market, argued that AT&T's marginal costs of offering an optional calling plan should include the full per-minute access price. Furthermore, Kelley (1985) noted that treating access charges as a fixed cost gave

[9]For the LECs an increase in the volume of IXC minutes of access will in the initial year result in an increase the access charge payments they receive from the pool.
[10]AT&T Transmittal No. 79, 1984, Sec. 5, pp. 20ff.

Table 10.2
Distribution of monthly usage

Type	Band	Percent of accounts	Average minutes	Assumed price elasticity
1	0-60	74.03	15	-.16
2	61-1000	25.47	160	-.16
3	1001-2000	0.26	1364	-.50
4	2001-7000	0.17	3548	-.50
5	7001-20000	0.05	11026	-.70
6	20000+	0.02	67425	-.98

Source: Heyman, Lazorchak, Sibley, and Taylor (1987).

the carrier with a large market share a cost advantage over smaller, equal-cost suppliers. The FCC, in deciding the complaint, stated that AT&T had correctly accounted for the nontraffic-sensitive access expense. AT&T had computed the net of the increase in charges resulting from stimulation and the decrease in charges to all AT&T minutes resulting from the lower access charge per minute.[11]

10.4 Nonlinear pricing of carrier access

The incentive effects of charging for carrier access by a uniform per-minute rate structure have hardly gone unnoticed by both carriers and regulators. Most of the discussion has focused on bypass, and several alternative rate structures have been suggested. Of particular interest are two proposals to recover the fixed (nontraffic-sensitive) costs by rates that are based on individual customers' calling volumes, and a recently revised access tariff in Massachusetts. These illustrate how one might implement the theoretical properties of nonlinear tariffs described in Section 5.6.

Our discussion is based on Heyman, Lazorchak, Sibley, and Taylor's analysis (1987). Using New York data, they divide final customers into six usage groups (types) shown in Table 10.2. Also shown are the price elasticities those authors assumed for the groups.

Both of NYNEX's operating companies (New England Telephone and New York Telephone) had proposed carrier access charges based on ta-

[11]FCC (1986), p. 1400.

Table 10.3
Two nonuniform-pricing access rates

Type	Tapered tariff $/min.	Two-Part Tariff monthly	Two-Part Tariff per min.
1	.0961	$ 0	$.0756
2	.0713	0	.0756
3	.0484	0.52	.0752
4	.0352	29.18	.0674
5	.0302	342.17	.0446
6	.0269	3495.58	.0238

Source: Heyman, Lazorchak, Sibley, and Taylor (1987).

pered per-minute rates. At the time, the Carrier Common Line access charge for recovery of nontraffic-sensitive costs was $0.0756 per minute (originating plus terminating). A stylized version of a tapered rate structure is shown in Table 10.3. Under the tapered plan, rates for the smallest users are increased, while larger users enjoy increasingly lower rates. Assuming a marginal access cost of $0.01 per minute and omitting WATS customers, Heyman *et al.* calculate that the tapered rate structure would increase total surplus by $1.13 per month per customer, almost all of which accrues to consumers.

As an alternative to the tapered rate structure, Heyman *et al.* calculate a profit-maximizing set of six two-part tariffs subject to the Pareto-domination constraint. By starting from the original $0.0756 per minute access rate for the smallest consumer group, they ensure that no customer pays a higher rate. The resulting tariff is also shown in Table 10.3. It realizes a somewhat smaller total surplus gain, $1.00 per customer per month.[12] In this tariff, the increased surplus is shared equally by producers and consumers. The FCC did not approve the NYNEX type of tapered tariffs, which were strongly opposed by the interexchange carriers. Tariffs based on individual customers' volumes would mean substantial changes in billing arrangements and presumably require IXCs to make much more customer-specific data available to the local carriers.

In the Eastern Massachusetts LATA (which includes Boston) a some-

---

[12] Their welfare analysis implicitly assumes that the differential rates to larger-volume business customers do not competitively disadvantage smaller firms.

what different form of nonlinear carrier access pricing was introduced by the local exchange carrier, New England Telephone, in October 1990. The Carrier Common Line access charge that an interexchange carrier pays to the LEC is billed on the basis of originating minutes of use in three time-of-day/weekend rating periods. During the day period the originating rate per conversation minute is $0.066; during other periods it drops to $0.014. This tariff is subject to a volume discount which applies to directly dialed, non-800-number calls. The IXC receives a $0.05 credit per conversation minute for the minutes exceeding 6000 minutes per month from a single end-user location.

11

Social tariffs

"Lifeline" programs subsidize telephone services for low-income subscribers. These programs have two distinct goals: to encourage universal access and to alleviate financial hardship. The first goal can be related to network externalities and to telephone access as an "economic right." The second objective has been alluded to earlier under the headings of customer-class pricing (Section 4.6) and discriminating two-part tariffs (Section 5.4). Note that the tariffs described in this chapter use household characteristics, such as income, as a discrimination device rather than the level of consumption, as in self-selecting two-part tariffs (Section 5.6.5).

11.1 Telephone penetration

The Communications Act of 1934, which created the Federal Communications Commission, officially endorsed wide availability of telephone service as a central aim of telecommunications regulation. From 1983 until March 1990, telephone penetration of US households increased from 91.6 percent to 93.3 percent, as measured by the presence of a telephone in the housing unit.[1] Although the average level of penetration is quite high, certain subsectors of the population experience much lower levels of telephone access.

Table 11.1 summarizes historical penetration rates and shows how those rates vary according to different demographic strata. Penetration rates in the southern United States tend to be below the national average; while penetration rates in the central and northeastern part of

---

[1] Data on household access to telephones is collected by the US Bureau of the Census as part of its Current Population Survey (CPS). CPS data are collected monthly to track demographic trends between the decennial censuses. Telephone access is measured in two questions – household access to a telephone, and the presence of a telephone in the household living unit. We tabulate the latter measure of penetration.

Table 11.1
Telephone penetration in US households (percent)

	1984	1990
National average	91.6	93.3

By State, Highs and Lows

	1984	1990
Connecticut	95.5	97.1
Washington	93.0	97.1
Mississippi	82.4	87.0
New Mexico	82.0	85.8

By Household size

	1984	1990
1 person :	88.3	90.9
2-3 persons :	93.2	94.7
4-5 persons :	92.5	93.6
6+ persons :	86.9	87.8

By Employment Category of Head of Household

	1984	1990
Employed	94.0	95.3
Unemployed	81.7	85.0

By Annual Income Level†

	Total 1984	Total 1990	Black 1990	Hispanic 1990
under $ 5,000 :	71.2	75.4	66.1	61.1
$ 5,000 - $ 7,499 :	83.3	82.6	74.9	66.7
$ 7,500 - $ 9,999 :	86.5	86.9	77.3	74.8
$10,000 - $12,499 :	89.7	88.9	81.9	74.1
$12,500 - $14,999 :	92.1	91.7	85.9	82.0
more than $15,000 :	>93.7	>93.3	>87.7	>85.1

By Age of Head of Household

	Total 1984	Total 1990	Black 1990	Hispanic 1990
16–24 years :	77.0	81.2	64.4	67.8
25–64 years :	93.8	94.7	86.4	87.5
65+ years :	>95.3	>96.3	>90.7	>90.7

Notes: Critical values for 95% confidence intervals associated with above data are usually in the range of 1% to 3%.

†Households with incomes which exceed $15,000 have penetration rates which exceed value shown, approaching 99% for highest income group.
Source: Federal-State Joint Board, Monitoring Report, (CC Docket No. 80-286, January 1991). Data are annual averages.

the country exceed the average. Lower-income households, households
which are either larger or smaller than the national average, households
headed by someone sixteen to twenty-four years old, and black and Hispanic households experience below-average telephone penetration rates.[2]
For example, black and Hispanic households with annual incomes under $15,000 experience penetration rates below 85 percent, as shown in
Figure 11.1.

Penetration increases with the age of the head of household in all
demographic groups. Elderly households are more likely to have telephones: in 1990, 96 percent of householders who were sixty or older had
telephones, while only 81 percent of householders who were between sixteen and twenty-four years did. Over time the same subgroups in the
population continue to experience lower (higher) than average penetration rates, as demonstrated by the comparison of 1984 and 1990 data in
Table 11.1.

Low-income households are an important target population for programs designed to encourage network subscription. The positive externality associated with increased subscribership (Sections 4.4.1 and 5.3)
may provide an economic justification for the subsidization (and/or cross
subsidization) of access for marginal subscribers.[3]

The desire to alleviate financial hardship also may justify subsidies
targeted at low-income households. Telephone services as an expenditure category are income-inelastic, so that the monthly telephone bill
represents a larger share of the total expenditures of the average low-
income household.[4]

---

[2] There is significant overlap across the different classifications which have below-
average penetration rates. For example, many of the households which are smaller or
larger than average are headed by a black or Hispanic and are classified as low-income
households.

[3] Implicit cross subsidies may be extracted from other telecommunications services
and/or local access subscribers by setting prices lower than incremental costs. For
example the costs of local access depend on the length of local loops, but local service
rates do not typically vary with loop length.

[4] In 1989, expenditures on telephone services represented 2.0 percent of total expenditures for the average household, but represented 3.1 percent of total expenditures
for households grouped in the lowest expenditure fifth according to data collected in
the Bureau of Labor Statistics Consumer Expenditure Survey. See FCC, Telephone
Rates Update (1991), Tables 6, 7.

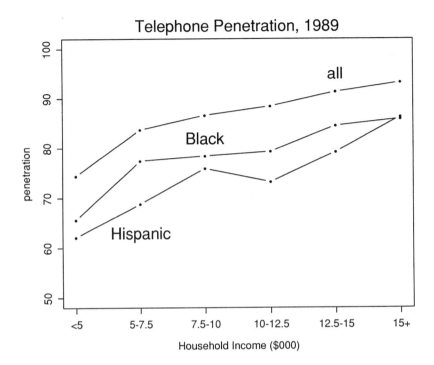

Figure 11.1
US telephone penetration

11.2   Goals of social tariffs

Subsidies which reduce the price of telephone service to inframarginal
subscribers (those who would continue to subscribe even in the absence
of such subsidies) support only the second goal of redistributing income.
Subsidies targeted at the marginal consumer, which lead to increased
subscribership, contribute to both goals. These two target populations
are different and the relative importance of each goal will affect the
design of an effective lifeline program. Johnson (1988) developed a useful
framework for evaluating and classifying different lifeline programs with
respect to which of the two goals appears more important.

For example, the increase in subscribership is relevant for evaluating the success of "universal access" programs; the level of program participation by income class is the appropriate criterion for evaluating "income redistribution" programs. Universal-access programs should not be restricted to the elderly (since they are more likely to have a telephone than the average household); however, the elderly and infirm may be targeted for income redistribution since we may believe that they are more dependent on telephone service.[5] It may be desirable to make universal access subsidies available only for local measured service, in order to screen out heavy users who are more likely to be flat-rate subscribers and to continue to subscribe in the absence of subsidies. On the other hand, poor consumers who are heavy users of the telephone suffer greater financial hardship from higher rates.

Finally, we might expect more extensive outreach efforts from a program whose chief aim was to encourage increased subscribership as opposed to redistributing income. The first goal seeks to target those who are not currently on the network; whereas the second may focus on current subscribers as the ones who are harmed most by rate increases. This second group may be reached via inserts mailed with the telephone bill.

11.3   The history of social tariffs

Historically, prices for telecommunications services have grown more slowly than prices in other sectors because of rapid productivity growth in information technologies (see Appendix). The benefits of this productivity growth have been unevenly distributed across the different telephone services. Although innovation had a greater impact on reducing the costs of long-distance transmission than on the costs of local access facilities, the relative prices of toll and local services showed little change for many years.

However, relative prices changed substantially in the early 1980s and following the divestiture of AT&T in 1984. Increased competition in toll markets and the regulatory-sanctioned reallocation of network costs led to a decline in toll rates and an increase in local calling rates. Federal

---

[5]The elderly may have fixed incomes or be less mobile and more likely to need emergency assistance. Ceteris paribus, one may argue that an older person values a telephone more and faces fewer alternatives to depending on a phone than a younger person. On the other hand, an unemployed young person may need a phone in order to find a job.

regulatory policy contributed to the increase in local rates by establishing the Subscriber Line Charge (SLC).

A number of states had established assistance programs to provide targeted subsidies to selected groups of telephone subscribers. In order to offset the negative impact of SLCs, to encourage subscriber access, and to reduce the financial hardship associated with higher local access rates, the FCC established the federal "Lifeline" program in December 1985 to provide subsidies to lower income households. In states with FCC-certified telephone rate discount programs, the FCC would match the monthly state-provided discounts to qualified subscribers (limited, however, so that the total federal subsidy per line did not exceed the amount of the federally mandated SLC).

In April 1987, the FCC introduced a second program, "Link-up America," that expanded telephone subsidies to low-income households. Under this program, federally coordinated funds from interexchange carriers pay for one-half of the connection charges for qualified[6] new subscribers (up to $30) and will subsidize the interest payments associated with deferred payment plans (for new service) implemented by certified states.[7] No matching state subsidy is required; as a consequence, the Link-up program has been adopted by more states than the lifeline program.

The federal component of both of these programs is funded by indirect taxes on interstate toll telephone services. Interexchange carriers are charged on the basis of their market share of presubscribed local-exchange access lines. The state subsidies are financed variously by general tax revenues and specific levies on telecommunications suppliers.

In most situations, the Link-up and lifeline programs are treated similarly at the state level, although their funding sources are separate. Both programs contribute to the same two goals discussed above; however, the Link-up programs place greater emphasis on the universal-access goal.

When households change their place of residence, they incur installation charges in order to restore their telephone service at the new location. Hence, we may expect Link-up subsidies to target both infra-

---

[6] The program is targeted at low-income and/or elderly households, but the specific eligibility criteria vary by state. See further discussion below.

[7] The subsidy will cover the interest accruing on service-establishment costs (up to $200) when they are included in a deferred payment plan.

marginal and marginal subscribers. Since lower-income households move more often than other households,[8] inframarginal subscribers need to pay installation charges more frequently. Thus, Link-up subsidies to the inframarginal households in this target population contribute to the distributional goals of social tariffs.

In areas served by small independent telephone companies there is an additional rate assistance program. Under the Universal Service Fund, telephone companies with especially high per-loop costs are allowed to allocate more of their loop costs to interstate services than other companies. As a result those companies obtain higher "settlement" revenues from long-distance calls and their subscribers realize lower local telephone rates than they would otherwise pay.

11.4   Description of state programs

As of January 1991, twenty-nine states and the District of Columbia have implemented certified lifeline programs; while forty-eight states, the District of Columbia and Puerto Rico participate in the Link-up America Program (Table 11.2).

Eligibility.   In each state, the Public Utility Commission or the Public Service Commission generally manages the program.[9] Eligibility in each of these programs is restricted to low-income households, which are identified typically in either of two ways:

1 Household income does not exceed the federal poverty level[10] (or some multiple of that level, such as 150 percent in California);

2 The household participates in one or more designated welfare programs (such as the Food Stamp Program, Aid for Dependent Children, the Fuel Assistance Program, etc.).

Eligibility may be self-certified (as in California) or may be verified by either the LEC (as in Indiana) or by the department responsible for ad-

---

[8] According to Census data, 26.3 percent of poverty households versus 15.6 percent of overall households had moved in the preceding twelve months in 1985. See US General Accounting Office (1987), p. 22.

[9] In a few cases such as Montana, New Mexico, and Wyoming, the LEC administers the program.

[10] The poverty level increases with household size.

Table 11.2
Eligibility in Lifeline and Link-up programs

State	Entity	Eligibility criteria	Income verification
Alabama	Public Service Commission	Recipient of: SSI, AFDC, or Food Stamps	Medicaid or Food Stamp card
Arizona	Corporation Commission	Lifeline: Income below 150% poverty Link-up: Income at or below poverty and participant in Senior-Telephone Discount Program	Arizona Dept. of Economic Security
Arkansas	Public Service Commission	Recipient of: SSI, AFDC HEAP, Food Stamps Medicaid, or Subsidized housing	Local Exchange Companies
California	Public Utilities Commission	Income at or below 150% poverty	Self certified
Colorado	Public Utilities Commission	Recipient of: SSI, Old Age Pension, Aid to the Blind, or Aid to the Needy & Disabled	Dept. Of Social Services
Connecticut	Dept. of Public utility Control	Eligible for any low-income assistance or energy assistance program administered by the CT Dept. of Human Resources or CT Dept. of Income Maintenance or SSI	Applicable agency of those listed
District of Columbia	Public Service Commission	Over age 65 & eligible for LIHEAP or Complementary Energy Assistance Program	D.C. Energy Office
Florida	Public Service Commission	Recipient of: Food Stamps or Medicaid	Dept. of Health & Rehabilitative Services

Eligibility in Lifeline and Link-up programs, cont.

State	Entity	Eligibility criteria	Income verification
Georgia	Public Service Commission	Recipient of: SSI, AFDC, and/or Food Stamps	Dept. of Human Resources
Hawaii	Public Utilities Commission	Age 60 or older or handicapped with annual household income $10,000 or less	Hawaiian Telephone Co.
Idaho	Public Utilities Commission	Recipient of: APDC: Food Stamps, Aid to the Aged, Blind & Disabled, or Medical Assistance	Medical Assistance or Food Stamp ID card
Illinois	Illinois Commerce Commission	Recipent of public assistance in programs administered by the Illinois Dept. of Public Aid	Dept. of Public Aid
Indiana	Utility Regulatory Commission	Recipient of: SSI, AFDC, HEAP, Medicaid, or Food Stamps	Local Exchange Companies
Iowa	State Utilities Board	Recipient of SSI, AFDC, LIHEAP, or Food Stamps	Local Exchange Companies
Kansas	Corporation Commission	Recipient of: SSI, AFDC, Food Stamps, Medicaid, or General Assistance	Local Exchange Companies
Kentucky	Public Service Commission	Recipient of: SSI, AFDC, Food Stamps, or Medical Assistance	Cabinet for human Resources
Louisiana	Public Service Commission	Recipient of: SSI, AFDC, or Food Stamps	Medicaid or Food Stamp card
Maine	Public Utilities Commission	Recipient of: SSI, AFDC, HEAP, Medicaid, or Food Stamps	Dept. of Human Services

Eligibility in Lifeline and Link-up programs, cont.

State	Entity	Eligibility criteria	Income verification
Maryland	Public Service Commission	Recipient of: General Assistance	Dept. of Human Resources
Massachusetts	Dept of Public Utilities	Recipient of: SSI, AFDC, General Public Welfare, Food Stamps, Medicaid, and Fuel Assistance	Depot of Public Welfare and/or Office of Fuel Assistance
Michigan	Public Service Commission	Income at or below 130% poverty	Dept. of Social Services or Office Services to the Aging
Minnesota	Public Utilities Commission	Age 65 or older or income level which meets state poverty levels	Dept. of Human Services
Mississippi	Public Service Commission	Recipient of: SSI, AFDC, or Food Stamps	Medicaid or Food Stamp card
Missouri	Public Service Commission	Recipient of: Medicaid	Dept. of Social Services
Montana	GTE, Inc.	Recipient of: SSI, AFDC, or Medicaid	Medicaid card Social & Rehabilitation Services
Nebraska	Public Service Commission	Recipient of: SSI, AFDC, Energy Assistance, Food Stamps, Medicaid, or Aid to the Aged, Blind or Disabled	Medicaid Agency or Dept. of Social Service or Food Stamp program
Nevada	Public Service Commission	Recipient of: SSI, AFDC, Energy Assistance, Food Stamps, Indian General Assist., Commodity Foods, or VA Improved Pension	Proof of enrollment in listed programs

Eligibility in Lifeline and Link-up programs, cont.

State	Entity	Eligibility criteria	Income verification
New Hampshire	Public Utilities Commission	Recipient of: SSI, AFDC, Food Stamps, Fuel Assistance, Old Age Assistance, Weatherization Assist., Aid to Permanently/ Totally Disabled, Women, infants & Children Feeding Program Welfare, Title XX, or Subsidized Housing	Respective donor agency
New Jersey	Board of Public Utilities	Recipient of: SSI, AFDC, HEAP, Pharmaceutical Assist. to the Aged, Welfare, ot Lifeline Credit	Local Exchange companies
New Mexico	Mountain Bell Tel.	Recipient of: SSI, AFDC, or LITAP	Medicaid card
	Continental Tel. Co.	Recipient of: SSI, AFDC, or Coordinated Community In-Home Care (CCIC)	Human Services Dept.
	Western NM Tel. Co.	Recipient of: SSI, AFDC, or CCIC	Human Services Dept.
New York	Dep t. of Public Services	Recipient of: SSI, AFDC, Food Stamps, Medicaid, or Home Relief	Administering Agency
North Carolina	Utilities Commission	Recipient of: SSI or AFDC	Dept. of Human Resources
North Dakota	Public Service Commission	Eligible for: Food Stamps	County Social Service Board
Ohio	Public Utilities Commission	Recipient of: HEAP or Ohio Energy Credits	Local Exchange Companies

Eligibility in Lifeline and Link-up programs, cont.

State	Entity	Eligibility criteria	Income verification
Oklahoma	Corporate Commission	Recipient of aid from state low income programs	Dept. of Human Services
Oregon	Public Utilities Commission	Eligible for: Food Stamps	Dept. of Human Resources
Pennsylvania	Public Utities Commission	Recipient of: SSI, AFDC, Food Stamps, General Assistance, or Blue Card Medical Ass. Medically Needy Only	Dept. of Public Welfare
Puerto Rico	PR Tel. Co.	Recipient of: Nutritional Assistance Program	Dept. of Social Services
Rhode Island	Public Utilities Commission	Recipient of: SSI, AFDC, General Assistance, or Medical Assistance	Dept. of Human Services
South Carolina	Public Service Commission	Recipient of: AFDC, Food Stamps, Medicaid, or Temporary Emergercy Food Assistance	Local Exchange Companies
South Dakota	Northwestern Bell	Recipient of: HEAP or Food Stamps	Dept. of Social Services
Tennessee	Public Service Commission	Recipient of: SSI, AFDC, Medicaid, or Food Stamps	Medicaid card or Food Stamp Notice of Disposition
Texas	Public Utilities Commission	Eligible for: SSI, AFDC, LIHEAP, Food Stamps, Medicaid, Medical Assistance, or Maternal Health Program	Local Exchange Companies

Eligibility in Lifeline and Link-up programs, cont.

State	Entity	Eligibility criteria	Income verification
Utah	Public Service Commission	Eligible for: SSI, AFDC, Food Stamps, General Assistance, Home Energy Assistance, Medical Assistance, Refugee Assistance, or Energy Work Programs	Local Exchange Companies
Vermont	Public Service Board	Recipient of: SSI, AFDC, Food Stamps, Medicaid; or Fuel Assistance	Dept. of Social Welfare
Virginia	Corporation Commission	Recipient of: Virginia Universal Service Plan	Dept. of Medical Assist. Services
Washington	Utilities Transportation Commission	Recipient of: SSI, AFDC, Food Stamps, Refugee Assistance, Chore Services, or Community Options Program Entry System	Dept. of Social & Health Services
West Virginia	Public Service Commission	Disabled or age 60 or older & receives SSI, AFDC or Food Stamps or is eligible for SSI	Dept. of Human Services
Wisconsin	Wisconsin Bell	Recipient of: AFDC, SSI, Food Stamps, Title 19 Medical and Energy Programs	Dept. of Health and Social Services
Wyoming	US West	Recipient of: SSI, AFDC, LIHEAP, or Food Stamps	Dept. of Health Social Services
	United Tel. Co.	Recipient of: SSI, AFDC, LIHEAP, Food Stamps, or Food Distribution Program	Dept. of Health & Social Services

Notes:
SSI — Supplemental Social Security Income
AFDC — Aid for Dependent Children
HEAP — Home Energy Assistance Program
LIHEAP — Low Income Home Energy Assistance Program
LIEAP — Low Income Energy Assistance Program

ministering the qualifying program (e.g., Department of Social Services in Colorado).

As a separate criterion for assistance, a number of states either extend eligibility to include the elderly (as in Minnesota) or limit participation to the elderly (as in the District of Columbia).

States vary with respect to their treatment of security deposits under the Link-up America program. For example, Arkansas and Texas do not require deposits; whereas Missouri and Kansas do. Consequently, the LECs in Arkansas and Texas face a much larger problem with uncollectible bills (Makarewicz, 1990).

Benefits. In addition to the sorts of differences cited above, the state programs differ with respect to the level of benefits they offer. California's lifeline program is noteworthy for being one of the earliest, largest, and more generous.[11] The California program covers both flat-rate and measured service. It provides a 50 percent discount for the SLC, the basic rate service charges,[12] and the installation fee.[13] Furthermore, the California program provides a $0.75/month credit to defray the expenses of phone equipment and a $0.25/month credit for maintenance of inside wiring. The credits appear on the monthly telephone bill. In order to obtain the service, one submits a signed form stating that one's household income does not exceed 150 percent of the household poverty level.[14]

In New York, there are two basic lifeline programs, both of which waive the entire SLC of $3.50 per month. Under the "basic" service op-

[11] Participants in California's lifeline program represent 65 percent of the national participation and 33 percent of the total eligible population. (New York and California together account for 52 percent of the total eligible population.)

[12] The 50 percent credit reduces the SLC from $3.50 to $1.75 per month. In Santa Monica, if you choose measured service lifeline you pay $2.62 per month (50 percent off the normal rate of $5.25) and you get sixty free local calls. Thereafter, you pay the normal $0.08 per local call measured-service rate. If you choose flat-rate service, you pay $4.87 per month (instead of $9.75) and get unlimited local calling. Optional features such as "touch tone" dialing add about a $1.00 to these rates. The actual rates vary across California, but the percentage discounts are the same.

[13] California does not participate in the federal Link-up America program; its program to subsidize installation fees was started before the federal program became available. Since the California program relies on self-certification of eligibility status, it has not been approved by the FCC, which requires the states to have certified verification procedures to participate in th͡ ͡nk-up program.

[14] A single person's household income may not exceed $13,600 per year. Exact verification procedures vary across the state. In some cases, the subscriber has to fill out detailed forms; in other cases, the subscriber has to sign a single form.

tion the subscriber pays $1.00 per month for network access and receives a 10 percent discount off usage charges for intra-LATA calls; under the "expanded" service option, the customer pays $10.00 for access and usage (up to $10.00 in usage).[15] In lieu of these subsidies, the subscriber would pay $3.80 for network access plus $3.50 for the SLC plus charges for usage.[16] To qualify for the program, one must receive benefits from one or more of the following programs: the Home Energy Assistance Program (HEAP); Supplemental Social Security; Aid for Dependant Children; Food Stamps; Home Relief; or Medicaid. The telephone company verifies the subscriber's eligibility with the agency that administers the program which is used to qualify the subscriber for the Link-up America or lifeline program.

In the Arkansas program, lifeline service is limited to the local measured-service rate (except in places where only flat-rate service is available), and provides a discount equal to one-third of the flat-rate charge (Makarewicz, 1990).

Participation. Such state-to-state differences help account for the wide dispersion in the sizes of the lifeline programs and the percentages of the eligible populations which participate (see Table 11.3).[17] Participation in lifeline averages 32 percent, while participation in the Link-up America program is lower, averaging 3 percent.[18] In many states, the eligibility criteria for the two programs are the same, although the states differ with respect to how the sizes of the eligible populations are reported in the FCC statistics. If, however, we assume that the eligible populations are the same, we would expect a lower participation rate for the Link-up programs since most of the eligible population already have

---

[15] In certain parts of New York there are special location charges, which for example may vary by the distance a customer is from the telephone office. These surcharges, which are waived for the Lifeline subscriber, provide an additional subsidy.

[16] There are a number of calling plans available to regular subscribers which provide volume discounts and/or special discounts for high volume or regional callers.

[17] There may be a number of data problems associated with the "Monitoring Report" data. For example, the overall participation rate is calculated by assuming a zero participation rate in states which did not report data. Furthermore, states differ with respect to how they compute eligibility statistics.

[18] The lifeline participation ranges from a low of 4 percent in Maryland to a high of 74 percent in Idaho. Participation in the Link-up America program ranges from a low of less than 0.01 percent in Nevada to a high of 56 percent in Nebraska. Since many of these state programs are relatively small and the target populations are hard to measure, there may be significant errors in the reported statistics. Furthermore, there are differences in the way states report their data.

a telephone service (and so do not need subsidies to defray installation charges). If we conservatively estimate that between 75 percent and 85 percent of the eligible Link-up population already have telephones, then the "true" participation rate would be between 12 percent to 20 percent (actual participants divided by estimated eligible population without telephones).

The attractiveness of the program: its age, local demand considerations, the choice of income verification scheme, the selection of eligible programs used to qualify lifeline participants, and the level of effort expended to publicize the program – all may be expected to influence the level of participation.

Limiting the program to a measured-service rate will tend to reduce participation rates. Since the existence of this limitation is more characteristic of programs whose primary aim is to encourage universal access, a low participation rate may not be a problem. It is an indication that the restriction is effectively screening-out low-income families who prefer flat-rate service and do not require subsidies to maintain their service connections.

11.5   The costs of social tariffs

As discussed by Johnson (1988), there are two sources of economic costs associated with telephone subsidies. The first stems from the direct administrative costs associated with implementing and managing the program. The second stems from any allocative inefficiencies which may be due to how the program is funded. If the program were funded by lump-sum poll taxes then there would be no allocative inefficiencies; however, the subsidy programs are funded by the use of excise taxes on other telephone services (such as interstate toll services). If demand for the taxed service is relatively inelastic, then the inefficiency associated with the tax is reduced.

The state lifeline programs are funded in a variety of ways. However, most approaches entail either a direct or indirect tax on other telephone services.[19] For example, California and Oregon tax intrastate toll messages; whereas Vermont taxes overall basic rate services. In Arkansas and New York the LEC absorbs the cost of the program, and will im-

[19] Johnson (1988) provides information for the source of funding for a selection of the programs.

Table 11.3
Enrollment in social tariffs

State	Lifeline			Link-up		
	Date implemented	Subscribers number	%	Date implemented	Subscribers number	%
Alabama				2/88	5,961	1.3
Arizona	11/86	8,826	24.8	11/86	5,961	1.6
Arizona - Pilot	11/86	3,446	64.6			
Arkansas	5/86	6,305	8.5	11/87	11,099	3.2
California	1/1/85	1,179,658	62.7			
Colorado	9/86	0	0.0	8/88	0	0.0
Connecticut				11/87	5,605	3.5
District of Columbia	3/86	3,793	6.8	8/87	1,602	2.9
Florida				10/88	5,689	22.8
Georgia				1/89	N/A	N/A
Hawaii	10/86	6,473	32.9	9/89	79	0.1
Idaho	8/87	8,212	73.5	(5/89)	5,579	7.0
Illinois				(9/89)	N/A	N/A
Indiana				1/89	1,272	2.0
Iowa				4/88	6,383	44.6
Kansas				2/88	1,272	49.8
Kentucky				1/88	1,631	0.4
Louisiana				(10/88)	11,140	2.0
Maine	1/88	33,908	49.5	1/88	7,913	26.9
Maryland	7/86	2,929	3.9	10/87	540	0.2
Massachusetts	(2/90)	N/A	N/A	2/90	2,542	0.6
Michigan	5/89	45,502	7.4	5/89	8,325	1.4
Minnesota	1/88	46,845	35.1	1/88	1,704	0.9
Mississippi				5/88	2,322	0.9
Missouri	10/87	14,727	58.8	4/88	1,945	1.9
Montana	4/88	5,348	5.9	4/88	2,125	2.3
Nebraska				6/88	495	56.1
Nevada	7/88	4,650	19.8	11/88	N/A	0.0
New Hampshire				12/88	361	0.9
Oregon	6/86	21,503	25.3	5/88	1,899	4.6
Pennsylvania				6/88	34,281	4.6
Puerto Rico				(11/88)	2,519	2.6
Rhode Island	11/88	14,056	30.4	11/88	853	1.9
South Carolina				2/88	8,988	2.3
South Dakota	6/88	4,653	53.8	6/88	1,038	1.4
New Jersey				1/88	1,673	4.4
New Mexico	7/87	11,729	33.5	3/88	2,548	1.2
New York	11/87	260,628	23.7	8/87	95,967	8.7
North Carolina	3/87	15,413	8.15	3/88	4.976	1.8
North Dakota	(12/89)	N/A	N/A	1/89	687	1.1
Ohio	4/87	12,095	10.07	12/87	10,115	8.4
Oklahoma				(4/90)	N/A	N/A
Tennessee				1/89	7,909	1.8

Enrollment in social tariffs, cont.

| State | Lifeline | | | Link-up | | |
	Date implemented	Subscribers number	%	Date implemented	Subscribers number	%
Texas	9/88	15,346	12.4	11/87	14,244	7.9
Utah	(12/86)	13,473	33.7	3/88	1,298	1.4
Vermont	10/86	17,250	47.9	(2/90)	N/A	N/A
Virginia	1/88	15,453	32.1	1/88	4,470	0.9
Washington	8/87	33,237	17.2			
West Virginia	10/86	6,060	13.8	10/87	2,113	18.1
Wisconsin				(7/89)	N/A	N/A
Wyoming				3/89	518	2.9
Totals		1,812,518	31.85		287,641	3.1

Notes: Other sources used where noted and required by the failure of certified states and LEC's to submit cost benefit reports. ( ) Date approved by FCC.
1 Data from Bell Communications Research.
2 As of 6/89 from Bell Communications Research.
3 Colorado's telephone assistance plan was discontinued in February, 1989. However, a new plan was certified in May 1990.

Source: Unless noted, FCC Form 496, State Telephone Assistance Report, filed May 1, 1990; data as of December 31, 1969.

plicitly recoup the program cost via higher rates for other services. In Hawaii the program is funded out of general tax revenues via a "public service tax." Since the price elasticity of demand for local access is lower than for toll calls, Vermont's approach may produce less inefficiency than California's for equal-size taxes. True interstate comparisons of the welfare losses associated with the distorting impact of different program features would need to consider the magnitude of the implicit tax and the particulars of state demand.

Table 11.4 summarizes the federal reimbursements associated with the lifeline and Link-up programs. The sum of the link-up transfers and twice the lifeline[20] transfers provides a (very rough) lower-bound estimate for the magnitude of the transfers associated with these programs. At the rate for the first six months of 1989 this amounts to about $100 million per year. Unfortunately, data on the full program expenditures

[20] Federal transfers match state subsidies up to a maximum equal to the level of the SLC.

Table 11.4
Reimbursements to local exchange companies

Period	Lifeline ($000)	Link-up ($000)
July-Dec., 1987	11,607	150
Jan.-June, 1988	14,402	1,085
July-Dec., 1988	17,672	913
Jan.-June, 1989	24,129	1,354
July-Dec., 1989	26,944	3,017

Source: *Monitoring Report* (CC Docket No. 87-339, January 1991).

for the various states are not available. One source reported that total program expenses (transfers plus administrative expenses) in California were expected to exceed $155 million in 1988 (US General Accounting Office, 1987).

Data on the direct administrative expenses of the state programs are also limited. Not all states report this information, and the coverage in those that do report data varies.[21] Table 11.5 summarizes the information contained in the "Monitoring Report." Based on these data, lifeline administrative costs range from a high of around $5.50 per month per participant in Maryland to a low of around $0.25 per month per participant in Hawaii, with an approximate average between $1.00 and $2.00 per month per participant. The relatively high costs experienced by certain states may be due to scale diseconomies for small programs. Start-up costs may include changes to billing systems, publicity, etc. There does not appear to be any discernible relationship between lifeline and Link-up cost data, which may be due simply to differences in reporting practices. The data in Table 11.5 are included only to give an indication of the relative magnitude of the direct costs associated with these programs; their precision is suspect.

[21] States in the federally sponsored lifeline and Link-up America programs must submit annual "496" forms which contain line items for reporting annual administrative exenditures as either start-up costs or monthly recurring costs.

Table 11.5
Administrative costs of state programs, 1989

	Startup costs ($000s)		Recurring costs ($/household/month)	
	Lifeline	Link-up[1]	Lifeline	Link-up[2]
Arizona	$ 60	$ 18	$ 4.95	$ 1.60
Hawaii	2		0.25	
Indiana		10		8.70
Iowa		7		0.90
Kansas		4		6.25
Maryland	45		5.50	
Missouri	5	8	2.10	3.75
Nebraska	22		1.50	
New York	274		1.00	
New Jersey		2		1.30
North Carolina	18	20	1.20	4.10
Ohio	268	67	22.16	7.25
Rhode Island	30		2.10	
South Carolina		22		5.10
Texas	29	26	2.15	2.05
West Virginia	32	2	5.30	1.00

Notes: [1]From Chart 2.1 (Lifeline) and from Chart 2.3 (Link-up America) start-up costs, which include such things as adjustments to billing systems, advertising, etcetera. Reporting errors ± $1,000.
[2]From Chart 2.2: (Lifeline) and Chart 2.4 (Link-up America) monthly recurring administrative costs per household. Computed by taking the State's reported monthly administrative costs and dividing by the number of participating households. Reporting errors ± $ 0.25.

Source: Federal-State Joint Board , Monitoring Report, (CC Docket No. 88-286, July 1990). Data have been extracted from charts included in the Monitoring Report which are difficult to read exactly and so there may be reporting errors. Also, the states may differ in the way they report data. Not all states report.

11.6 The welfare impact of social tariffs

In order to evaluate the welfare impact of the lifeline and Link-up programs, we need to decide on an appropriate baseline. Assume that the primary motivation behind the lifeline programs was the desire to neutralize the potential negative impact of SLCs on low-income subscribers (i.e., to foster universal access and avoid cost increases at low incomes). Taking this view, Larson, Makarewicz, and Monson (1988) analyzed the impact of the SLCs on the average consumer and found that the rate rebalancing which SLCs facilitated led to significant welfare gains. For

44 percent of the consumers living in low-income areas, the combined effect of higher SLCs and lower toll rates reduced monthly telephone bills by over $10.00; while the 56 percent of the consumers whose bills increased suffered only a $1.92 average increase.

This analysis of the effect of SLCs on the average subscriber ignores the impact of certain events. For example, higher SLCs contributed to the shift in relative rates between local and toll telephone services. SLCs increased local rates and helped facilitate lower toll rates; however, in the absence of SLCs, we would have expected lower toll rates due to the increased interstate toll competition following AT&T's divestiture. Lower average rates have been accompanied by improvements in the quality of telephone services. New services are available such as information services and optional calling features.[22] We would like to identify the portion of the improvements in service quality and the reduction in toll rates which would have occurred without SLCs and use this as the baseline against which to assess the welfare effect of SLCs and lifeline programs.

Although the above effects may change the welfare impact of SLCs, the lower toll rates are likely to offset at least part of the negative welfare impact imposed on the subscriber whose local rates increase. It is clear that any household that participates in a lifeline program, which subsidizes the entire SLC, is unambiguously better off as a result of the somewhat lower toll rates due to the SLCs. On the other hand, if the subsidy offsets only a fraction of the SLC, customers who are not heavy toll callers may be worse off after the imposition of SLCs. However, Larson *et al.* (1988) analyzed Southwestern Bell's regional traffic data and found that from 1983 to 1988, long-distance usage increased significantly faster for lower income users than for the average residential subscriber. In addition, Makarewicz (1990) found that the average lifeline customer and the average residential customer spent approximately the same share of their total telephone bill on toll services (approximately 57 percent) after accounting for the lifeline subsidy provided to participating Southwestern Bell subscribers.

As Johnson (1988) points out, if the goal of social tariffs were merely

---

[22]New calling features include such options as call-blocking and call-forwarding services. The new "976-" numbers offer information services where the caller is billed a per minute rate to access an information service. These have been used for dial-up sex lines, joke lines, and even for crossword puzzle help lines.

to effect income redistribution, the transfer might have been accomplished by increasing the benefits for those programs which are used to qualify participants in lifeline programs (e.g., increasing the food stamp allowance by the amount by which the telephone service bills increased would leave the subscriber unambiguously better off). To address the effectiveness of these programs in encouraging the second goal of universal access we would need to separate the participants into marginal and inframarginal subscribers. The inframarginal subscribers are "free-riders" with respect to the goal of encouraging universal access. Makarewicz (1990) examines data on discretionary telephone expenditures by lifeline participants and designates those whose discretionary telephone expenditures are more than twice the size of the lifeline discount as free-riders. He found only about 20 percent free-ridership.

Further evidence that these programs do encourage additional subscribership is provided by the higher than average turnover rates observed for Colorado lifeline participants after the program was interrupted for ten months in August, 1989. Lifeline subscribers who disconnected their service following this were queried regarding the reasons for their action. The local exchange carrier (US West) found that about 3 percent of the households who subscribed to lifeline service (and had not moved or died) had disconnected, a rate double the disconnection rate for subscribers with regular service.

IV

SYNTHESIS

12

Synthesis of theory and practice

This study has provided an overview of recent developments in the economic theory of pricing and the innovative practice of setting telecommunications tariffs in the United States. In this final chapter we recapitulate the principal linkages between theory and practice and suggest how these tools can be applied to new pricing problems.

12.1 Lessons from pricing theory

12.1.1 Overview of theory

The benchmark for all public utility tariffs is *marginal-cost prices*, which are exemplified in telecommunications under the heading of *peak-load pricing*. Under the appropriate conditions marginal-cost prices are welfare maximizing; they are firmly based on cost; and they, and the rationale behind them, are easily understood. However, the simplicity of marginal-cost prices hides major conceptual difficulties, measurement problems, and potential inefficiencies. Potential inefficiencies of marginal-cost pricing can arise because marginal-cost prices, due to long-run excess capacity or due to economies of scale and scope, rarely cover total cost of service.

Most of the literature assumes that the firm's pricing must cover its total costs without external subsidies. Budget constraints on the regulated telecommunications carrier or differentiated welfare weights in the objective function then lead to various versions of *Ramsey pricing* and of the inverse elasticity rule. This rule says that relative markups of prices over marginal costs for the various services offered should deviate in inverse proportion to the respective demand elasticities. This rule can be adapted in various ways to cases of interdependent demands, competitive situations, situations involving consumption externalities, and dynamic settings. Also, it holds for both welfare-maximizing and profit-maximizing behavior. Thus the inverse elasticity rule, properly interpreted, is a surprisingly robust concept. Consumption externalities and learning-by-doing, however, lead to additional terms in the pricing equation under welfare maximization, terms that are absent under profit maximization.

In general, Ramsey prices differ from marginal-cost prices. At the margin, one could increase social surplus (or Pareto-improve welfare) by selling additional units closer to, or at, marginal cost. This approach – selling different units of the same service to the same consumer at different prices – is called *nonlinear* (or *nonuniform) pricing*. Nonlinear prices are widely applied in telecommunications. Their main advantage is that they can improve on Ramsey prices, yet allow the firm to raise enough revenue to cover costs. Their main disadvantage is that their derivation requires more detailed information about individual demands.

The simplest types of nonlinear prices are *two-part tariffs*, consisting simply of a (fixed) entry fee E and a (marginal) price p. The entry fee may exclude some customers from purchasing the service at all and can lead to a major inefficiency or unfairness even if the marginal units of the service are sold at marginal cost. However, if everyone continues to purchase the commodity in spite of the fixed fee imposed under a two-part tariff, then the marginal-cost price can be charged and the firm's budget can be covered simultaneously. Such first-best two-part tariffs are called *Coase tariffs*.

Since Coase tariffs are infeasible for most services, even two-part tariffs will contain distortions. We may be able to reduce the distortions by increasing the nonlinearity of the tariffs, the extreme refinement being a *smooth nonlinear tariff* that changes continuously with the quantity purchased. Smoothness may actually make such a tariff analytically and conceptually more tractable than the *multipart tariffs* that lie between the two-part and the smooth tariff. Multipart tariffs are hard to handle because the number of parts and their ranges have to be determined simultaneously.

The analysis and implementation of nonlinear tariffs substantially increases the informational, computational, and conceptual requirements for the tariff-setting firm or regulator. In particular, market demand as the basis for tariff setting loses much of its usefulness. Instead, either individual consumer demands are ranked by consumer types or the different purchase quantities of individual consumers are aggregated as separate markets. Surprisingly, the inverse elasticity rule as the main result of Ramsey pricing carries over to nonlinear pricing. Under nonlinear pricing there is some presumption that larger consumers receive lower marginal and average prices than smaller consumers. This is certainly true if nonlinear tariffs take the form of sets of optional two-part tariffs.

To this point the theory relates cost and demand in order to maximize efficiency defined as some weighted sum of consumer and producer welfare. A rather different emphasis is the compatibility of prices and cost, rather than the maximization of such an objective function. The necessity for such compatibility is justified by issues of fairness and competition. The traditional approach is one of *fully distributed-cost pricing*. In contrast, modern concepts of cost-based pricing are developed based on *cost-axiomatic, subsidy-free, sustainable* and other game-theoretic approaches.

The concept of fully distributed-cost pricing appears to be the least satisfactory one – it has only limited fairness properties, is quite fragile in situations of competitive entry, and is totally unrelated to efficiency. The other concepts are better rooted in fairness and, in some cases, are quite compatible with competition and efficiency. In particular, their properties emphasize the concepts of anonymous equity, sustainability, and the second-best core.

12.1.2 Similarity between theoretical and actual tariffs

US telephone rates have in the past been heavily influenced by federal and state regulators. While one could argue that welfare maximization has been the guiding principle of these institutions, most economists agree that regulators are mostly influenced by political considerations (Peltzman, 1976). As a result, cross subsidization to politically influential user groups is cited much more heavily as the outcome of rate innovation than efficient pricing. Empirically, this assertion is backed by the study of Kaserman, Mayo, and Flynn (1990).

It appears that the burst in tariff innovations occurred only after US regulators reduced their influence on tariff setting in favor of more competitive pricing by the dominant carriers and their potential competitors and bypassers. This suggest that the guiding principle of the tariff innovations described in Chapters 7–10 has been profit maximization.

How is that compatible with welfare maximization? As we have seen in Chapters 4–5, profit-maximizing price schedules in oligopoly are likely to show shapes and structures similar to welfare-maximizing prices. It is the *level* of prices charged that will differ in a welfare-maximizing regime. Hence, we expect that under profit maximization the tariff innovations will be quite similar to those required under welfare maximization. However, profits exceeding competitive levels would indicate deviations from welfare-optimal pricing.

12.2   Assessing practice in light of theory

In Chapter 1 we sketched different sequences in which innovations in theory and practice may by connected. What, then, is the empirical evidence about their relationship in the United States? Here we attempt to link together the theory and practical implementation of telecommunications pricing to propose some tentative answers to these questions: Which types of theoretical innovations have led to tariff implementations? And which of those implementations have been successful? What factors prevent theory from being successfully translated into practice?

12.2.1   Overview of US practice

For many years, the policy of federal and state regulators and the interests of AT&T supported revenue transfers from long-distance to local telephone services.[1] The policy of maintaining low prices for network access served the objective of encouraging universal service. Using class-of-service pricing, state regulators charged business subscribers higher rates, in order to further reduce the access price for residential consumers.

With the achievement of nearly universal penetration and the increasing disparity between long-distance rates and falling costs for trunk calls, the toll-to-local transfer policy lost much of its justification. However, because rate restructuring would not be Pareto improving, it was politically important to develop targeted subsidies to assist groups who would otherwise be disadvantaged. State and federal regulators created

---

[1] Although this has been widely referred to as the local-service subsidy, the rate structure may nevertheless have been subsidy free. Trunk-call rates were substantially higher than marginal costs, but they may not have exceeded the stand-alone costs of long-distance service.

a series of social lifeline tariffs to subsidize access and local usage for low-income and elderly groups.

The emergence of vigorous national competition in interexchange markets has put strong pressure on all firms to weed out inefficient operations and increase productivity. It has increased the importance of marketing efforts and the differentiation of services and rate structures.

Driving forces. During the last decade or so the remarkable changes in US telecommunications pricing have been driven by several factors. The settlement of the US antitrust suit that resulted in the divestiture of AT&T in 1984 broke the internal link between the supply of local and long-distance services. This change compelled a new policy for pricing both consumer access to the network and interexchange carrier access to those consumers. Increasing competition in the supply of intercity service, coupled with the feasibility of self-supply by larger business customers, generated strong pressures for rate reductions in vulnerable market segments.

Rapid advances in technology have driven down costs and expanded the possibilities for matching services to customer needs. These developments have in turn increased the degree of market segmentation. Wholesale services, particularly, are being closely tailored to market segments, through volume discounting, private networks, and toll-free services.

The formerly widespread reliance on fully distributed-cost pricing has waned, and with the recent replacement of cost-of-service regulation by price caps further pricing flexibility has become possible for the dominant intercity carrier, AT&T, and for access rates charged by local carriers. This could lead to further changes in price structures in the future.

This period has also seen vigorous innovation in the economic theory of pricing, with major progress in nonlinear pricing and the relationship between prices and costs in multiproduct firms. Some of these discoveries may have stimulated the introduction of new rate structures and revised regulatory procedures. And, as we noted in Chapter 1, innovations that first appear in market practice can conversely lead to new theoretical understandings.

Hindering forces. Despite the extensive pressures for rate restructuring, substantial institutional forces in the United States shackle innovation and delay change. Past pricing practices have created vested interests in the status quo and the expectation that prices are set through political processes. State regulators are especially loath to increase the residential access price, and the unique division of power between American state and federal authorities makes status quo prices especially powerful.

Federal regulators seem to have become more favorable to pricing innovation, yet FCC attempts to give AT&T greater pricing flexibility are hobbled by a judicial preoccupation with the dangers of predation and a resistance to demand-based pricing.

Alternatively, regulators can be viewed as pursuing a policy of fostering competition per se, and seeking to protect recent entrants at the cost of greater pricing efficiency.

A decade's innovations in telecommunications pricing has brought US consumers generally lower price levels and a substantially wider set of service choices. Within the basic restructuring of long-distance and local rates, overall telephone prices have fallen at both the retail and wholesale levels for most services (see Appendix). And for most major services residential and business subscribers have several suppliers and rate plans from which to choose. This broader set of possibilities, combined with the separation of carriers for local service and interexchange service comes at a real price. Consumers now confront increased transactions costs in ordering what were formerly integrated services and in choosing among suppliers. Particularly in the period of transition, the total costs of service for some subscribers may have increased.

12.2.2 Empirical evidence

In broad perspective, US rates have been relatively high for long-distance trunk calls and quite low for network access and local calls. Differential rates of technological change, divided federal/state regulatory authority, divestiture of AT&T, and a growing pro-competitive policy for intercity service have gradually rebalanced the spread between trunk and local rates.

Rate rebalancing. Quantitative empirical studies would be necessary to assess whether actual prices have moved in the direction of welfare optimization. Some work to this effect has been done for the 1960s and

1970s. The studies by Littlechild and Rousseau (1975), Rohlfs (1979), and Marfisi *et al.* (1981) are particularly noteworthy.

Littlechild and Rousseau (1975) constructed a mathematical programming model of a regional telephone carrier and obtained profit- and welfare-maximizing prices for local, intrastate, and interstate trunk calls by time of day. The observed 1967 prices, including price discrimination in favor of large users, are best explained as the result of welfare maximization subject to separate constraints on intrastate and interstate profit levels.

Rohlfs (1979) examined interstate trunk, intrastate trunk, and local rates for the nearly nationwide Bell System. His study, based on extensive estimates of marginal costs, included measures of network externalities. Rohlfs computed the Ramsey prices implied by these data and found that major efficiency gains would be achieved by reducing longer-distance trunk rates.

The Marfisi *et al.* (1981) study is noteworthy for its explicit attention to welfare effects resulting from business firms' demands for telephone service, the presence of competitive suppliers, and redistributive effects by income, age, and urban/rural residence. Its TELPOL model computed the indirect effects of telephone price changes on firms' final prices and profits for eleven income groups, and by age and location. By incorporating cross elasticities of demand between different WATS tariffs, retail MTS rates, and private-line service it allows the user to evaluate nonlinear tariffs.

It is our view that it would be particularly worthwhile to conduct similar studies for the pricing developments of the past ten years.

Peak-load pricing. Trunk calls have been subject to time-of-day and weekend peak-load pricing for many years. For interstate rates AT&T has adjusted both the hours and the percentage discount for the off-peak periods on several occasions. For the most part, intrastate trunk rates follow the same hours, but with varying discount periods. Only a few local rates include peak-load pricing.

Park and Mitchell (1987) investigated the efficiency of peak-load rates for local service with explicit consideration of non-price rationing and constraints on the number of tariff periods. They found that in some cases flat rates, with a zero price per call and some degree of congestion,

are more efficient than time-of-day rates with a feasibly small number
of pricing periods.

Exploiting the very low marginal costs during periods of excess
telecommunications capacity, rate structure innovations have focused
on optional calling plans and other types of off-peak rates to stimulate
increased calling among targeted consumer groups. Such market segmentation may continue to develop alongside standard rate structures
based on peak-load pricing for broad, regular daily and weekly pricing
periods. However, dynamic, real-time pricing based on the actual extent
of excess capacity has yet to emerge.

Local service rates and access rates. In the United States, residential customers' access to the network has largely been bundled with
local calling and included in a single monthly flat-rate price. Increasingly, however, local exchange carriers have been offering unbundled
measured service rates as an option for residential customers, and as a
requirement in many areas for businesses. Access rates vary significantly
by state, and within many states by size of community.

Mitchell (1978) measured the efficiency tradeoff between measured-
rate pricing and the costs of metering and billing. He found that with
US call-ticketing technology (rather than periodic pulses) measured rates
yield greater welfare than flat rates only in exchanges served by electronic switches.

Daly and Mayor (1980) examined the welfare gains achievable by pricing a particular local service – directory assistance, a labor-intensive
service that had long been provided without charge by most local carriers. They established that the distribution of monthly calls for "information" is very skewed, and that, with its significant variable cost
per call, pricing this service would increase welfare and sharply reduce
usage. LECs that use directory-service rates have frequently established
a nonlinear tariff with an allowance of one to three free calls per month.

Park and Mitchell (1989) investigate both efficiency and distributive
effects of various combinations of flat, measured, and lifeline rates for
local service. They confirm that discounted rates that are targeted to
low-income consumers are effective at maintaining penetration in the
face of higher general price levels and are more efficient than an optional
measured-service rate.

US practice has long adopted class-of-service pricing to discriminate between residential and business consumers for network connections and ongoing access. Otherwise, services are available to all consumers at non-discriminatory rates (not withstanding the common practice of referring to high-volume rate structures as "business" tariffs). Moreover, US pricing does not discriminate by type of use, so that a customer may use the same service to transmit both data and voice applications.

On balance, it is our assessment that US practice has been moving toward more efficient rate structures. The basic rebalancing of long-distance and local rates and the establishment of a fixed entry fee for network access is in accord with the structure of telecommunications costs. This change has been facilitated by social tariffs that provide targeted subsidies to marginal consumers. Significant rate reductions have been achieved in the more price-elastic longhaul markets. The distance elements of toll rate structures have adjusted, reflecting the reduced importance of distance in the cost structure of the latest technology. Finally, the growing use of volume discounts and optional rate structures with lower marginal prices at high usage levels enables suppliers to discriminate among customers by reducing prices to users with high elasticities.

12.2.3 The United States as laboratory

Throughout this book we have sought to elucidate the linkages between economic theory and business practice. New theoretical discoveries in Ramsey and nonlinear pricing and the analysis of cross subsidies have been followed in practice by new tariffs and new regulatory tests. Conversely, in the fray of market competition, pricing innovations have arisen that have stimulated theoretical analysis.

The fundamental structural changes in US telecommunications that have been proceeding over the last decade make American experience a unique laboratory for observing the workings of these new telecommunications pricing arrangements. In many instances, economic theory establishes that profit-maximizing and welfare-maximizing behavior leads to similar price structures. Hence, the experience observed in increasingly competitive US markets has broad inferential value for other economies, including those in which publicly directed monopoly supply pertains. Although this experience is most directly relevant in the telecommunications sector, in many instances both theory and practice have a considerably wider compass.

We have, for example, alluded to some differences between pricing in electricity and telecommunications. At the same time, the pricing problems of these two sectors share many technical features, such as high sunk costs, nonstorability of output, and demand relationships that reflect daily load patterns. Comparable similarities to telecommunications emerge in other energy and transportation sectors.

Some of the pricing innovations observed in practice result from American institutional and market conditions, and not all US rate structure developments will be immediately transferable to other economies. In particular:

- Some pricing results may explicitly depend on a rate-of-return-regulated and privately owned monopoly rather than the alternative assumption of a public enterprise.

- US services are often supplied under conditions of excess capacity, whereas networks in other countries are subject to greater congestion at some hours. As a result, US tariff innovations may emphasize demand stimulation rather that rationing of scarce capacity.

- Competitive supply of many network services in the United States may limit the range of theoretical pricing results that can be observed in practice to just the sustainable subset of tariffs. On the other hand, competition may stimulate some tariff innovations.

- The US geographic areas for local calls have fixed boundaries, and customers near a boundary are charged trunk rates to call nearby locations in adjacent communities. This type of inequity leads to a multiplicity of local rate options and large local calling areas. Such complexities do not arise, for example, in countries that have a "sliding" local geographic area.

12.3   Pricing and the future

One of the most obvious opportunities for pricing theory to influence practice arises when a completely new pricing problem emerges, due to either technological or institutional change. The introduction of price caps by the FCC is an example of recent institutional change (see Section 7.3). This decision was preceeded by an intensive theoretical debate about the pricing consequences of price caps as a regulatory mechanism and of specific features of the price cap ruling under discussion.

One important change, both technological and institutional, is the establishment of open network architecture (ONA) arrangements that will unbundle access, transport, switching, and other network components. In Chapter 6 we have alluded to possible ONA pricing implications, including multiproduct nonlinear pricing and vertical pricing issues.

A second, rapidly emerging area is the development of personal communications networks (PCNs) based on lightweight portable pocket-telephone sets. PCN technology portends competitive entry into local exchange markets and raises a host of pricing issues for incumbent carriers and entrants alike.

A third technological advance which is likely to have especially strong pricing consequences will be the introduction of a broadband network. Some of these pricing issues will arise first in the context of introducing a narrowband integrated services digital network (ISDN). ISDN, which will also represent a significant technological advance, will be a much smaller increment in network capacity and occur in an evolutionary manner. In this synthesis we concentrate on broadband pricing as an open problem which could be analyzed with a large number of the theoretical tools developed in this study.

12.3.1 Pricing a new broadband network

Network characteristics. The relevant characteristics of a broadband network appear to be the following. The technology involves strong economies of scale, a long life time and therefore large, lumpy, and sunk investments. We can expect that capital costs will be very high, while variable costs will be virtually zero. Initially, there will be excess capacity at almost all locations where broadband has been introduced. It will, however, be introduced gradually, moving from high-density to low-density areas over time. It will thereby absorb the existing network rather than coexist side by side with it. In terms of outputs, broadband will provide the traditional telecommunications services at enlarged capacity and allow for completely new applications.

Broadband networks raise once again the issues of natural monopoly that seem to have gradually vanished from telecommunications, first in the trunk network and then increasingly in the local network. While we believe that a broadband network will have natural monopoly properties

for subsets of services and for some geographical areas, this will definitely not be true for telecommunications services in general. There is
enough intermodal competition from microwave transmission and other
technologies in place.

Pricing issues. From these characteristics it is clear that a large number of pricing issues have to be solved either simultaneously, or before,
the introduction of broadband.[2] We will pose these issues in the form
of broad questions with some tentative answers.

How should the appropriate budget constraint be set, given that there
is likely to be large initial overcapacity? Even if capital costs are going
to be spread over many years (through low depreciation rates), it may
be impossible to break even on the broadband investment in the initial
years. The question then is whether investment should be deferred until there is sufficient demand that breaking even becomes possible. We
believe that a multiperiod budget constraint is preferable, due to anticipated network growth and due to the presence of multiple network
externalities.

The relevant network externalities manifest themselves in the availability of communication partners for enhanced services along with the
availability of new types of hardware and (increasingly) software as the
basis for the creation of these enhanced services. In this connection it
may be worth considering whether there are advantages from vertical
integration by the broadband network provider, or if there are opportunities and justifications for the network provider to collect fees from the
suppliers of hardware, software, and value-added services. Conversely,
one has to consider the unbundling of services provided by the network
supplier in the form of ONA. It is here that the problems of ONA pricing
would have to be integrated with the problems of broadband pricing.

The fact that a service cannot initially break even is no clear indication
that its introduction should be deferred. As should have become clear
from our discussion of externality pricing in Chapters 4–5, it may be difficult to reach a critical mass of network subscribers. Initial deficits may
be the appropriate way to achieve that, although such deficits would also
increase the investment risk in view of continued technological change.
As has become evident from the introduction of cellular telephone serv-

---

[2]Levin (1988) raised some of the issues discussed in the following paragraphs.

ice, the telecommunications carrier can expect to be able to finance these deficits in the capital market. Such financing would, however, become harder if regulators imposed depreciation rules and fully distributed-cost pricing rules that would prevent the network supplier from recovering investment costs over time.

Given that there should be a multiperiod budget constraint, how should the burden of capital costs be spread over consumers of existing and new services? In answering this question one could bring to bear a plethora of insights from our theory chapters. Since this is a task for future research, we can only raise the issues rather than give the answers. We proceed by taking up the various objectives and discussing their relevance in the current context.

In many instances the pricing of new services does not raise severe fairness problems, because usually all consumers are made better off. However, this is unlikely to hold for broadband because the old network will gradually be supplanted, so that the old services will also be supplied in the new network. This raises issues of status quo fairness, cross subsidization, anonymous equity, etc. We suggest that any pricing scheme proposed for broadband be checked against these concepts. This is important, because consumers of the old services could, in principle, continue to be served by the old network. However, do they currently pay their stand-alone costs? Given that incremental costs of additional traffic under the broadband network would be close to zero, should consumers simply continue to pay what they paid before? If so, how should this price be adjusted over time? This begs questions for the basis of current pricing and its further justification. In particular, one might want to consider the effects of broadband as a network parallel to the existing one. In this case, high-use customers would be the first to join the broadband network, bypassing the old network and necessitating price increases for the remaining customers. On the other hand, with only the broadband network in place incentives and opportunities may remain for some customers to bypass the (broadband) network, by taking cheaper low-quality alternatives.

Under the efficiency goal, it becomes most important initially that capacity utilization be increased. To that end, peak-load pricing techniques discussed in Chapter 4 deserve attention. Although peak-load pricing may be more of an issue in the later stages of broadband penetration, the availability of new techniques, for instance, of priority pricing may allow one to tailor better the initial capacity of the broadband network to demand. Linear Ramsey prices and constrained optimal two-part tariffs are likely to be somewhat more promising initially than peak-load pricing. Given that marginal costs of usage are close to zero, however, more sophisticated nonlinear pricing schemes, with very low marginal prices, will have to be considered. This would place the burden of raising the necessary funds for meeting the (intertemporal) budget constraint on the inframarginal price. The curvature of the nonlinear outlay function will be restricted by the (legal) possibility for resale. This possibility gives increased importance to club-related pricing through various aggregators. Hence, it can be expected that network providers will sell a smaller fraction of their services directly to final consumers.

The costs of the broadband network provider change with the expansion of the network as it penetrates the market, but they do not change with an increase of usage. As a consequence, the commodity that should be priced becomes a decision variable. From a cost point-of-view the unit of output becomes irrelevant. What matters most is its relationship to the consumer's willingness-to-pay. Pricing by type of service may be difficult because it cannot be monitored by the network supplier. However, there appear to be other opportunities to develop rate elements based on such factors as the occupancy of the data frame, the type of routing and switching, and additional processing provided by the network (Levin, 1988).

Besides price structures at any point in time, it is the intertemporal trajectory of prices that makes broadband pricing a challenging theoretical problem. Here we can apply the lessons from intertemporal pricing models such as those by Faulhaber and Boyd (1989), Salant and Woroch (1989), and Dhebar and Oren (1985a, 1985b). We have sketched a simple approach for a one-time investment at the end of Section 4.7.3. This would have to be enhanced by incorporating aspects of gradual market penetration, intermodal competition, and consumption externalities − something we hope to do in the future. Gradual penetration raises issues such as: Should prices differ at any point in time for old and new subscribers of the network? Also, we would expect that, due to the network externality effect, prices could be increased over time. In contrast, some expect prices to fall because an increase of penetration means reaching out for subscribers with lower willingness-to-pay (Levin, 1988).

12.3.2   Institutional factors.

In addition to these theoretical insights, we can bring to bear lessons from US pricing practice that relate to institutional factors:

- Innovations in the normative theory of tariffs are driven by economy-wide considerations of economic welfare, whereas implementation decisions tend to be dominated by political sensitivity to individual interest groups (as treated in the positive economic theory of tariffs, e.g., Peltzman, 1976). We would expect that Pareto-improving tariffs are politically easier to implement than are tariffs that represent merely *potential* Pareto improvements. Applied to broadband this means that existing tariffs may have to continue as an option.

- We also expect that tariff innovations that would lead to major setbacks for small interest groups would either be watered down or would be accompanied by compensating tariff changes elsewhere. This calls for consideration of "basic" lifeline programs under broadband.

- We expect that the type of regulation will affect the pace and direction of implementable tariff innovations. For example, rate-of-return regulation *versus* price caps can influence the application of peak-load pricing and of Ramsey pricing.

- Implementation could depend on the simplicity and intuitive rationale of a tariff innovation. For example, nonlinear tariffs for multiple commodities are quite complicated, while the principles of peak-load pricing are simple. Ramsey prices rank in between.

The rapid pace of technological advance in telecommunications will surely continue. Now coming into view are the opening of the telephone network architecture to new suppliers, personal portable telephones, and broadband networks of great capacity and versatility. Yet fairness and efficiency will remain the fundamental goals challenging researchers and practitioners as they seek to apply pricing tools to these and still unforeseen developments. The questions raised here show that the field is ripe for further innovations in both the theory and practice of telecommunications pricing.

Appendix

US telephone price indexes

There are two primary sources of publicly available information regarding trends in the prices for US telecommunications services: the Bureau of Labor Statistics (BLS) telephone indexes, and the tariff filings associated with the price cap regulation of AT&T's long-distance telephone services, which we have already described in Section 7.3. In this appendix we first examine the BLS indexes[1] and then compare those data with the AT&T indexes. More technical details of the AT&T price cap formulas follow in the final section.

A.1 Bureau of Labor Statistics (BLS) price indexes

A.1.1 Price indexes and US experience

The United States government's Bureau of Labor Statistics (BLS) compiles statistics on the overall economy, with numerous subindexes devoted to specific sectors. The BLS maintains two different indexes which include price changes in domestic telecommunications services. The first is the Consumer Price Index (CPI), which reports changes in the prices of retail goods and services purchased by the typical consumer; the second is the Producer Price Index (PPI) which tracks trends in firms' sales prices. Both are chained Laspeyres indices that are infrequently reweighted; thus, they overstate the inflation which would be estimated by an ideal price index. Recent trends in these indexes are shown in Figure A.1.

Both indexes separate local and toll telephone services. In the United States, the domestic market is geographically divided into Local Access Transport Areas (LATAs) which in most cases correspond to metropolitan areas. With few exceptions, LATAs do not cross state lines. Local and intraLATA calls are handled by the Local Exchange Carrier (LEC),

---

[1] The BLS section is based on Lande and Wynns (1987).

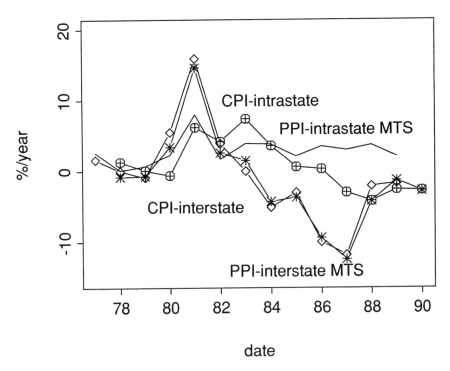

Figure A.1
Interstate and state prices

either a Bell Operating Company or an indepedent telephone company. Toll calls between LATAs may be either interstate or intrastate. Toll calls are originated and terminated in LATAs by the LECs over access circuits leased by the toll carrier. Since the divestiture of AT&T in 1984, the interLATA toll market has become increasingly competitive. AT&T is regulated as the dominant carrier in this market.

Differences in the level of competition, and between state and federal regulations, mean that the markets for local, intrastate, and interstate toll services are each distinct markets, with separate pricing structures. Since a significant share of toll revenues are used to pay for local access facilities, changes in local regulation (e.g., cost allocation decisions) can have significant exogenous effects on the toll rates charged by individual companies.

International calling is proportionately less important in the United States than it is in European markets. International rates are affected by exchange agreements between domestic US interexchange carriers and (in most cases) foreign Postal, Telephone, and Telegraph (PTT) monopolies.

A.1.2   How are the indexes calculated?

Consumer price index (CPI).   The CPI reports changes in the purchase price for a market basket chosen to reflect the consumption expenditures of a typical US household. It is a price index only for residential services, which estimates what consumers actually pay. The composition of the market basket is determined in the base year; changes in the cost of purchasing that basket of services are reported monthly.

The composition of the market basket is based on periodic Consumer Expenditure Surveys (CES). There are seven major categories of expenditures. Telephone services are included within the category of "fuel and other utility" expenditures. The expenditure share in the base year for each of the telephone categories is used for weighting in the construction of composite indexes.[2] Prior to 1987, the market basket was based on 1972-3 expenditure weights; thereafter, 1983-4 weights have been used. When the weights change, the BLS does not restate the earlier indexes according to the new weights; the new weights are used only prospectively.

The CPI tracks three separate categories of telephone service prices, shown in Figure A.2:

- Local Services (27011)

- Intrastate Toll (27051)

- Interstate Toll (27061)

The local service (27011) price index is based on a sampling of rates for urban areas.[3] Data are provided by the LECs who are responsible for maintaining the local access facilities (i.e., local loops and network

---

[2]For example, for construction of the "fuel and other utility" subindex and the overall CPI index.

[3]Until 1986, a panel of 85 cities was used. They are defined as Standard Metropolitan Statistical Areas (SMSA) which include over 81 percent of total US population. In January 1987, the panel was reselected and the total number of cities expanded to 91.

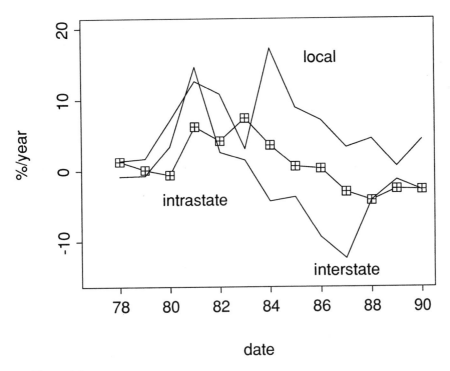

Figure A.2
CPI price indexes

facilities used to provide local services and access to the interexchange carriers). BLS collects the rates for a selection of services in two clusters: main station charges[4] and other local charges.[5] The composite local service index is constructed by weighting the particular services according to LEC-reported revenue shares. The basket of services is repriced each month. The CPI includes both monthly recurring and one-time charges.

Prices for intrastate (27051) and interstate (27061) toll calls are based on a representative sample of actual calling data provided by the LECs

[4] These include cost of telephone sets and the basic service charge for local telephone service. In addition, Subscriber Line Charges, taxes, etc. are included.
[5] These include charges for special options and installation.

and AT&T.[6] The sample contains the price for each call identified by city of origination, city of termination, time of day, duration, and the day of the week. Calls in the five largest cities are repriced monthly, while the remaining cities are divided into two groups which are sampled on alternating months. As a result changes in toll prices can take two months to be fully reflected in the CPI.

The entire sample of price sources for telephone services was reselected in 1986-7, both with respect to which companies are reporting and which services/calls are included. This new sample was first used in the January 1987 indexes. In the future, one-fifth of the toll sample will be reselected each year and the entire local sample will be reselected every five years.

Producer price index (PPI). The PPI reports selling prices for a representative sample of firms.[7] The PPI is a revenue price index that measures what firms charge (which may differ from what consumers pay). As with the CPI, a base year basket of services is repriced monthly to determine the change in the price index. The PPI tracks telephone services separately and does not include these in the composite PPI index. The PPI reports two separate telephone indexes: Local Service (4811-1) and Toll Service (4811-2). Each of these is further subdivided into a number of component indexes, including separate indexes for residential and commercial services. These are combined to form overall indexes using the total value of base year service revenues as weights.

Local services, based on nineteen companies,[8] are reported in four separate categories:

1 Residential Recurring (4811-111)

2 Business Recurring (4811-112)

3 Optional Additional Service (4811-113)

4 Coin (4811-114)

Toll Service, shown in Figure A.3, is subdivided into four categories:

---

[6]The other interexchange carriers were first included in the sample of interstate toll calling in 1987.

[7]Only interindustry sales are reported; intraindustry sales are excluded.

[8]If a LEC is active in more than one state which was sampled, then it is included as more than one company in the sample. For coin-operated telephone services only nine companies were sampled.

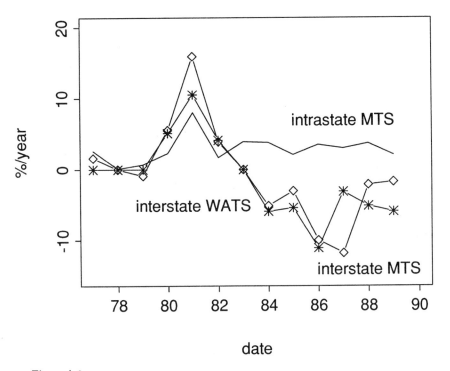

Figure A.3
MTS and WATS prices

1 Intrastate Message Telephone Service (MTS) (4811-211)

2 Interstate MTS (4811-212) [9]

3 International MTS (4811-213)

4 Wide Area Telephone Service (WATS) (4811-214), with two subindices:

- Intrastate WATS (4811-214-11)
- Interstate WATS (4811-214-12)

[9] The PPI interstate toll index is based on AT&T data. BLS is currently updating the sampling weights. It is no longer reported by the FCC in its summary statistics.

Since 1987, the base year for all but WATS services was 1972; since 1987, the indexes are based on 1982 sample data, except that the WATS sample was based on 1975 data. BLS anticipates updating the weights to 1987 in January 1991. Component indexes are constructed from a census of all services provided in the base year and then weighted by revenue. For example, interstate MTS rates are computed using information for all rate classes and mileage bands and then combining these using revenue shares. The PPI, as a revenue index, excludes nonrecurring charges (e.g., installation), special fees (e.g., subscriber line charges), and taxes. This is different from the CPI, which is a purchase price index that includes these charges.

The BLS also reports a Private Line index in the PPI, but the sample has not kept pace with the dramatic explosion of new services and pricing in this market segment. The FCC no longer includes this index in its summary reports.

A.1.3 Analysis and comparison of the CPI and PPI

The CPI and PPI share important similarities:

- Both indexes are Laspeyres indexes, which measure the change in prices in a base year basket of services. Composite indexes use base year revenue/expenditure shares for weights.

- Both indexes rely on a sampling of data provided by LECs and AT&T.

- Both indexes are broad, national indexes which average across states and firms. They average across rate classes which vary by origination, destination, distance, duration, time of day and day of week. They also may vary by customer calling volume (e.g., when there are block calling discounts).

- Both indexes report separate subindexes for local telephone service, intrastate, and interstate toll services.

- Through 1986, both use base year baskets from the early 1970s (before AT&T's 1984 divestiture radically changed the industry's structure).

However, in other respects the two indexes have major differences, which are summarized in Table A.1.

Table A.1
Differences between CPI and PPI telephone indexes

CPI	PPI
Index measures prices paid by urban residential consumers.	Index measures prices charged by providers of telephone services. Separate subindexes report rates charged residential and business customers.
Sample consists of specific items as they might appear on the customer bill (e.g., a 5 minute call from New York to Los Angeles at 3 p.m. Saturday). The selection of these reflects base period usage.	Sample consists of all rate classes, weighted by the base period usage.
Refunds appear in the month that they occur.	Previous data are revised to reflect impact of refunds on month when originally collected.
Local service includes equipment, installation, and maintenance charges.	Local service is based on monthly recurring charges only. Excludes equipment, installation, and maintenance charges.
Excludes coin telephone usage.	Includes coin telephone usage.
Includes Subscriber Line Charges.	Prior to 1987, Subscriber Line Charges excluded.
Includes surcharges and excise taxes	Excludes surcharges and excise taxes.
Prices for local services are updated monthly (1/3rd at start, middle, and end of each month). Half of toll prices for smaller cities are updated in alternating months, so changes can be spread over two months.	Prices are updated monthly, using mid-month prices. Toll price changes are reflected in a single month.

SOURCE: Lande and Wynns (1987), Table 1.1, p. 9.

Table A.2
Consumer Price Index data

Date (December)	All goods & Services	All telephone Services	Interstate local services (27011)	Toll service (27061)
1970	39.8	59.6		
1971	41.1	62.7		
1972	42.5	65.9		
1973	46.2	69.0		
1974	51.9	69.9		
1975	55.5	73.8		
1976	58.2	75.3		
1977	62.1	75.7	69.2	83.4
1978	67.7	76.4	70.2	82.7
1979	76.7	76.9	71.4	82.1
1980	86.3	80.4	76.4	84.9
1981	94.0	89.8	86.0	97.3
1982	97.6	96.3	95.3	99.8
1983	101.3	99.8	98.3	101.3
1984	105.3	109.0	115.2	96.9
1985	109.3	114.1	125.5	93.3
1986	110.5	117.2	134.4	84.5
1987	115.4	115.7	138.9	74.0
1988	120.5	117.2	145.2	70.9
1989	126.1	116.9	146.0	70.0
1990	133.8	116.4	147.5	67.4

Source: Bureau of Labor Statistices data as provided by James
Lande, Common Carrier Bureau, Federal Communications Commission.

In spite of the differences, Lande and Wynns (1987) found that the
CPI and PPI series correlate quite well. This correlation is stronger
when the indexes are corrected to reflect known differences. Neither
index is able to track the effects of the AT&T divestiture because of
accounting changes and other one-time-only adjustments which occurred
at divestiture. The imposition of Subscriber Line Charges (SLC) [10] after
1984 and the detariffing of Customer Premise Equipment (CPE)[11] are

[10] SLCs are federally mandated fixed monthly charges designed to assign an increasing
portion of Nontraffic Sensitive (NTS) local loop costs to residential subscribers. In the
past, these costs had been covered largely by access charges paid by the interexchange
carriers. See the discussion of SLCs in Chapter 11.
[11] Prior to divesture, most households leased telephone equipment from AT&T. These
lease expenditures for CPE are included in the CPI but excluded from the PPI. In
1983/4, the FCC detariffed CPE and much of the equipment was sold in-place, but
the market basket still reflected 1973/4 pre-divestiture leasing trends. The sale of
this equipment produced a jump in the index in 1983/4 and the increase in AT&T's

Table A.3
Producer Price Index data

Date (December)	Local services 4811-1	Local residential services 4811-111	Local business services 4811-112	Local optional additional usage 4811-113
1971		97.70		
1972		100.7	100.9	
1973		106.7	107.3	
1974		109.7	113.4	
1975		116.2	120.5	
1976		119.6	124.5	
1977		120.5	123.4	
1978		124.2	128.8	
1979		126.2	131.6	
1980		135.1	139.2	
1981		156.2	161.0	
1982		170.2	170.3	
1983	164.8	170.6	174.1	127.0
1984	187.6	188.4	216.0	122.5
1985	204.8	211.7	228.0	130.2
1986	216.8	230.5	233.6	131.5
1987	219.3	236.6	231.8	127.7
1988	226.4	247.4	233.0	127.7
1989	229.4	252.2	234.5	127.5
1990	231.4	256.0	234.6	126.1

Source: Bureau of Labor Statistices data as provided by James Lande, Common Carrier Bureau, Federal Communications Commission.

the two most important examples.

Both indexes reflect broad averages that are appropriate for tracking general trends in the prices for telecommunications services, but do not readily yield information on how relative prices for different services and the introduction of new services have changed the industry. Although total consumption of telecommunications services has grown substantially, they have remained a fairly constant share of total household expenditures, averaging less than 2 percent per year.[12] Telecommunication prices have tended to grow more slowly than overall prices, but

lease rates in 1986 increased the CPI still further. Lande and Wynns (1987) estimate that the change in lease rates increased the overall CPI for telephone services by 1.7 percent in 1986 (Lande and Wynns, Appendix I, p. 23).

[12]Telecommunications services represented 1.6 percent of total household expenditures included in the CPI in both 1977 and 1986. See Lande and Wynns (1987), Table 2.1, p. 30.

Producer Price Index data, cont.

Date (December)	Toll service 4811-2	Intrastate MTS 4811-211	Interstate MTS 4811-212	International MTS 4811-213
1972	100.7	101.8	100.0	99.4
1973	104.3	106.3	103.1	99.4
1974	105.1	109.1	102.9	99.4
1975	114.8	119.3	113.5	98.3
1976	122.0	128.6	120.0	100.5
1977	124.3	132.0	121.9	98.7
1978	123.9	132.1	121.9	84.0
1979	123.3	131.2	120.8	91.4
1980	128.3	134.2	127.4	96.2
1981	142.1	144.9	147.7	83.5
1982	147.5	147.4	153.4	92.3
1983	149.8	153.2	153.4	92.7
1984	147.4	159.0	145.6	86.8
1985	146.2	162.4	141.3	86.5
1986	136.0	156.7	127.1	84.1
1987	125.2	152.0	112.1	83.8
1988	122.3	146.3	109.7	83.8
1989	122.2	149.3	107.8	83.8
1990	120.0	142.8	107.7	83.4

have been more volatile. Interstate toll rates have been more volatile than intrastate toll rates.

Examination of the component indexes reflects the dramatic readjustment in relative rates for local and toll services. For the past several decades, technological innovation has been more rapid in telecommunications than in the economy as a whole. The FCC reviewed a number of studies and determined in its Price Cap order that AT&T has experienced between 2-3 percent per year faster productivity growth than the overall economy.[13]

Under the terms of pre-divestiture regulation, toll revenues were shifted to local services to cover the relatively higher local transport costs. Beginning before divestiture (in anticipation thereof) local rates rose relative to toll rates, reflecting the reallocation of costs. This trend accelerated after 1985 with the imposition of FCC-mandated Subscriber Line Charges (SLCs).[14] Since future increases in the SLC are not antic-

[13]See Federal Communications Commission (1989), pp. 103-30 and section A.2 below.

[14]The SLC rose from $1.00 per residential subscriber in mid-1985 to the present maximum value of $3.50.

Producer Price Index data, cont.

Date (Dec.)	WATS 4811-214	Interstate WATS 4811-214-11	Intrastate WATS 4811-214-12	Interstate private line 4811-311
1971				
1972		100.0		100.1
1973		102.0		99.6
1974		100.3		99.5
1975		102.9		107.0
1976		105.1		108.3
1977		105.1		108.6
1978		105.1		108.6
1979		105.1		108.3
1980		110.5		110.8
1981		122.1		154.5
1982		127.1		156.9
1983	133.7	127.1	151.1	158.4
1984	127.8	119.6	149.6	163.1
1985	123.3	113.1	150.3	168.3
1986	113.3	100.6	146.9	
1987	110.1	97.5	143.4	
1988	102.7	92.5	129.7	
1989	98.8	87.0	130.1	
1990	97.8	87.0	126.1	

ipated, toll rates will decline less rapidly relative to local rates. Overall telephone rates should increase less rapidly than overall inflation because of higher than average expected productivity increases.

Until 1987, the interstate toll component of the CPI was based on AT&T data. Since then the sample has included other interexchange carriers. However, the PPI is still based only on AT&T data.[15] In 1980, AT&T supplied 95 percent of the interstate toll market; by 1986, its share had fallen to 77 percent.[16] Exclusion of other carriers which generally have lower rates leads to a higher index.

Neither the BLS PPI nor the CPI indexes provide much insight into the plethora of new tariff offerings which have emerged since divestiture in 1984. These have been especially important with large commercial customers. New centrex services, digital voice, and data services such

[15] The samples on which the CPI is based were reselected in 1986-7. The CES for 1982-4 provided new expenditure share data. These new weights and new samples were first used in January 1987. The PPI resampled but has not finished developing new weights and so the indexes have not been updated yet to reflect new weights.
[16] See Perl (1988), p. 1.

Table A.4
Interstate and state share of total minutes

Date	Subscriber line usage		
	Total minutes	Interstate share	State share
1980	1,650,394	7.6%	7.8%
1981	1,696,565	7.9%	8.1%
1982	1,751,114	8.1%	8.2%
1983	1,808,023	8.3%	8.3%
1984	1,894,437	9.2%	9.1%
1985	1,977,159	10.6%	9.6%
1986	2,019,982	11.0%	9.9%
1987	2,069,860	11.9%	10.3%
1988	2,185,955	12.7%	10.4%
Growth Rate			
1980 to 1988	3.6%	10.4%	7.4%

Note: All minutes are Tier1A minutes. A Tier 1 carrier is a local exchange carrier that has $100 million or more annually in rev-
enue from regulated telecommunications services for five consecutive
years. Tier 1A minutes are from companies for which data was available for all years. Tier1A represent 94% of the total Subscriber Line
Usage minutes.

Source: Federal-State Joint Board,Monitoring Report, (CC Docket
No. 80-286,July 1990).

as virtual private network services, and special customer-specific tariffs
are not reflected in the BLS statistics.

The 1972 weights which were used until 1987 in the CPI did not
account for the dramatic increase in toll calling which accompanied the
rebalancing of toll and local rates discussed above.[17] An index based on
current market weights would therefore have shown lower average prices
during the period. Toll and special commercial services have become
proportionately more important since 1984, and so the BLS indexes
weights which are based on 1984 data continue to lag current trends.
(See Table A.4 for data on minutes by type of traffic.)

A.2   AT&T price cap indexes

In Section 7.3 we investigated the introduction of price caps for AT&T's
major services as a regulatory innovation affecting US pricing practice.

[17]According to one estimate, the decline in toll rates between 1984 and 1987, "stimulates 19.8 billion minutes of additional calling" (Perl, 1988) p. 10.

Table A.5
Consumer Price Index: annual growth rates (percent)

Period	All goods & services	All telephone services	Local services	Interstate toll service	Intrastate toll service
'76–'77	6.7	0.5			
'77–'78	9.0	0.9	1.4	-0.8	1.3
'78–'79	13.3	0.7	1.7	-0.7	0.1
'79–'80	12.5	4.6	7.0	3.4	-0.6
'80–'81	8.9	11.7	12.6	14.6	6.2
'81–'82	3.8	7.2	10.8	2.6	4.2
'82–'83	3.8	3.6	3.1	1.5	7.4
'83–'84	3.9	9.2	17.2	-4.3	3.6
'84–'85	3.8	4.7	8.9	-3.7	0.6
'85–'86	1.1	2.7	7.1	-9.4	0.3
'86–'87	4.4	-1.3	3.3	-12.4	-3.0
'87–'88	4.4	1.3	4.5	-4.2	-4.2
'88–'89	4.6	-0.3	0.6	-1.3	-2.6
'89–Jun '90	6.1	1.9	4.4	-2.8	-2.7
'77–Jun '90	6.1	3.6	6.3	-1.5	0.9
'79–'83	7.2	6.7	8.3	5.4	4.2
'84–Jun '90	3.9	1.5	4.8	-6.0	-1.9

Note: Growth rates are annualized. Growth rates are for December to December, except as noted for December 1989 to June 1990.

Source: Bureau of Labor Statistices data as provided by James Lande, Common Carrier Bureau, Federal Communications Commission, August 1990.

Here we compare the price indexes generated by price caps in terms of other indexes of telecommunications prices.

A.2.1   Comparison with British Telecom price index

The United Kingdom was the first to institute price cap regulation of its monopoly telephone company, British Telecom. The UK's $RPI - X$ approach helped inspire the move towards price cap regulation in the United States; but the British approach is somewhat different.

The $RPI - X$ approach uses the "Retail Price Index" to track general inflation, and reduces this to account for expected productivity growth. This is similar to the AT&T price cap regulation. The two approaches differ in three major respects:

1 British Telecom is both a local and long-distance telephone company.

Table A.6
Producer Price Index: annual growth rates (percent)

Period	Local services 4811-1	Local residential services 4811-111	Local business service 4811-112	Local optional services 4811-113	Local coin service 4811-114
'76–'77		0.8	-0.9		
'77–'78		3.1	4.4		
'78–'79		1.6	2.2		
'79–'80		7.1	5.8		
'80–'81		15.6	15.7		
'81–'82		9.0	5.8		
'82–'83		0.2	2.2		
'83–'84	13.8	10.4	24.1	-3.5	38.3
'84–'85	9.2	12.4	5.6	6.3	2.8
'85–'86	5.9	8.9	2.5	1.0	0.5
'86–'87	1.2	2.6	-0.8	-2.9	-0.2
'87–'88	3.2	4.6	0.5	0.0	5.0
'88–'89	1.3	1.9	0.6	-0.2	0.2
'89–Jun '90	0.0	0.5	-0.3	-2.2	0.0
'77–Jun '90	n/a	6.1	5.3	n/a	n/a
'79–'83	n/a	7.8	7.2	n/a	n/a
'84–Jun '90	3.7	5.5	1.5	0.5	1.5

2 The $RPI-X$ formula has two service-specific baskets (the second one for private lines was added in 1989).

3 Other services are unregulated.

This allows a greater degree of pricing flexibility under the $RPI-X$ approach than under the AT&T price cap approach. Rates across services can be rebalanced more easily.

A.2.2   Comparison with BLS price indexes

We also can compare the AT&T price cap indexes with the BLS CPI and PPI indexes, although there are a number of important differences. The AT&T index is company-specific, but it is comprehensive for the services that are included. In contrast, the BLS indexes are industry-wide and are based on sampled data. The weights used to construct composite BLS indexes are updated relatively infrequently. This means that pricing innovations are reflected in the BLS indexes only with a lag; whereas, the AT&T price cap indexes will facilitate more current tracking. However, the AT&T indexes only cover long-distance services; whereas the BLS

Producer Price Index: Annual growth rates (percent), cont.

Period	Toll service 4811-2	Intrastate MTS 4811-211	Interstate MTS 4811-212	International MTS 4811-213
'76–'77	1.9	2.6	1.6	-1.8
'77–'78	-0.3	0.1	0.0	-14.9
'78–'79	-0.5	0.7	-0.9	8.8
'79–'80	4.1	2.3	5.5	5.3
'80–'81	10.8	8.0	15.9	-13.2
'81–'82	3.8	1.7	3.9	10.5
'82–'83	1.6	3.9	0.0	0.4
'83–'84	-1.6	3.8	-5.1	-6.4
'84–'85	-0.8	2.1	-3.0	-0.3
'85–'86	-7.0	3.5	-10.0	-2.8
'86–'87	-7.9	3.0	-11.8	-0.4
'87–'88	-2.3	3.7	-2.1	0.0
'88–'89	-0.1	2.1	-1.7	0.0
'89–Jun '90	-1.8	4.0	0.2	-1.0
'77–Jun '90	-0.2	0.8	-1.0	-1.3
'79–'83	5.0	4.0	6.2	0.4
'84–Jun '90	-3.5	-1.5	-5.3	-0.7

indexes also cover local telephone services. The supporting information which is included in AT&T's price cap tariff filings is not standardized, and so the information may vary year-to-year.[18]

Table 7.9 summarizes AT&T price cap index experience, and includes BLS indexes (from Tables A.2 and A.3) to facilitate comparisons. Table A.7 provides a side-by-side comparison of AT&T and BLS data and illustrates the difficulties of comparing these indexes directly.

AT&T's Basket #1 API may be compared with the CPI's and PPI's interstate toll indexes (series #28061 and series 4811-212, respectively). Since January 1987, the CPI indexes have included AT&T's long-distance competitors, the other interexchange carriers; but the PPI indexes are still being updated. Since AT&T is still the dominant carrier its prices should dominate movements in the BLS indexes. However, the lag in adjusting weights in the BLS indexes causes these indexes to understate actual decline in MTS toll rates. Furthermore, since the CPI index is based on a representative sample of actual calls, it does not reflect volume discounts which are associated with a consumer's total toll

---

[18]For example, in the first annual filing, AT&T reported service specific revenue shares; whereas in the second annual filing, AT&T only reported total service revenues for each basket.

Producer Price Index: annual growth rates (percent), cont.

Period	WATS 4811-214	Interstate WATS 4811-214-11	Intrastate WATS 4811-214-12
'76–'77		0.0	
'77–'78		0.0	
'78–'79		0.0	
'79–'80		5.1	
'80–'81		10.5	
'81–'82		4.1	
'82–'83		0.0	
'83–'84	-4.4	-5.9	-1.0
'84–'85	-3.5	-5.4	0.5
'85–'86	-8.1	-11.1	-2.3
'86–'87	-2.8	-3.1	-2.4
'87–'88	-6.7	-5.1	-9.6
'88–'89	-3.8	-5.9	0.3
'89–Jun '90	-0.6	0.0	-2.1
'77–Jun '90	n/a	-1.5	n/a
'79–'83	n/a	4.9	n/a
'84–Jun '90	-4.6	-5.6	-2.7

usage. The AT&T indexes reflect the growth in evening and night traffic and the introduction of new volume discount services such as the Reach Out America program, which are not captured by the BLS indexes.

A.3   AT&T price cap formulas

This section is based on information contained in the FCC's 1989 *Report and Order*.[19] Page references are to the relevant sections in that document.[20]

A.3.1   Price cap index (PCI) formula

$$PCI_t = PCI_{t-1}[1 + w(\text{GNP-PI} - X) + dY/R + dZ/R],$$

where:

$PCI_t =$ price cap

[19] See FCC (March 16, 1989).
[20] FCC (1989), pp. 155-6.

Table A.7
Changes in AT&T price cap indexes and BLS indexes, July 1988 to July 1989

AT&T		BLS indexes	
Residential Services			
Residential Only	-3.7%	CPI-Interstate Toll	-1.2%
		CPI-Intrastate Toll	-2.2%
		PPI-Interstate Toll	-0.1%
		PPI-Intrastate Toll	-4.8%
(largest Basket #1 reductions)			
Domestic Evening MTS	-7.6%		
Reach Out America	-7.1%		
Commercial Services			
Pro WATS	-5.0%	PPI-Overall WATS	-0.8%
AT&T WATS	-0.1%	PPI-Interstate WATS	0.0%
Megacom	-4.4%	PPI-Intrastate WATS	-2.4%
International Services			
International MTS	-3.5%	PPI-International MTS	-0.5%

Sources: For AT&T data: 7/1/89 data, see AT&T Revised Tariff Submittal No. 1618
Exhibit #4. For 7/1/90 data, see Transmittal No. 2396, Exhibit #5.
For CPI and PPI Price Index Data: Bureau of Labor Statistics data provided by
James Lande, Common Carrier Bureau, FCC, August 1990. CPI/PPI Growth rates
are for June 1989 to June 1990.

$R =$ Base period quantity of rate element i times its price when PCI_{t-1} computed.

$w =$ $\left[R - \left[\begin{array}{c}\text{access rates in} \\ \text{effect at } t-1\end{array} \times \begin{array}{c}\text{base period} \\ \text{demand}\end{array}\right] + dZ\right] \Big/ R$

w reflects the share of revenue (base period quantities priced at $t-1$) for which changes are not due to changes in access rates. Exogenous cost changes are included so that the inflation adjustment is applied to these.

GNP-PI =   Percent change in Gross National Product Price Index, the general fixed-weighted price index published by the US Department of Commerce's Bureau of Economic Analysis. Included annually in PCI on July 1. Percentage change calculated from fourth quarters of the current and preceeding years. Uses index published seventy-five days after relevant quarter.

$X =$ Productivity factor adjustment, 3 percent, which includes 0.5 percent "Consumer Productivity Dividend" added to encourage pass through of additional productivity gains expected to occur.

$$dY = \left[\begin{array}{ccc} \text{New access} & - & \text{Prior period} \\ \text{rate} & & \text{access rate} \end{array} \right] \times \begin{array}{c} \text{base period} \\ \text{demand} \end{array}$$

$dZ =$ Dollar effect of current regulatory changes when compared to regulations in effect when PCI_{t-1} computed, measured at base period level of operations.

Discussion of Key Terms

GNP-PI

The Gross National Product Price Index (GNP-PI) is used as a measure of general inflation, a broadly based index that reflects investment good prices as well as final goods prices (the CPI tracks only final goods). There was no obvious way to choose amongst the PPI subindexes, which in any case only track changes in manufactured goods and neglect retail trade, construction, services, etc. Certain parties argued for other measures of inflation. For example, BellSouth argued that the GNP-PI contains many elements which are not relevant for carriers and preferred the CPI which tracks labor contracts (and grows faster than GNP-PI). The NTIA argued for use of the "implicit GNP deflator" since it correlated well with pre-divestiture cost index data. Still others argued for some industry-specific index.

Productivity

The price index is adjusted downward to account for greater technological progress in telecommunications than experienced by the economy as a whole. There was discussion of using the BLS productivity index, but the FCC felt it was not specific enough and again faced the difficulty of choosing amongst subindexes. The FCC examined a number of independent studies of historical rates of productivity in telecommunications *vis-à-vis* all US industry and selected 2.5 percent per year as representative.

Consumer Productivity Dividend (CPD)
The GNP-PI is reduced by an additional 0.5 percent as a Consumer Productivity Dividend. This CPD guarantees that inflation adjusted rate
reductions will exceed historical levels in this new regulatory regime.

Exogenous Costs
The PCI is adjusted to account for costs which change due to changes
in laws, regulations, or rules beyond a carrier's control. These include
changes in access charges paid by AT&T; changes in expense levels due
to the expiration of current amortization programs; and changes due
to Part 36 of the FCC's rules (the Jurisdictional Separations Manual).
Depreciation changes are not considered exogenous costs. The Commission regards them as under the carrier's control since the carrier decides
when to replace physical plant. There is a required downward adjustment to reflect expiration of current amortization programs to correct
reserve imbalances, however.

The FCC rejected US West's suggestion that price caps be adjusted
downward to reflect bypass savings since the FCC does not believe
AT&T could successfully manipulate the access charge portion of the
price cap.

A.3.2   Operation of the price cap

AT&T price caps will be adjusted on an annual basis, with the exception of FCC-mandated Subscriber Line Charge (SLC) increases. These
price cap changes will become effective on the dates that scheduled SLC
increases become effective.

The GNP-PI$-X$ component is the same across all baskets. The dY
and dZ components will vary.

Exogenous nontraffic-sensitive access costs must be allocated across market baskets based on the proportion of total base period nontraffic-
sensitive minutes of access (both originating and terminating) associated
with each basket. Allocation of change in traffic-sensitive access costs is
based on each basket's base period share of traffic-sensitive minutes.

The dZ costs must be allocated on a "cost causative basis" (p. 157).

A.3.3 Baskets and bands

(i). *Residential and small business basket* is divided into six narrow service categories:

1 domestic day

2 domestic evening

3 domestic night/weekend

4 international MTS

5 operator and credit card services

6 Reach Out America.

AT&T forfeits streamlined treatment if it raises the rates of Domestic evening or Domestic night/weekend by more than 4 percent or any other service category in the basket by more than 5 percent relative to the change in the basket's PCI. In addition, average residential rates cannot rise by more than 1 percent per year relative to the PCI. Finally, service-specific rates may not decline by more than 5 percent relative to the PCI in one year. (This last restriction is intended to discourage predatory pricing.) WATS is excluded from this basket to avoid cross subsidization.

(ii). *800 Service Basket* is separate because there are special entry barriers in this business. Until 1986, AT&T was sole provider of these services. There are four services included:

1 Readyline 800

2 AT&T 800

3 Megacom 800

4 all other 800.

There is a 5 percent upper and lower band on each service.

(iii). *Business Services Basket* has seven service categories:

1 PRO WATS

2 WATS

3 Megacom

4 SDN

5 other switched

6 voice grade private line and below

7 other private line

There is a 5 percent upper and lower band on each service.

A.3.4   Actual price index (API) formula

$$API_t = API_{t-1} \sum_i v_i (\frac{p_2}{p_1})_i,$$

where:

API_{t-1}	is prior period Actual Price Index
API_t	is new Actual Price Index
p_1	existing price for rate element i.
p_2	proposed price for rate element i.
v_i	current estimated revenue weight for rate element i, calculated as the ratio of base period demand for the rate element i priced at the existing rate, to the base period demand for the entire basket of services priced at existing rates.

Source: FCC (1989), pp. 197-9.

Bibliography

Acton, Jan P. and Ingo Vogelsang (1989). Introduction (to Symposium on Price-Cap Regulation). *RAND Journal of Economics*, 20:369–72.

(February 1990). Telephone Demand Over the Atlantic – Evidence from Country-Pair Data. Technical Report R-3715-NSF/MF, RAND, Santa Monica.

Adams, W. J. and J. L. Yellen (1976). Commodity Bundling and the Burden of Monopoly. *Quarterly Journal of Economics*, 90:475–98.

American Telephone and Telegraph Co. (April 23, 1984). Optional Calling Plan Filing, Transmittal No. 79.

(September 30, 1987). Reach Out America Quarterly Tracking Report, File No. E-85-11.

(May 17, 1989). Revised Tariff Filing, Transmittal No. 1618.

(August 31, 1989). Revised Tariff Filing, Transmittal No. 1762.

(June 28, 1990). Revised Tariff Filing, Transmittal No. 2396.

(July 13, 1990). Revised Tariff Filing, Tariff No. 1.

Auerbach, A. J. and A. J. Pellechio (1978). The Two-Part Tariff and Voluntary Market Participation. *Quarterly Journal of Economics*, 92:571–87.

Aumann, R. J. and L. S. Shapley (1974). *Values of Non-Atomic Games*. Princeton University Press, Princeton, NJ.

Averch, H. and L. L. Johnson (1962). Behavior of the Firm under Regulatory Constraint. *American Economic Review*, 52:1053–69.

Bacharach, M. (May 1985). Some Extensions of a Claim of Aumann in an Axiomatic Model of Knowledge. *Journal of Economic Theory*, 37:167.

Bain, Joe S. (1956). *Barriers to New Competition*. Harvard University Press, Cambridge, MA.

Baron, David P. (1989). Design of Regulatory Mechanisms and Institutions. In Schmalensee, R. and R. D. Willig, editors, *Handbook of Industrial Organization: Vol. II*, pages 1347–447. North-Holland, Amsterdam.

Baron, David P. and R. B. Myerson (1982). Regulating a Monopolist with Unknown Cost. *Econometrica*, 50:911–30.

Baumol, William J. (1968). Reasonable Rules for Rate Regulation: Plausible Policies for an Imperfect World. In Phillips, Almarin, editor, *Prices: Issues in Theory, Practice and Public Policy*. University of Pennsylvania Press, Philadelphia, PA.

(1982). Productivity Incentive Clauses and Rate Adjustments for Inflation. *Public Utilities Fortnightly*, 110:11–18.

(1986). *Superfairness*. MIT Press, Cambridge, MA.

Baumol, William J., E. E. Bailey, and R. D. Willig (1977). Weak Invisible Hand Theorems on the Sustainability of Prices in a Multiproduct Natural Monopoly. *American Economic Review*, 67:350–65.

Baumol, William J. and D. F. Bradford (1970). Optimal Departures from Marginal-Cost Pricing. *American Economic Review*, 60:265–83.

Baumol, William J., W. F. Koehn, and R. D. Willig (September 3, 1987). How Arbitrary is Arbitrary, or: Towards the Desired Demise of Full Cost Allocation. *Public Utilities Fortnightly*, 120 (5):16–21.

Baumol, William J., J. C. Panzar, and R. D. Willig (1982). *Contestable Markets and the Theory of Industry Structure.* Hartcourt Brace Jovanovich, New York.

Belinfante, Alexander (May 1990). Telephone Subscribership in the United States. Technical report, Federal Communications Commission, Common Carrier Bureau.

Bell Canada (April 5-7, 1989). *Telecommunications Costing in a Dynamic Environment,* San Diego CA. Bell Canada/Bell Communications Research.

Bell Communications Research (1984). The Impact of End-User Charges on Bypass and Universal Telephone Service. Technical report, Bell Communications Research, Livingston, NJ.

Berg, S. V., editor (1983). *Innovative Electric Rates: Issues in Cost-Benefit Analysis.* Lexington Books, Lexington MA.

Berg, S. V. and J. Tschirhart (1988). *Natural Monopoly Regulation.* Cambridge University Press, Cambridge, England.

Besanko, D. and D. E. M. Sappington (1987). *Designing Regulatory Policy with Limited Information,* volume 20 of *Fundamentals of Pure and Applied Economics.* Harwood Academic Publishers, Chur, Switzerland.

Billera, Louis J. and David C. Heath (February 1982). Allocation of Shared Costs: A Set of Axioms Yielding a Unique Procedure. *Mathematics of Operations Research,* 7(1):32–9.

Billera, Louis J., David C. Heath, and Joseph Raanan (November-December 1978). Internal Telephone Billing Rates–A Novel Application of Non-Atomic Game Theory. *Operations Research,* 26(6):956–65.

Billera, Louis J., David C. Heath, and Robert E. Verrecchia (Spring 1981). A Unique Procedure for Allocating Common Costs from a Production Process. *Journal of Accounting Research,* 19(1):185–96.

Bohn, Roger, M. Caramanis, and Fred Schweppe (1984). Opimal Pricing in Electrical Networks over Space and Time. *RAND Journal of Economics,* 15(3):360–76.

Boiteux, M. (1964). Peak-Load Pricing. In Nelson, J., editor, *Marginal Cost Pricing in Practice,* chapter 3. Prentice Hall, New York. Reprinted in *Journal of Business,* April 1960.

Bonanzinga, Patrizia and Claudio Leporelli (1988). Dynamic Cooperative Supply Policies for the Diffusion of a New Telecommunication Service. Working paper 6t24489, Fondazione Ugo Bordoni, Rome, Italy.

Bös, D. (1983). Public Pricing with Distributional Objectives. In Finsinger, J., editor, *Public Sector Economics,* pages 171–88. MacMillan, London and Basingstoke.

  (1985a). Means-Tested Public Pricing. Discussion paper no. A-22, Projektbereich A, Sonderforschungsbereich 303, Bonn University.

  (1985b). Public Sector Pricing. In Auerbach, A. J. and M. Feldstein, editors, *Handbook of Public Economics,* pages 129–211. North Holland.

Bös, D. and G. Tillmann (1983). Cost-Axiomatic Regulatory Pricing. *Journal of Public Economics,* 22:243–56.

Braeutigam, Ronald R. (1979). Optimal Pricing with Intermodal Competition. *American Economic Review,* 69:38–49.

(1980). An Analysis of Fully Distributed Cost Pricing in Regulated Industries. *Bell Journal of Economics*, 11(1):182–96.

(1984). Socially Optimal Pricing with Rivalry and Economies of Scale. *RAND Journal of Economics*, 15:127–34.

(1985). Efficient Pricing with Rivalry between a Railroad and a Pipeline. In Daughety, Andrew F., editor, *Analytical Studies in Transport Economics*, pages 207–20. Cambridge University Press.

Braeutigam, Ronald R. and J. C. Panzar (1989). Diversification Incentives Under "Price-Based" and "Cost-Based" Regulation. *RAND Journal of Economics*, 20:373–91.

Brander, James A. and Barbara J. Spencer (1985). Ramsey Optimal Two Part Tariffs: The Case of Many Heterogeneous Groups. *Public Finance-Finances Publiques*, 40:335–46.

Brandon, Belinda B., editor (1981). *The Effect of the Demographics of Individual Households on their Telephone Usage*. Ballinger, Cambridge, MA.

Brennan, Timothy J. (1989). Regulating by Capping Prices. *Journal of Regulatory Economics*, 1:133–48.

Brock, W. and J. Scheinkman (1983). Free Entry and the Sustainability of Natural Monopoly: Bertrand Revisited by Cournot. In Evans, D., editor, *Breaking Up Bell*. North-Holland, Amsterdam.

Brock, W. A. and W. D. Dechert (October 1985). Dynamic Ramsey Pricing. *International Economic Review*, 26(3).

Brown, D. J. and G. Heal (1980). Two-Part Tariffs, Marginal Cost Pricing and Increasing Returns to Scale in a General Equilibrium Model. *Journal of Public Economics*, 13:25–49.

Brown, Stephen J. and David S. Sibley (1986). *The Theory of Public Utility Pricing*. Cambridge University Press.

Browning, Edgar K. (1976). The Marginal Cost of Public Funds. *Journal of Political Economy*, 84:283–98.

(1987). On the Marginal Welfare Cost of Taxation. *American Economic Review*, 77:11–23.

Cabe, R. (1988). *Two Essays on the Regulation of Multiproduct Firms*. PhD thesis, University of Wyoming.

Cabral, L. M. B. (February 1990). Optimal Pricing of the Portuguese Telephone Service. *Applied Economics*, 22(2):211–20.

California Public Utilities Commission (June 6, 1990). Investigation on the Commission's own motion into the regulation of cellular radiotelephone utilities, Decision 90-06-025.

Carbajo, J., D. De Meza, and D. J. Seidman (March 1990). A Strategic Motivation for Commodity Bundling. *Journal of Industrial Economics*, 38(3):283–98.

Chao, Hung-Po and Robert Wilson (December 1987). Priority Service: Pricing, Investment and Market Organization. *American Economic Review*, 77(5):899–916.

Coase, R. H. (1946). The Marginal Cost Controversy. *Economica*, 13:169–82.

Cohen, G. (March 1977). Measured Rates Versus Flat Rates: A Pricing Experiment. Paper presented at Fifth Annual Telecommunications Policy Research Conference.

Cole, L. P. (1981). A Note on Fully Distributed Cost Prices. *Bell Journal of Economics*, 12:329–34.

Cooper, Mark N. and Mitchell Shapiro (October 1986). Low Income Households in the Post-Divestiture Era: A Study of Telephone Subscribership and Use in Michigan. Technical report, The Michigan Divestiture Research Fund.

Crew, Michael A. and Paul R. Kleindorfer (1976). Peak Load Pricing with a Diverse Technology. *Bell Journal of Economics*, 7:207–31.

(1979). *Public Utility Economics*. St. Martin's Press, New York.

Curry, B. and K. D. George (March 1983). Industrial Concentration: A Survey. *Journal of Industrial Economics*, 31:203–55.

Daly, George and Thomas Mayor (April 1980). Estimating the Value of a Missing Market: The Economics of Directory Assistance. *Journal of Law and Economics*, pages 147–66.

Dansby, Robert E. (January 1983). Spatial Considerations in Public Utility Pricing. Technical Report 265, Bell Laboratories, Economics Discussion Paper.

Dhebar, A. and S. S. Oren (1985a). Optimal Dynamic Pricing for Expanding Networks. *Marketing Science*, 4 (a).

(1985b). Dynamic Nonlinear Pricing in Networks with Interdependent Demand. *Operations Research*, 34:384–94.

Dierker, Egbert (1991). The Optimality of Boiteux-Ramsey Prices. *Econometrica*, 59(1):99–121.

Ebrill, Liam P. and Steven M. Slutsky (1990). Production Efficiency and Optimal Pricing in Intermediate-Good Regulated Industries. *International Journal of Industrial Organization*, 8:417–42.

Eckel, Catherine C. (1985). A General Model of Customer-Class Pricing. *Economics Letters*, 17:285–9.

Eckel, Catherine C. and William T. Smith (April 20, 1990). Multiproduct Pricing and Capacity Choice with Correlated Demands. Technical report, Department of Economics, Virginia Polytechnique Institute and State University, Blacksburg, VA.

Egan, Bruce (March 1987). Costing and Pricing the Network of the Future. In *Internal Switching Symposium*, Phoenix, AZ.

Einhorn, Michael A. (1987). Optimality and Sustainability: Regulation and Intermodal Competition in Telecommunications. *RAND Journal of Economics*, 18(4).

(1990). Regulatory Biases in Network Pricing with Access and Usage Externalities. mimeo.

Ellis, Randall P. (Summer 1986). Rational Behavior in the Presence of Coverage Ceilings and Deductibles. *RAND Journal of Economics*, 17(2):158–75.

Faulhaber, Gerald R. (1975). Cross-subsidization: Pricing in Public Enterprises. *American Economic Review*, 65:966–77.

Faulhaber, Gerald R. and William J. Baumol (1988). Economists as Innovators. *Journal of Economic Literature*, 26:577–600.

Faulhaber, Gerald R. and James W. Boyd (1989). Optimal New-Product Pricing in Regulated Industries. *Journal of Regulatory Economics*, 1(4):341–58.

Faulhaber, Gerald R. and S. B. Levinson (1981). Subsidy-Free Prices and Anonymous Equity. *American Economic Review*, 71:1083–91.

Faulhaber, Gerald R. and J. C. Panzar (1977). Optimal Two-Part Tariffs with Self-Selection. Economic Discussion Paper 74, Bell Laboratories.

Federal Communications Commission (April 24, 1984). Memorandum Opinion and Order, Volume Discount Guidelines, CC Docket No. 79-246.

    (October 17, 1985). Memorandum Opinion and Order, OCP Guidelines Order, CC Docket No. 84-1235.

    (July 2, 1986). Memorandum Opinion and Order, File No. E-85-11.

    (March 16, 1989). Report and Order and Second Further Notice of Proposed Rulemaking in the Matter of Policy and Rules Concerning Rates for Dominant Carriers, CC Docket 87-313.

    (June 8, 1990). Memorandum Opinion and Order.

    (January 30, 1991). Telephone Rates Update, Common Carrier Bureau, Industry Analysis Division.

    (February 28, 1991). Trends in Telephone Service.

Federal-State Joint Board (July 1990). Monitoring Report, CC Docket No. 86-286.

    (January 1991). Monitoring Report, CC Docket No. 86-286.

Feldstein, Martin S. (1972a). Equity and Efficiency In Public Sector Pricing: The Optimal Two-Part Tariff. *The Quarterly Journal of Economics*, 86.

    (1972b). Distributional Equity and the Optimal Structure of Public Prices. *American Economic Review*, 62:32–6.

Finsinger, J. and K.-H. Neumann (April 1981). Wirtschaftspolitische Massnahmen und die Opposition der Verlierer. Discussion paper IIM/IP 81-9, International Institute of Management, Berlin.

Finsinger, J. and I. Vogelsang (1982). Performance Indices for Public Enterprises. In Jones, L. P., editor, *Public Enterprise in Less-Developed Countries*, pages 281–96. Cambridge University Press, Cambridge.

Fuss, M. A. and L. Waverman (1981). Regulation and the Multiproduct Firm: The Case of Telecommunications in Canada. In Fromm, G., editor, *Studies in Public Regulation*, pages 277–313. MIT Press, Cambridge, MA.

Gale, William A. and Roger Koenker (undated). Pricing Interactive Computer Services: A Rationale and Some Proposals for Unix Implementation. Technical report, Bell Laboratories.

Goldman, M. B., H. E. Leland, and D. S. Sibley (1984). Optimal Nonuniform Pricing. *Review of Economic Studies*, 51:305–19.

Griffin, James M. and Thomas H. Mayor (October 1987). The Welfare Gain From Efficient Pricing of Local Telephone Services. *Journal of Law & Economics*, 30.

Guesnerie, Roger (1975). Pareto-Optimality in Non-Convex Economies. *Econometrica*, 43:1–29.

Hagerman, James (1990). Regulation by Price Adjustment. *RAND Journal of Economics*, 21(1):72–82.

Harberger, Arnold C. (1964). Taxation, Resource Allocation and Welfare. In *The Role of Direct and Indirect Taxes in the Federal Revenue System*, number 3 in Other Conference Series. University Microfilms.

Harris, J. G. and E. G. Wiens (1980). Government Enterprise: An Instrument for the Internal Regulation of Industry. *Canadian Journal of Economics*, 13:125–32.

Hausman, Jerry A. (February 1989). Competition In Telecommunications. Technical Report MIT-TEP 89-001, Massachusetts Institute of Technology, Telecommunication Economics Program.

Henriet, D. and D. Vayanos (June 1988). Some Results on Network Externalities. Paper presented at ITS Conference.

Heyman, D. P., J. M. Lazorchak, D. S. Sibley, and W. E. Taylor (July 1987). An Analysis of Tapered Access Charges for End Users. Technical Report Economics Discussion Paper No. 31, Bell Communications Research.

Jackson, C. L. and J. H. Rohlfs (1985). Access Charging and Bypass Adoption. Technical report, Shooshan and Jackson, Inc., Washington D. C.

Johnson, Leland L. (February 1988). Telephone Assistance Programs for Low-Income Households: A Preliminary Assessment. Technical Report R-3603-NSF/MF, RAND.

Jones, L. P., P. Tandon, and Ingo Vogelsang (1990). *Selling Public Enterprises: A Cost-Benefit Methodology*. MIT Press, Cambridge, MA.

Kahn, Alfred E. and William B. Shew (1987). Current Issues in Telecommunications Regulation: Pricing. *Yale Journal on Regulation*, 4(2):191–256.

Kaserman, David L. and John W. Mayo (1991). Regulation, Advertising and Economic Welfare. *Journal of Business*, 64(2):255–67.

Kaserman, David L., John W. Mayo, and Joseph E. Flynn (1990). Cross-Subsidization in Telecommunications: Beyond the Universal Service Fairy Tale. *Journal of Regulatory Economics*, 2:231–49.

Kay, J. A. (October 1979). Uncertainty, Congestion and Peak Load Pricing. *Review of Economic Studies*, pages 601–11.

Kelley, Daniel (1985). AT&T Optional Calling Plans: Promotional or Predatory? In Mann, Patrick C. and Harry M. Trebbing, editors, *The Impact of Deregulation and Market Forces on Public Utilities: The Future Role of Regulation*. Institute of Public Utilities, Michigan State University, East Lansing, MI.

Knieps, G. and Ingo Vogelsang (1982). The Sustainability Concept under Alternative Behavioral Assumptions. *Bell Journal of Economics*, 13:234–41.

Laffont, Jean-Jacques, E. Maskin, and J.-C. Rochet (1987). Optimal Nonlinear Pricing: The Case of Buyers with Several Characteristics. In Groves, T., R. Radner, and S. Reiter, editors, *Information, Incentives and Economic Mechanisms: In Honor of L. Hurwicz*. University of Minnesota Press.

Laffont, Jean-Jacques and Jean Tirole (1990a). The Regulation of Multiproduct Firms. Part I: Theory. *Journal of Public Economics*, 43:1–36.

  (1990b). The Regulation of Multiproduct Firms. Part II: Applications to Competitive Environments and Policy Analysis. *Journal of Public Economics*, 43:37–66.

Lande, James L. (February 9, 1990). Telephone Rates Update. Technical report, Federal Communications Commission, Common Carrier Bureau.

Lande, James L. and P. Wynns (April 1987). Primer and Sourcebook on Telephone Price Indexes and Rate Levels. Technical report, Federal Communications Commission, Industry Analysis Division, Common Carrier Bureau.

Larson, A. and Dale Lehman (February 1987). Asymmetric Pricing and Arbitrage. Technical Report TM-NPL-008597, Bell Communications Research.

Larson, A., T. Makarewicz, and C. Monson (December 1988). The Effect of Subscriber Line Charges on Residential Telephone Bills. *Telecommunications Policy*, 13 (4).

Larson, Alexander C., Calvin S. Monson, and Patricia J. Nobles (December 1989). Competitive Necessity and Pricing in Telecommunications Regulation. *Federal Communications Law Journal*, 42:1–49.

Levin, Stanford L. (October-November 1988). The Economics and Pricing of Broadband. Presented at Sixteenth Annual Telecommunications Policy Research Conference.

Littlechild, S. C. (June 1970). Marginal-Cost Pricing with Joint Costs. *Economic Journal*, 80:323–35.

(1975). Two-Part Tariffs and Consumption Externalities. *Bell Journal of Economics*, 6:661–70.

(1983). Regulation of British Telecommunications' Profitability, Report to the Secretary of State, Department of Industry.

Littlechild, S. C. and J. J. Rousseau (1975). Pricing Policy of a US Telephone Company. *Journal of Public Economics*, 4:35–56.

Loeb, M. and W. Magat (1979). A Decentralized Model of Utility Regulation. *Journal of Law and Economics*, 22:399–404.

Mackie-Manson, Jeffrey K. (1990). Optional Time-of-use Pricing Can be Pareto Superior or Pareto Inferior. *Economics Letters*, 33:363–7.

Makarewicz, T. (May 10, 1990). The Effectiveness of Low-Income Telephone Assistance Programs: Southwestern Bell's Experience. Revenues and Public Affairs Department, Southwestern Bell Telephone Co.

Marchand, M. G. (1973). The Economic Principles of Telephone Rates Under a Budgetary Constraint. *Review of Economic Studies*, 40:507–15.

Marfisi, E. P., K. J. Murphy, M. M. Murphy, J. H. Rohlfs, and D Silverstein, (December 1981). Telecommunications Policy Model: Evaluating Changes in Telecommunications Policies: Whose Ox Will Be Gored? Technical report, American Telephone and Telegraph Co., Microeconomic Analysis Group.

Maskin, E. and J. Riley (1984). Monopoly with Incomplete Information. *RAND Journal of Economics*, 15:171–96.

Mathios, Alan D. and Robert P. Rogers (November 1988). The Impact of State Price and Entry Regulation on Intrastate Long Distance Telephone Rates. Technical report, Federal Trade Commission.

(1989). The Impact of Alternative Forms of State Regulation of AT&T on Direct-Dial Long-Distance Telephone Rates. *RAND Journal*, 20:437–53.

McAfee, R. Preston, John McMillan, and Michael D. Whinston (May 1989). Multi-product Monopoly, Commodity Bundling, and Correlation of Values. *Quarterly Journal of Economics*, pages 371–83.

McFadden, Daniel (1975). The Revealed Preference of a Government Bureaucracy: Theory. *Bell Journal of Economics*, 6:401–16.

McGraw-Hill (1989). Datapro Reports on Telecommunication.

Mirman, Leonard J. and David Sibley (1980). Optimal Nonlinear Prices for Multiproduct Monopolies. *Bell Journal of Economics*, 11(2):659–70.

Mirman, Leonard J., Y. Tauman, and I. Zang (1985a). Supportability, Sustainability, and Subsidy Free Prices. *RAND Journal of Economics*, 16:114–26.

(1985b). Monopoly and Sustainable Prices as a Nash Equilibrium in Contestable Markets. In Feiwel, G. R., editor, *Issues in Contemporary Microeconomics and Welfare*, pages 328–39. State University Press of New York, Albany, New York.

(1986). Ramsey Prices, Average Cost Prices, and Price Sustainability. *International Journal of Industrial Organization*, 4:123–40.

Mirrlees, John A. (1976). Optimal Tax Theory: a Synthesis. *Journal of Public Economics*, 6:327–58.

Mitchell, Bridger M. (1978). Optimal Pricing of Local Telephone Service. *American Economic Review*, 68(4):517–37.

(1979). Pricing Policies in Selected European Telephone Systems. In Dordick, H., editor, *Proceedings of the Sixth Annual Telecommunications Policy Research Conference*. Lexington Books, Lexington, MA.

(1979). Telephone Call Pricing in Europe: Localizing the Pulse. In Wenders, J. T., editor, *Pricing in Regulated Industries: II*. Mountain States Telephone and Telegraph Co., Denver, CO.

(1980). Alternative Measured-Serviced Structures for Local Telephone Service. In Crew, M. A., editor, *Issues in Public Utility Pricing and Regulation*, pages 107–23. Lexington Books, Lexington, MA.

(1983). Local Telephone Costs and the Design of Rate Structures. In Courville, L., A. De Fontenay, and R. Dobell, editors, *Economic Analysis of Telecommunications: Theory and Applications*. Elsevier Science Publishers, Amsterdam.

(April 1988). The Market Equilibrium of Optional Time-of-Day Tariffs. Presented to the Conference on Utility Regulation, Center for Economic Policy Research, Stanford University, Stanford CA.

(July 1990). Incremental Costs of Telephone Access and Local Use. Technical Report R-3909-ICTF, RAND.

Mitchell, Bridger M., W. G. Manning, and J. P. Acton (1978). *Peak-Load Pricing: European Lessons for US Energy Policy*. Ballinger Publishing Company, Cambridge, MA.

Mulgan, Geoffrey J. (June 1988). Costs and Tariffs in ISDN and Broadband Networks: A Case of Whatever You Can Get Away With? Technical report, Center for Communication and Information Studies, London.

Neu, Werner (1988). A Theoretical Look at Price Capping Mechanims: Some Clarifications and One Recommendation. Technical Report 47, WIK, Bad Honnef, Germany, Diskussionsbeiträge zur Telekommunikationsforschung.

Neumann, K.-H. (1984). *Gebührenpolitik im Telekommunikationsbereich*. Nomos, Baden-Baden.

Neumann, K.-H. and C. C. von Weizsäcker (1982). Tarifpolitik bei Mietleitungen und Nebenstellenanlagen unter volkswirtschaftlichen Gesichtspunkten. In *Jahrbuch der Deutschen Bundespost*. Deutsche Bundespost, Bonn.

Neumann, K.-H. and B. Wieland (1986). Competition and Social Objectives: The Case of West German Telecommunications. *Telecommunications Policy*, 10:121–31.

Ng., Y. and M. Weisser (1974). Optimal Pricing with a Budget Constraint – The Case of the Two-Part Tariff. *Review of Economic Studies*, 41:337–45.

Noll, Roger G. and Susan Riely (1988). The Laboratory of the States: Local Service Prices Before and After Divestiture. Technical report, Stanford University.

Noll, Roger G. and Susan R. Smart (May 1989). The Political Economics of State Responses to Divestiture and Federal Deregulation in Telecommunications. Technical report, Workshop on Applied Microeconomics, Industrial Organization, and Regulation, Stanford University, Discussion Paper No. 148.

Oi, Walter Y. (1971). A Disney Land Dilemma: Two-Part Tariffs for a Mickey Mouse Monopoly. *Quarterly Journal of Economics*, 85:77–96.

Ordover, J. A. and J. Panzar (1980). On the Nonexistence of Pareto Superior Outlay Schedules. *Bell Journal of Economics*, 11:351–4.

Oren, Shmuel, Stephen Smith, and Robert Wilson (May 1982). Nonlinear Tariffs in Markets with Interdependent Demand. Technical report, Program in Information Policy, Stanford University.

    (1983). Competitive Nonlinear Tariffs. *Journal of Economic Theory*, 29:49–71.

    (May 1985). Capacity Pricing. *Econometrica*, 53(3).

Owen, Bruce M. and Ronald R. Braeutigam (1978). *The Regulation Game: Strategic Use of the Administrative Proces*. Ballinger, Cambridge, MA.

Palmer, Karen (December 1989). Using an Upper Bound on Stand-alone Cost in Tests of Cross-subsidy. Technical Report Discussion Paper QE90-07, Resources for the Future, Washington DC.

Panzar, John C. (1976). A Neoclassical Approach to Peak Load Pricing. *Bell Journal of Economiocs*, 7:521–30.

    (1980). Sustainability, Efficiency and Vertical Integration. In Mitchell, Bridger M. and Paul R. Kleindorfer, editors, *Regulated Industries and Public Enterprise*, pages 171–85. Lexington Books, Lexington, MA.

Panzar, John C. and A. W. Postlewaite (1984). Sustainable Outlay Schedules. Technical Report Discussion Paper No. 626S, The Center for Mathematical Studies in Economics and Management Science, Northwestern University.

Panzar, John C. and Robert D. Willig (1977). Free Entry and the Sustainability of Natural Monopoly. *Bell Journal of Economics*, 8:1–22.

Park, Rolla Edward (1989). Incremental Costs and Efficient Prices with Lumpy Capacity: The Single Product Case. Technical Report R-3723-ICTF, RAND.

Park, Rolla Edward and Bridger M. Mitchell (March 1987). Optimal Peak-load Pricing for Local Telephone Calls. Technical Report R-3404-1-RC, RAND.

    (June 1989). Local Telephone Pricing and Universal Telephone Service. Technical Report R-3724-NSF, RAND.

Park, Rolla Edward, Bridger M. Mitchell, and Bruce M. Wetzel (1980). Demographic Effects of Local Calling under Measured vs. Flat Rate Service: Analysis of Data from the GTE Illinois Experiment. In *Pacific Telecommunications Conference Proceedings*. Pacific Telecomunications Conference '80, Honolulu.

Park, Rolla Edward, Bridger M. Mitchell, Bruce M. Wetzel, and James H. Alleman, (1983). Charging for Local Telephone Calls: How Household Characteristics Affect the Distribution of Calls in the GTE Illinois Experiment. *Journal of Econometrics*, 22:339–64.

Park, Rolla Edward, Bruce M. Wetzel, and Bridger M. Mitchell (1983). Price Elasticities for Local Telephone Calls. *Econometrica*, 51(6):1699–1730.

Peltzman, S. (1976). Towards a More General Theory of Regulation. *Journal of Law and Economics*, 19:211–40.

Perl, Lewis J. (April 1984). A New Study of Economic and Demographic Determinants of Residential Demand for Basic Telephone Service. Presented to the Telecommunications Policy Research Conference, Airlie, VA.

(June 1988). Welfare Consequences of Competition in Telecommunications. Presented to the Seventh International Conference of the International Telecommunications Society, Cambridge, MA.

Perry, Motty (1984). Sustainable Positive Profit Multiple-Price Strategies in Contestable Markets. *Journal of Economic Theory*, 32:246–65.

Peters, Wolfgang (1988). Cost Inefficiency and Second Best Pricing. *European Journal of Political Economy*, 4, special issue(1):29–45.

Phlips, Louis (1983). *The Economics of Price Discrimination*. Cambridge University Press, Cambridge.

Pousette, Tomas (1982). Technology, Pricing and Investment in Telecommunications. Working Paper 71, The Industrial Institute for Economic and Social Research.

Pyatt, Graham (September 1972). Some Economics of Public Utility. Technical report, University of Warwick and Cooper Brothers.

Ramsey, Frank (1927). A Contribution to the Theory of Taxation. *Economic Journal*, 37:47–61.

Rawls, John A. (1971). *A Theory of Justice*. Harvard University Press, Cambridge, MA.

Rees, Ray (1976). *Public Enterprise Economics*. Weidenfeld and Nicolson, London.

(1986). Indivisibilities, Pricing and Investment: The Case of the Second Best. *Journal of Economics*, Suppl. 5:195–210.

Roberts, K. (1979). Welfare Considerations of Nonlinear Pricing. *Economic Journal*, 89:66–83.

Rohlfs, J. (1974). A Theory of Interdependent Demand for Telecommunications Service. *Bell Journal of Economics and Management Science*, 5:16–37.

(January 1979). Economically-Efficient Bell-System Pricing. Discussion Paper 138, Bell Laboratories.

Roscitt, Richard R. (September 30, 1985a). Statement, Federal Communications Commission File No. E-85-11.

(October 15, 1985b). Statement, Federal Communications Commission File No. E-85-11.

Ross, T. W. (1984). Uncovering Regulator's Social Welfare Weights. *RAND Journal of Economics*, 15:152–5.

Rosse, J. N. (August 1978). The Sustainability of Natural Monopoly. Mimeo, Department of Economics, Stanford University, Stanford CA.

Salant, David J. and Glenn A. Woroch (1989). Trigger Price Regulation. Technical report, GTE Laboratories.

Salant, Stephen W. (1989). When is Inducing Self-Selection Suboptimal for a Monopolist? *Quarterly Journal of Economics*, pages 391–7.

Sappington, David (1980). Strategic Firm Behavior under a Dynamic Regulatory Adjustment Process. *Bell Journal of Economics*, 11:360–72.

(1983). Optimal Regulation of a Multiproduct Monopoly with Unknown Technological Capabilities. *Bell Journal of Economics*, 14:453–63.

Sappington, David and David Sibley (1988). Regulating without Cost Information: The Incremental Surplus Subsidy Scheme. *International Economic Review*, 29:297–306.

Schmalensee, Richard (1981). Monopolistic Two-Part Tariff Arrangements. *Bell Journal of Economics*, 12:445–66.

(1982). Commodity Bundling by a Single-Product Monopolist. *Journal of Law and Economics*, 25:67–71.

(1984, Supplement). Gaussian Demand and Commodity Bundling. *Journal of Business*, 57:S211–35.

(1989). Good Regulatory Regimes. *RAND Journal of Economics*, 20:417–36.

Schultz, Richard J. (February 1989). United States Telecommunications Pricing Changes and Social Welfare: Causes, Consequences and Policy Alternatives, Department of Consumer and Corporate Affairs, Government of Canada.

Science (April 14, 1989). PARC Brings Adam Smith to Computing. *Science*, pages 14–15.

Sharkey, William W. (1982). *The Theory of Natural Monopoly*. Cambridge University Press, Cambridge.

(July 1988). Supportability of Network Cost Functions. Economics Discussion Paper 41, Bell Communications Research.

(May 1990). Cores of Games with Fixed Costs and Shared Facilities. *International Economic Review*, 31(2):245–62.

Sharkey, William W. and David S. Sibley (December 1985). Applications of Public Utility Pricing Theory to BOC Pricing Issues. Economics Discussion Paper 11, Bell Communications Research.

(March 1991). Optimal Non-linear Pricing with Regulatory Preference over Customer Types. Bellcore economics discussion paper, Bell Communications Research.

Sharkey, William W. and Lester G. Telser (1978). Supportable Cost Functions for the Multiproduct Firm. *Journal of Economic Theory*, 18:23–37.

Sherman, Roger (1989). *The Regulation of Monopoly*. Cambridge University Press.

Sherman, Roger and A. George (1979). Second-Best Pricing for the US Postal Service. *Southern Economic Journal*, 45:685–95.

Sherman, Roger and Michael L. Visscher (1978). Second Best Pricing with Stochastic Demand. *American Economic Review*, 68 (1):41–53.

(1979). Rate-of-Return Regulation and Price Structure. In Crew, M. A., editor, *Problems in Public Utility Economics and Regulation*, pages 119–32. D. C. Heath, Lexington, MA.

(1982). Nonprice Rationing and Monopoly Price Structure When Demand is Stochastic. *Bell Journal of Economics*, 13:254–62.

Sibley, David (1989). Asymmetric Information, Incentives and Price Cap Regulation. *RAND Journal of Economics*, 20:392–404.

Sievers, Mark (May 1989). The Law and Economics of Intralata Competition: 1+ Issues and Access Charge Imputation. Presented at Rutgers University Advanced Workshop in Regulation and Public Utility Economics, Newport RI.

Simnett, Richard E. (1989). Contestable Markets and Telecommunications. In Crew, M. A., editor, *Deregulation and Diversification of Utilities*, pages 127–42. Kluwer Academic Publishers.

Spence, M. (1977). Nonlinear Prices and Welfare. *Journal of Public Economics,*
7:1–18.

(1980). Multi-Product Quantity-Dependent Prices and Profitability Constraints.
Review of Economic Studies, 47:821–41.

Spencer, B. J. and J. A. Brander (1983). Second Best Pricing of Publicly Produced
Inputs: The Case of Downstream Imperfect Competition. *Journal of Public
Economics,* 20:113–19.

Spulber, Daniel F. (1986). Second-best Pricing and Cooperation. *RAND Journal of
Economics,* 17:239–50.

(1989a). *Regulation and Markets.* MIT Press, Cambridge, MA.

(1989b). The Second Best Core. *International Economic Review,* 30:623–31.

Squire, L. (1973). Some Aspects of Optimal Pricing for Telecommunications. *Bell
Journal of Economics,* 4:515–25.

Srinagesh, Padmanabhan (1990). Why Marginal Prices are Below Marginal
Cost: Mixed Linear-Nonlinear Pricing. Bellcore Economics Discussion Paper
LCC3B234, Bell Communications Research.

Starrett, David A. (June 1978). Marginal Cost Pricing of Recursive Lumpy Investments. *Review of Economic Studies,* XLV (2)(140):215–27.

Stolleman, Neal C. (June 29, 1988). A Generalized Non-Linear Pricing Structure
With Application To Open Network Architecture. Presented at International
Telecommunications Society Seventh International Conference.

(October 1990). Intertemporal Pricing for a New Service. Mimeo.

Stolleman, Neal C. and Whitney Hatch (February 1986). Bypass of the Public
Switched Network: Cause, Potential Exposure, Regulatory Response. Paper
presented at the Twelfth Annual Rate Symposium, University of Missouri.

Taylor, Lester D. (1980). *Telecommunications Demand: A Survey and Critique.*
Ballinger, Cambridge, MA.

ten Raa, T. (1983). Supportability and Anonymous Equity. *Journal of Economic
Theory,* 31:176–81.

(1984). Resolution of Conjectures on the Sustainability of Natural Monopoly.
RAND Journal of Economics, 15:135–141.

Tirole, J. (1988). *The Theory of Industrial Organization.* MIT Press, Cambridge,
MA.

Train, Kenneth E., M. Ben-Akiva, and T. Atherton (1989). Consumption Patterns
and Self-selecting Tariffs. *Review of Economics and Statistics,* pages 62–73.

US Bureau of Labor Statistics (1991). Consumer Expenditure Survey: Telephone
Rates Update.

US Bureau of the Census (1991). Current Population Survey.

US General Accounting Office (September 1987). Telephone Communications: Cost
and Funding Information on Lifeline Telephone Service, GAO/RCED-87-189.

US West (June 12, 1990). Colorado Lifeline Disconnect Study, Submitted in Federal
Communications Commission CC Docket No. 87-339.

Vickrey, W. (1971). Responsive Pricing of Public Utility Services. *Bell Journal of
Economics and Management Science,* 2 (1):337–46.

Viswanathan, N. and Edison T. S. Tse (February 1989). Monopolistic Provision of Congested Service with Incentive-Based Allocation of Priorities. *International Economic Review*, 30(1):153–74.

Vogelsang, Ingo (1989). Two-Part Tariffs as Regulatory Constraints. *Journal of Public Economics*, 39:45–66.

(1990a). *Public Enterprise in Monopolistic and Oligopolistic Industries*, volume 36 of *Fundamentals of Pure and Applied Economics*. Harwood Academic Publishers, Chur, Switzerland.

(1990b). Optional Two-Part Tariffs Constrained by Price Caps. *Economics Letters*, 33:287–92.

Vogelsang, Ingo and J. Finsinger (1979). A Regulatory Adjustment Process for Optimal Pricing by Multiproduct Monopoly Firms. *Bell Journal of Economics*, 10:157–71.

von Weizsäcker, Carl Christian (1986). Free Entry into Telecommunications. In Snow, M. S., editor, *Marketplace for Telecommunications*, New York and London. Longman.

Wall, Gerald W., Leonard Waverman, and Lester D. Taylor (December 27-29, 1988). Equity Consideration and Ramsey Pricing in Telecommunications. Presented at Association of Managerial Economists, ASSA Meetings.

Ware, R. and R. A. Winter (1986). Public Pricing Under Imperfect Competition. *International Journal of Industrial Organization*, 4:87–8.

Weismann, Dennis (1988). Default Capacity Tariffs: Smoothing the Transitional Regulatory Asymmetries in the Telecommunications Market. *Yale Journal on Regulation*, 5(1):157–61.

Wellicz, S. H. (1963). Regulation of Natural Gas Pipeline Companies: An Economic Analysis. *Journal of Political Economy*, 55:30–43.

Westfield, F. (1965). Regulation and Conspiracy. *American Economic Review*, 55:424–43.

Willig, Robert D. (1978). Pareto-Superior Nonlinear Outlay Schedules. *Bell Journal of Economics*, 9:56–69.

(1979). The Theory of Network Access Pricing. In Trebing, H., editor, *Issues in Public Utility Regulation*, pages 109–52. Michigan State University, East Lansing.

Willig, Robert D. and Elizabeth E. Bailey (1977). Ramsey-Optimal Pricing of Long Distance Telephone Services. In Wenders, J. T., editor, *Pricing in Regulated Industries: Theory and Application*, pages 68–97. The Mountain States Telephone and Telegraph Company, Denver, CO.

Wilson, Robert (1989a). Efficient and Competitive Rationing. *Econometrica*, 57(1):1–40.

(1989b). Nonlinear Pricing. Book manuscript, Graduate School of Business, Stanford University.

(1991). Multiproduct Tariffs. *Journal of Regulatory Economics*, 3(1):5–26.

Woroch, Glenn A. (November 1985). On Pricing with Lumpy Investment: Boiteux's Two Problems. Technical report, University of Rochester.

(September 1987). The Economics of Bypass in a Simple Model of the Telephone Network. Technical report, GTE Laboratories, Waltham, MA.

(October 1989). Consistent Pricing of Access to a Network Service. Mimeo.

Xie, Jinhong and Marvin A. Sirbu (December 1988). Estimation of a Market Growth Model With Network Externalities and Dynamic Pricing Using an Extended Kalman Filter. Technical report, Carnegie Mellon University, Pittsburgh, PA.

Zajac, E. E. (1979). Dupoit-Marshall Consumer's Surplus, Utility, and Revealed Preference. *Journal of Economic Theory*, 20:260–70.

(January 1982). Toward a Theory of Perceived Economic Justice in Regulation. Economic Discussion Paper 235, Bell Laboratories.

(1985). Perceived Economic Justice: The Example of Public Utility Regulation. In Young, H. P., editor, *Cost Allocation: Methods, Principles and Applications*. North-Holland, Amsterdam.

Zupan, M. A. (April 1990). On Cream Skimming, Coase, and the Sustainability of Natural Monopoly. *Applied Economics*, 22(4):487–92.

Index

Selected List of RAND books

Alexiev, Alexander R. and S. Enders Wimbush (eds.) (1988). *Ethnic Minorities in the Red Army: Asset or Liability?* Boulder, CO: Westview Press.

Builder, Carl H. (1989). *The Masks of War: American Military Styles in Strategy and Analysis* Baltimore, MD: The Johns Hopkins University Press.

Chassin, Mark R. *et al.* (1989). *The Appropriateness of Selected Medical and Surgical Procedures: Relationship to Geographical Variations* Ann Arbor, MI: Health Administration Press.

Gustafson, Thane (1989). *Crisis Amid Plenty: The Politics of Soviet Energy under Brezhnev and Gorbachev* Princeton, NJ: Princeton University Press.

Hosmer, Stephen T. (1987). *Constraints on U.S. Strategy in Third World Conflicts* NY: Taylor & Francis.

Kanouse, David E. *et al.* (1989). *Changing Medical Practice Through Technology Assessment: An Evaluation of the NIH Consensus Development Program* Ann Arbor, MI: Health Administration Press.

Korbonski, Andrzej and Francis Fukuyama (eds.) (1987). *The Soviet Union and the Third World: The Last Three Decades* Ithaca, NY: Cornell University Press.

Levine, Robert A. (1990). *Still the Arms Debate* Aldershot, England: Dartmouth Publishing Company Limited; and Brookfield, VT: Gower Publishing Company.

Morrison, Peter A. (ed.) (1990). *A Taste of the Country: A Collection of Calvin Beale's Writings* University Park, PA: The Pennsylvania State University Press.

Nerlich, Uwe and James A Thomson (eds.) (1988). *Conventional Arms Control and the Security of Europe* Boulder, CO: Westview Press.

Ross, Randy L. (1988). *Government and the Private Sector: Who Should Do What?* NY: Crane, Russak & Company.

(1988). *Markets or Governments: Choosing Between Imperfect Alternatives* Cambridge, MA: The MIT Press.

Wolf, Charles Jr. (1991). *Linking Economic and Foreign Policy* New Brunswick, NJ, Transaction.